Helion & Company Limited
Unit 8 Amherst Business Centre
Budbrooke Road
Warwick
CV34 5WE
England
Tel. 01926 499 619
Email: info@helion.co.uk
Website: www.helion.co.uk
Twitter: @helionbooks
Visit our blog http://blog.helion.co.uk/

Text © Kenton White 2021
Photographs © as individually credited
Artworks by David Boquelet, Renato
    Dalmaso and Tom Cooper 2021
Maps drawn by George Anderson and
    Anderson Subtil © Helion & Company
    2021

Designed and typeset by Farr out
    Publications, Wokingham, Berkshire
Cover design Paul Hewitt, Battlefield Design
    (www.battlefield-design.co.uk)

Every reasonable effort has been made to
trace copyright holders and to obtain their
permission for the use of copyright material.
The author and publisher apologise for any
errors or omissions in this work, and would
be grateful if notified of any corrections that
should be incorporated in future reprints or
editions of this book.

ISBN 978-1-914377-08-2

British Library Cataloguing-in-Publication
    Data
A catalogue record for this book is available
    from the British Library

All rights reserved. No part of this
publication may be reproduced, stored in a
retrieval system, or transmitted, in any form,
or by any means, electronic, mechanical,
photocopying, recording or otherwise,
without the express written consent of
Helion & Company Limited.

We always welcome receiving book
proposals from prospective authors.

# CONTENTS

**MAP OF EUROPE 1945–1992**

Note: In order to simplify the use of this book, all names, locations and geographic
designations are as provided in *The Times World Atlas*, or other traditionally accepted major
sources of reference, as of the time of described events.

## DEDICATION

To Professor Beatrice Heuser and the late Professor Colin S Gray

# ABBREVIATIONS

| | |
|---|---|
| **1 (BR) Corps** | 1st British Corps; the combat element of the British Army of the Rhine |
| **1 (GE)** | 1st German Corps |
| **2ATAF** | 2nd Allied Tactical Air Force |
| **AAA** | anti-aircraft artillery |
| **ACCHAN** | Allied Command Channel |
| **ACE** | Allied Command Europe |
| **ACHDF** | Air Commander Home Defence Forces |
| **AD-70** | Alliance Defence in the Seventies |
| **AEW** | Airborne Early Warning |
| **AFNORTH** | Allied Forces Northern Europe |
| **APDS** | Armour Piercing Discarding Sabot |
| **ASM** | Air-to-Surface Missile |
| **ASW** | Anti-Submarine Warfare |
| **ATGW** | Anti-Tank Guided Weapon |
| **BALTAP** | Baltic Approaches |
| **BAOR** | British Army of the Rhine |
| **CDI (I)** | Conventional Defence Improvement Initiative |
| **CDS** | Chief of the Defence Staff |
| **CF** | Covering Force |
| **CinC** | Commander-in-Chief |
| **CINCEASTLANT** | Commander-in-Chief East Atlantic |
| **CINCNAVHOME** | Commander-in-Chief Naval Home Command |
| **CINCUKAIR** | Commander-in-Chief United Kingdom Air Forces |
| **CINCUKLF** | Commander-in-Chief United Kingdom Land Forces |
| **CND** | Campaign for Nuclear Disarmament |
| **COS** | Chiefs of Staff Committee |
| **DOAE** | Defence Operational Analysis Establishment |
| **EASTLANT** | Eastern Atlantic Area |
| **FOFA** | Follow-on Forces Attack |
| **FRG** | Federal Republic of Germany (West Germany) |
| **GDP** | Gross Domestic Product |
| **GDP** | General Defence Plan |
| **GWB** | Government War Book |
| **HCDC** | House of Commons Defence Committee |
| **HESH** | High Explosive Squash Head |
| **IGB** | Inner German Border (sometimes also Inter or Intra) |
| **JIC** | Joint Intelligence Committee |
| **LSG** | Logistic Support Group |
| **LTDP** | Long Term Defence Programme |
| **MBT** | Main Battle Tank |
| **MDA** | Main Defence Area |
| **MNC** | Major NATO Commanders |
| **MoD** | Ministry of Defence |
| **NAC** | North Atlantic Council |
| **NATO** | North Atlantic Treaty Organisation |
| **NORTHAG** | Northern Army Group |
| **POL** | Petrol, Oil and Lubricants |
| **RAF** | Royal Air Force |
| **RAF(G)** | Royal Air Force (Germany) |
| **REFORGER** | Reinforcement/Return of Forces in/to Germany |
| **RM** | Royal Marines |
| **RN** | Royal Navy |
| **RORO** | Roll On Roll Off ferry |
| **RRP** | Rapid Reinforcement Plan |
| **SACLANT** | Supreme Allied Commander Atlantic |
| **SAM** | Surface to Air Missile |
| **SDE** | Statement on Defence Estimates |
| **SGN** | Standing Groups in NATO |
| **SSBN** | Nuclear-powered ballistic missile submarine |
| **TA** | Territorial Army |
| **TAVR** | Territorial Army Volunteer Reserve |
| **UK/NL** | United Kingdom/Netherlands (usually referring to the joint amphibious group) |
| **UKADGE** | United Kingdom Air Defence Ground Environment |
| **UKLF** | United Kingdom Land Forces |
| **UKMF** | United Kingdom Mobile Force |
| **UKWMO** | United Kingdom Warning and Monitoring Organisation |
| **UN** | United Nations |
| **USAF** | United States Air Force |
| **USSR** | Union or Soviet Socialist Republics (Soviet Union) |
| **WMR** | War Maintenance Reserve |
| **WP** | Warsaw Pact (colloquial name for the Warsaw Treaty Organisation) |
| **WTO** | Warsaw Treaty Organisation |

# PREFACE

This book is derived from my PhD thesis which was entitled, 'British Defence Planning and Britain's NATO commitment, 1979 – 1985'. I have extended the period of research from the adoption of the NATO Strategic Concept known as 'Flexible Response' in 1967 to the end of the fall of the Berlin Wall in 1989. I have also tried to make this a less academic piece of work, hopefully with appeal to those with an interest in British defence policy during the last stages of the Cold War.

I began my research to the sound of several respectable academics – leaders in their fields – telling me to do a different subject. I was told either to concentrate on statistics, or to look at the development of doctrine. I chose to do neither, and without the financial support of any charity, agency or other organisation, ploughed what was at times a lonely furrow.

In my research I have attempted to let those taking part speak for themselves, and to use information from the participants of the time, rather than interpretations of that information. I have sought to return to original sources, and to present the events based on them. This does lead to some conclusions which are at odds with the accepted history. Where information is available both in the archives and published sources, I have endeavoured to cite both, so that you may avail yourself of the same material.

# ACKNOWLEDGEMENTS

Despite the isolation, several people actively encouraged and helped me in my endeavours. I would like to thank those people who have helped me complete this work. Without the following people, so much of this work would have remained unresearched:

Professor Colin Gray, Professor Beatrice Heuser, Dr Geoffrey Sloan, and Dr Adam Humphries have all influenced my work, contributed to or supported my research at various times, and provided direction when needed.

The following serving or retired officers have provided unstinting support and aided my work enormously; Lieutenant Colonel Matthew Whitchurch MBE RE, Colonel Mike Crawshaw OBE, Major General Christopher Elliott CB MBE, Major General Mungo Melvin CB OBE MA, General Sir Rupert Smith KCB, DSO & Bar, OBE, QGM, Captain Dr David Reindorp RN, Major Michael Tickner and Air Vice Marshal Michael Harwood CB CBE MA.

Finally, my family provided me with not only psychological and physical support, but the time and space to enable me to work. Thank you, Joel, Nathan, Christian, James, Elizabeth and William. To my wife, Rhona, without whom none of this would have been possible, thank you for your love and support.

# INTRODUCTION

This is an analysis of the conventional defence planning of the UK, its relationship to the policy, and their possible and actual execution.

Under the NATO strategy known as 'Flexible Response' Britain committed almost 120,000 ground troops and almost the entire Royal Navy and Royal Air Force to NATO's defence of Western Europe. 100,000 troops were assigned to Home Defence, and Britain would act as a staging post for foreign troops on their way to the front. Did Britain really have the means to mobilise, transport and supply these forces, and defend itself, in the event of war?

Deterrent plans were aimed at the perceived threat: planning for the manifestation of that threat, and implementing those plans, is analysed in detail. These plans relate intimately to NATO's 'Flexible Response' strategy and the desire to raise the nuclear threshold enabling NATO to stop a WTO attack by conventional means. Analysing the plans for mobilisation, and comparing them to the forces and facilities available, this book demonstrates whether the UK Government fulfilled its obligation, not only to NATO, but also to the Armed Forces and British public.

There are some, academic, military and political, who believe the NATO strategy worked and caused the fall of the Soviet Union. This thinking persists in policy, that funding can be cut, that military forces can be made more 'efficient' and 'effective' in peacetime. With the increasing tensions in Eastern Europe and the Pacific, and the British Armed Forces at their smallest for over a century, this post hoc analysis is dangerous. Strategy and policy makers ignore the lessons of history at their peril.

# 1

# GEOPOLITICS AND THE COLD WAR

The North Atlantic Treaty states that the basic aim of the Alliance is to safeguard the freedom, common heritage, and civilisation of the peoples of the NATO countries. To this end, a collective defence system has been built up for the purpose of averting war. This purpose cannot be fulfilled unless the potential aggressor is confronted by NATO with forces which are so organized, disposed, trained and equipped that he will conclude that the chances of a favourable decision are too small to be acceptable and that fatal risks would be involved if he launched or supported an armed attack, even with superior numbers and the advantage of surprise.

Part II – The Directive to the *NATO Military Authorities* from The North Atlantic Council

13th December 1956

## Introduction

With NATO's adoption of a new strategy in 1967 in document MC 14/3, commonly known as Flexible Response, was Britain fully committed to the demands placed upon it?[1] This book looks at the key areas of strategy – ends, ways, means, assumptions and risks. MC 14/3 was seen as an attempt to counteract the dangers of the low nuclear threshold of the 'Trip-Wire'.

Britain's NATO commitment was seen to be synonymous with BAOR. An article for the Journal of Strategic Studies published in 2008 states, 'During the Cold War the UK's principal military role was its commitment to the North Atlantic Treaty Organisation (NATO) through the British Army of the Rhine (BAOR) …'[2] In fact, the commitment was much larger, as this study will show. Britain committed forces to the UK base, the Channel, the Eastern Atlantic and the mobile and specialist reservist forces. In addition, Britain was committed not only to providing a substantial military contingent to NATO, but also to supporting the organisation of the main staging point and rear area in time of war. There has been much written of Britain and NATO in the 1950s and 60s, of the nuclear deterrent and tripwire strategy,[3] but little regarding Britain's conventional defence plans and their integration into NATO in the late 70s and early 80s. Britain's home defence (as opposed to civil defence) has been almost completely neglected, except for a recent surge in interest in Cold War architecture. The research that has been done has not been tied-in to its place in the Government plans. If Britain had been mobilised in times of crisis or war the true implications have not been investigated. Were the ends achievable with the ways and means available?

The research is approached such that the 'ends' are described by the political objectives set by NATO and the British Government. The strategy is encapsulated in MC 14/3 and the Government Defence White Papers. The 'ways' are how the ends were to be achieved. This is demonstrated in NATO document MC48/3[4] and the British Government War Book (GWB). It also includes the actions of the Transition to War Committee (TWC) and other planning documents. The 'means' includes the employment of military force to achieve the strategy objectives. This includes the MoD War Book, deployment plans, and operational and tactical doctrine to be employed in times of war, the use of military forces to support civilian organisations (for example Military Aid to the Civil Ministry (MACM)). It also involves the employment of civilian personnel, organisations, infrastructure and equipment to support military actions or to protect against attack. The assumptions

made will also be tested, which will identify the risks taken for defence in Europe. 'Assumptions' are those views which are held to make the policy and strategy valid, such as the assumption of long warning periods during a crisis. These include assumptions about the intent of the Warsaw Treaty Organisation as well as its capability. Finally, the risks the strategy brought about will be identified, and assessed considering the other aspects of strategy. In the end the question is: would the strategy have worked in the real world?

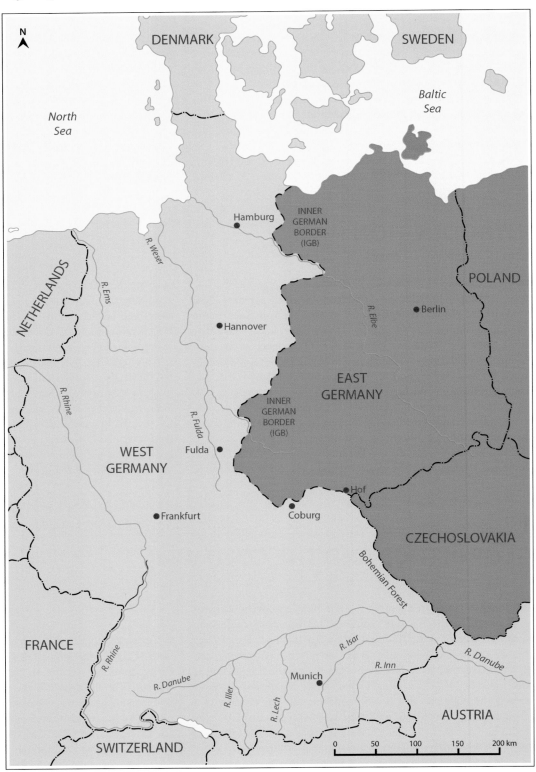

The line of the Inner German Border, dividing the Nation into East and West. (Map by George Anderson)

## Background

Following the end of the Second World War, a series of political crises in and around Europe culminated in the Soviet blockade of Berlin between 1948 and 1949. Ernest Bevin, British Foreign Secretary, became increasingly aware of Soviet hostility to the West, and aimed to bring the US militarily closer to Europe to balance this threat. Responding to the fears of an invasion, in 1948 the Ministry of Defence (MoD) Joint Planning Staff (JPS) reported that the Soviet Union could attack in West Germany with up to 45 divisions.[5] The increasingly difficult relationships between the Soviet Union and Western Europe prompted the establishment of the North Atlantic Treaty Organisation (NATO) in 1949, a collective defence region including the USA and some Western European allies. Article 3 of the North Atlantic Treaty, which deals with developing the, '… individual and collective capacity to resist armed attack'[6] and Article 5, which defines the policy of collective response, are probably the most well-known features of the Treaty. It was not until 1950 that the foreign ministers of the member countries agreed to, '… the establishment at the earliest possible date of an integrated force under centralized command, which shall be adequate to deter aggression and to ensure the defence of Western Europe.'[7] The Supreme Headquarters Allied Powers Europe (SHAPE) was formed under General Eisenhower to establish the means by which the different military forces of the member nations could be brought under a unified command.

The threat posed by the Soviet Union was described by NATO in the following terms:

At the close of World War II Soviet forces were not demobilized to the same extent as were those of the Western Powers. Instead, a considerable programme of reorganization and training was initiated. As a result, the Soviet Union now has in being a powerful military machine. These forces, in contrast to the combined forces of the Western Powers, are controlled by a unified command and a single staff system.[8]

NATO members feared aggression by the Soviet Union, exploiting its superiority in conventional forces to attempt to spread communism into the capitalist West by force. This fear was to persist for the next four and a half decades.

MC14, the first of the NATO Strategic Guidance documents, laid the foundation of NATO military planning until the end of the Cold War; 'Precise Soviet intentions are not known and cannot be predicted with reliable accuracy. For military planning purposes, however, it is essential to consider maximum intentions and capabilities.'[9]

The guidance described the possibility of a full-scale offensive operation launched pre-emptively, leading to world-wide conflict, rather than confined to the European and North Atlantic areas.[10] The Soviet Union was expected to wage a blitzkrieg style attack against Western Europe, accompanied by, '… a heavy aerial bombardment, including atomic attack, minelaying and submarine operations against the British Isles with their drive in Western Europe.'[11] Initially, NATO strategy spoke of holding a Soviet attack as far to the east in West Germany as possible and that, '… All types of weapons, without exception, might be used by either side.'[12]

Very quickly NATO policy established a central principle of Western European defence which remained part of the threat assessment throughout the Cold War: the enemy would have numerical superiority in conventional forces. The solution was explained in the NATO Medium Term Plan;

To compensate for the numerical inferiority of the armed forces of the North Atlantic Treaty nations by establishing and maintaining technical superiority, by developing and using modern combat methods, by providing training facilities capable of expansion, and by achieving close coordination of effort.[13]

Anti-armour missile development was an example of the technical superiority which would be relied upon. This would be given high priority, '… as the availability of such equipment is likely to change materially the nature of the defensive battle.'[14] The Medium Term Plan explained the reason behind the need for a strong conventional defence:

For the defense [sic] of Western Europe, and particularly Continental Europe, it will be necessary to make a maximum initial effort with all available resources even though it may not be possible to sustain this effort, provided, by so doing, sufficient delay may be achieved to allow for reinforcement, and for the strategic air offensive to take effect.[15]

The reinforcement of Europe relied on firm control of the sea lanes of the Atlantic and English Channel. Although the WTO did not initially possess a strong surface fleet to threaten the reinforcement by sea, it developed a powerful submarine force which NATO believed would endanger their maritime freedom. This idea of sustaining the initial defence to allow the military build-up remained at the heart of NATO strategy throughout the Cold War.

At sea, the North Atlantic Ocean Group possessed, '… the principal means of controlling and securing the ocean lines of communication …'[16] The great naval strength of the Western powers was important because of the reliance on maritime communications and trade. Thus, the concepts of sea control and sea denial were vital for NATO. These eventually replaced command of the sea as the objective of the NATO navies. Much of the output of the Royal Navy was aimed at countering the threat from WTO interference with specialist Anti-Submarine Warfare ships and technology.

Under NATO's Medium Term Plan of 1950, the timescale for the achievement of the required levels of military forces was set at 1 July 1954. These timescales were reviewed following the outbreak of war in Korea, and new Force Goals were set at the Lisbon Conference in 1952.[17] The Korean War raised fears that Western Europe, divided like Korea, would be the next target of Communist aggression, and so NATO began to re-assess its strategy. Reliance on US nuclear weapons was no longer sufficient for the defence of Europe. The 1952 NATO document MC14/1 sought to expand on MC14, taking into account the strategic and political changes since 1949. The evolving threat was considered to be a strike by the USSR and its allies using its preponderance in land forces, and NATO did not consider itself to be vulnerable to sea action. Because of this re-evaluation, and the need to expand considerably the conventional forces of NATO, the timescales for readiness of increased and improved NATO conventional forces were moved to 1956. However, it was clear that the NATO countries could not afford the increase in conventional capability, and an alternative was sought.

In 1954, NATO document MC 48 identified the threat as being one of, '… Communist aggression either intentional or as a result of miscalculation.'[18] MC 48 was interim guidance pending a review of MC 14/1. Although the early NATO documents mentioned the use of atomic weapons, their relative scarcity limited what the planners expected of them. Atomic weapons had been mentioned in MC14 but in reference to an attack on the US in an attempt, '… to disrupt

Until the introduction of Polaris, the iconic Vulcan bomber formed the backbone of Britain's strategic nuclear deterrent and would have delivered part of NATO's 'massive retaliation' in response to any large Warsaw Pact act of aggression. (US DoD)

and rely on nuclear weapons for deterrence.[21] Because of the increased availability of nuclear weapons to both sides, the strategy sees an escalation to nuclear exchange as inevitable:

Since NATO would be unable to prevent the rapid overrunning of Europe unless NATO immediately employed nuclear weapons both strategically and tactically, we must be prepared to take the initiative in their use.

14. In case of general war, therefore, NATO defense [sic] depends upon an immediate exploitation of our nuclear capability, whether or not the Soviets employ nuclear weapons.[22]

the flow of reinforcements to Europe and to cause maldeployment of U.S. forces.'[19] In the early 1950s the US developed low-yield nuclear warheads which promised tactically useful weapons although the necessary doctrines and theory for their use would take time to mature. Subsequently, the operational availability of thermo-nuclear weapons to both the USA and Soviet Union, with their enormous increase in destructive power, meant that the defence of Western Europe became a different exercise, and brought about the idea of a total nuclear response to any Soviet military action.

The solution proposed to convince the Soviet Union that they could not win a war, and would be subject to a '... devastating counter-attack employing atomic weapons.'[20] Events were to quicken in the latter half of the 1950s which prompted the North Atlantic Council to prioritise a reassessment of the Soviet threat. The ferocious suppression of the Hungarian Uprising in 1956 did little to quell Western fears about the readiness of the Soviet Union to use force. The Suez Crisis of 1956 had also prompted a direct threat from the Soviet Union against Britain and France, encouraging the need to maintain the collective defence arrangements. In the following year the launch of the first artificial satellite, Sputnik, raised fears that the Soviet Union was now capable of launching devastating attacks on both Europe and the USA with little or no warning.

WTO troops were trained extensively to fight in a nuclear, biological and chemical (NBC) contaminated environment, and NATO commanders feared that the WTO would attack using a first strike of chemical and nuclear weapons, neutralising the NATO conventional forces before reinforcements could arrive. To address this concern, MC14/2, or what has been termed 'massive retaliation' or 'Trip-Wire' was adopted in 1957. While the numerical superiority that the WTO enjoyed in conventional forces was, for a while, countered by the threat of nuclear retaliation from NATO, the lead was reduced as the Soviet Union developed its own nuclear strike capability.

Although this has been termed 'Flexible Response 1' or 'Differentiated Response' the intent on the part of the US and British Governments was to limit the need for conventional forces

NATO's strategy, therefore, was one of massive retaliation, relying on the swift use of nuclear weapons to counter any aggression by the WTO. Conventional forces were to act as a trip wire, but,

… in developing the pattern of NATO military strength which would be most effective in the type of war envisaged and which would be within the available resources, priority must be given to the provision of forces-in-being capable of effectively contributing to success in the initial [nuclear] phase.[23]

With rising tension in Europe, especially over Berlin, in the late 50s and early 60s, there was disillusionment with the 'Trip-Wire' strategy for dealing with low-level, non-nuclear, or intensifying, crises. The 1961 Vienna Summit caused consternation in the West because of the threats to Berlin by the Soviet Union: in October 1961, US and Soviet tanks confronted one another at Checkpoint Charlie in Berlin: three days later, the Soviet Union exploded a 58-megaton thermonuclear weapon, the largest ever detonated.[24]

The building of the Berlin Wall in 1961 and the Cuban Missile crisis of 1962 demonstrated the additional concern that a crisis could move to war rapidly. The threat of air delivered thermonuclear weapons, and their attendant devastating power, meant countries like the UK could be devastated in days by a small number of successfully delivered weapons, possibly even hours by the new range of WTO bombers with sufficient range to directly attack the UK mainland.

The fears of starting a war through miscalculation, as the Cuban Missile Crisis so nearly demonstrated, forced the problem of nuclear reliance into the forefront of strategic policy and planning. If the WTO countries were to forcibly deny Western access to Berlin again, what strategy was available to NATO with which to respond? Soviet 'salami-slicing' techniques – small incursions or actions which could not be answered with nuclear weapons – meant the likelihood of smaller, quicker attempts to gain an advantage might increase. An all-out nuclear attack could not be countenanced for something low-level, so corresponding strategies needed to be developed. The

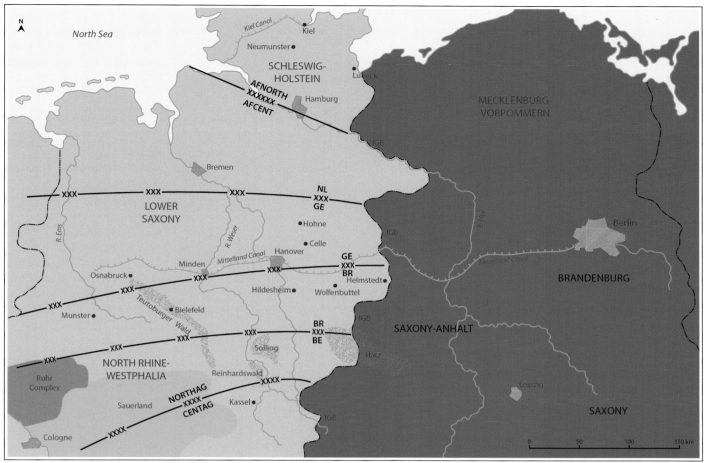

The north–south arrangement of Corps in AFCENT was commonly referred to as the 'Layer Cake'. 1 (BR) Corps formed part of NORTHAG, with 1 (GE) Corps to the north and 1 (BE) Corps to the south. It was widely thought that any major offensive in Europe by WTO ground forces would fall on the relatively open NORTHAG sector. (Map by George Anderson)

answer originated with the idea of graduated deterrence, relying ultimately on a US nuclear guarantee to the European states. This strategy promoted greater freedom of action in response to any level of aggression by the WTO. A period of warning of attack was postulated, with a conventional response to conventional attack, and a war whose duration could not be predicted.

## British Defence Policy

British post-war defence policy was a balancing act between providing for a shrinking overseas commitment and an increasing European one. Recovering from the effects of Second World War, with an underperforming economy, the cost of defence was a large part of Government spending. All the political parties looked for ways to reduce the burden on the nation. The cost of policing the Empire would need to be reduced, accomplished by divesting Britain of its colonies and overseas dominions. Membership of NATO seemed to answer the problem of preventing a new European war.

With the adoption of MC 14/3 in 1967, the NATO members had committed to increase their capability to answer conventional threats from the Warsaw Pact with a greater range of responses than had been available previously. This new posture demanded, '… sufficient ground, sea and air forces in a high state of readiness, committed to NATO for prompt, integrated action in times of tension or against any limited or major aggression.'[25] The initial post-war demand for large conventional forces was reduced by the change to massive retaliation. A great fear was that the development of a second-strike capability by the Soviet Union would mean that the USA would not be prepared to risk its own survival to defend

Europe. The answer to this was the adoption of flexible response to raise the nuclear threshold, and to tie the US more closely with the conventional defence of Europe.

The response from the UK Government was, outwardly, unstinting support of NATO and its strategy. Internally, however, the policy of the UK Government wavered as successive Governments applied different national policies, reduced the overall defence budget, and disputed the focus of the policy. Several Defence Reviews have taken place since the Second World War, most notably the Sandys, Healey, Mason and Nott reviews of 1957, 1965-68, 1974-75 and 1981 respectively. Following the withdrawal of most British forces from 'East of Suez' announced in the 1968 SDE, the focus of policy shifted to become collective defence in the shape of NATO with minimal Out-Of-Area commitments.

Evaluation of the air threat to the UK Home Base meant air defence of the UK was adopted as a NATO Region. The home islands themselves were not a NATO Region, and therefore came under national control. Some 100,000 personnel were allocated to defence of the UK. Policy for the UK looked to defend the nuclear deterrent first, with all conventional facilities in second place.

The geographical extent of Britain's standing commitment to NATO was:

**Northern Army Group (NORTHAG)**
- British Army of the Rhine (BAOR) and RAF (Germany) which was part of 2 Allied Tactical Air Force (2ATAF)

**Allied Forces Northern Europe (AFNORTH)**

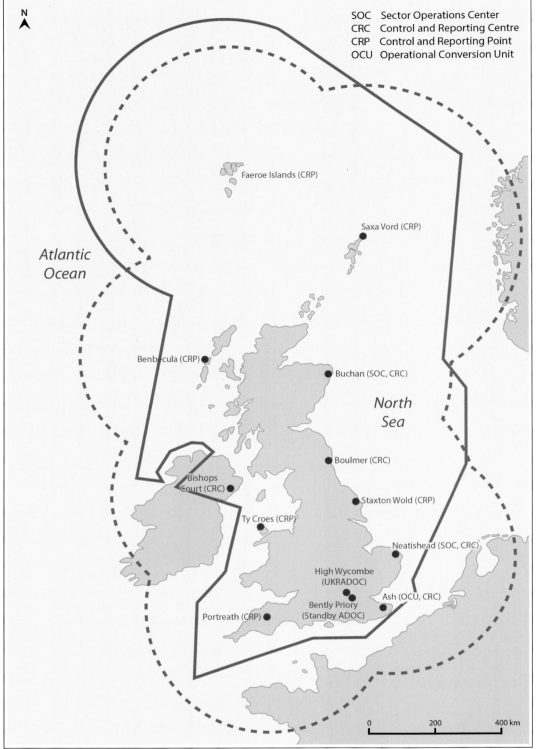

N

SOC  Sector Operations Center
CRC  Control and Reporting Centre
CRP  Control and Reporting Point
OCU  Operational Conversion Unit

Faeroe Islands (CRP)

Saxa Vord (CRP)

Atlantic
Ocean

Benbecula (CRP)

Buchan (SOC, CRC)

North
Sea

Boulmer (CRC)

Bishops
Court (CRC)

Staxton Wold (CRP)

Ty Croes (CRP)

Neatishead (SOC, CRC)

High Wycombe
(UKRADOC)

Ash (OCU, CRC)

Bently Priory
(Standby ADOC)

Portreath (CRP)

0        200        400 km

The radar cover (dotted line) and Major command posts of the United Kingdom Air Defence Region (solid line).
(Map by George Anderson)

### United Kingdom Air Defence Region (UKADR)

• RAF with UK Land Force component. Contained UKADGE (United Kingdom Air Defence Ground Environment)

Britain provided: the Deputy Supreme Allied Commander Europe (DSACEUR) who was a British General. This role was shared for a time with a German General; Commander-in-Chief, Eastern Atlantic Area (CINCEASTLANT) who was also CinC Home Fleet; CinC NORTHAG was the commanding General of BAOR.

The aim of British defence policy within NATO was to maintain deterrence for allies as well for the home islands. It was in Britain's interests to be part of an alliance that provided friendly space immediately adjacent to the British Isles. In pursuit of that policy, Britain committed nuclear and conventional forces to NATO in and around continental Europe. According to MC 48/3, the British Isles had a role in NATO to provide a base for, '… strategic counter-offensive forces and support of NATO forces in Europe.'[26] This meant that Britain's contribution was not only military personnel and weaponry, but locations, routes, ports, airports and other facilities which would be made available in times of crisis.

Britain did not face a serious military emergency following the Sandys' review of 1957, and the subsequent Labour Government felt confident in reducing the defence budget by minimising as far as possible Britain's overseas commitments. Labour's Denis Healey conducted another Defence Review between 1965 and 1968 which indicated, 'There has been no real attempt to match political commitments to military resources, still less to relate the resources made available for defence to the economic circumstances of the nation.'[27] The review sought to achieve '… a major cut in expenditure without any loss in military efficiency …'[28] Significant equipment purchases and research were cancelled. There were some dissenting voices to the manner of cuts being undertaken.

• UK Mobile Force and Royal Marine Commando Reinforcements to Denmark and Norway

### Eastern Atlantic Area (EASTLANT)

• Eastern Atlantic; Norwegian Sea. Royal Navy (RN). Commanded by Royal Navy Admiral based at Northwood. Included Standing Naval Force Atlantic (STANAVFORLANT) and Allied Command Channel (ACCHAN) which covered the English Channel and North Sea

This CVR(T) Scimitar is seen in Norway during Exercise Cold Winter '87. The British commitment to the AMF(L) included a medium reconnaissance squadron equipped with several variants of the CVR(T) family of vehicles. Although lightly armoured they also had an exceptionally low ground pressure and demonstrated excellent cross-country mobility in all ground conditions. (US DoD)

The cuts had a demonstrable effect on the capability of Britain's armed forces to fulfil their NATO obligation, but continued attempts were made to obfuscate them by Ministers and civil servants. A telling comment in a memorandum by the Secretary of State for Defence regarding the NATO report says, 'I believe … we can circumvent the difficulties over the cost of the LTDP, at any rate for the purposed of the Summit, without undertakings about the future level of the Defence Budget.'[34] This position was reinforced in a memorandum to the Defence Secretary from Michael Quinlan which identified some of the proposals in the LTDP which could be accepted, as they were, '… covered by existing plans or will cost little …'[35] The invasion of Afghanistan in 1979 gave pause, and was for some politicians and analysts confirmation of Soviet aggressive intentions. It also called into question the past decades of falling defence spending, and moved conventional defence back into the political spotlight. This came at about the same time as the broadening debate around the deployment of nuclear weapons in Europe. In Britain it provided a focus on the defence of the UK, as well as membership of NATO. CND membership rose, with the debate about nuclear disarmament extending to conventional forces, with a large minority urging the disengagement of Britain from NATO. Economically Britain was no longer strong; its aims must be planned in accordance with the available resources.

The Conservative Government of 1970-1974 made few changes to Healey's defence budget, but on Labour's return to power in 1974 a new review was announced. Labour's Defence Secretary Roy Mason conducted a review in 1975 which announced it would '… safeguard the essential security interests of Britain and her Allies …'[29] whilst reducing specialist forces (logistics, engineers and medical) and transport. The review would, '… give effect to the Government's pledge to achieve savings on defence expenditure of several hundred million pounds per annum over a period while maintaining a modern and effective defence system.'[30] Some £3,200 million would be saved in the following ten years from the equipment budget alone. However, The Expenditure Committee warned:

In the public debate on defence, the view is often expressed that the defence budget can safely be cut, with instant savings or other benefits to the economy, and with acceptable consequences for national security. Our examination of a wide range of subjects has convinced us that this view is largely fallacious.[31]

In early 1976, the Expenditure Committee of the House of Commons noted, 'The defence review decisions directly affecting the British contribution to NATO … reduce significantly some planned improvements in quantity or quality to major equipment. Not surprisingly, these measures created a good deal of concern within NATO …'[32] The effects of this were seen at the end of 1976 when the British representative at NATO was summoned by the Secretary General of NATO, Dr Joseph Luns and given what can only be described as a reprimand. Luns reminded the British Government of its obligation to notify NATO before making any cuts to defence spending, as:

… [Her Majesty's Government] had up until now asserted that cuts made were not having a quantitative or qualitative effect on our NATO contribution, but it was no longer possible for the Alliance to take the British Government's word for this.[33]

Fred Mulley, Labour's Defence Secretary between 1976 and 1979, referred to the defence budget cuts made under Healey as 'crazy' and which had left the home islands almost undefended. John Nott later said that, '… it could be argued … that the reviews of the '60s and '70s went too far …'[36] Following the election of Margaret Thatcher's Conservative Government in 1979, and in line with its monetarist policies, the 1981 Defence Review reported, '… hard decisions … reflect our resolve to give defence the resources Britain's security demands … in accordance with realistic, unsentimental and up-to-date judgement of what will be most relevant and effective in future years.'[37] The Royal Navy surface fleet was to suffer the most from the 1981 review, but the effects of the Falklands War in 1982 reversed some of the cuts, however briefly.

Concerns were raised about maintaining an effective force in Germany because of the cuts and relocation of some units and headquarters back to the UK. The House of Commons Defence Committee (HCDC) reported in 1982 that, 'It is accepted in BAOR that some of the economies must affect efficiency, although in general it is claimed that operational effectiveness should be maintained if not enhanced.'[38] The Chiefs of the Defence Staff expressed their concern in a meeting with the Prime Minister: 'The Soviet threat had increased. NATO had not succeeded in improving its position. The resolve of its members seemed, if anything, to have weakened … This was no time for Britain to be planning reductions.'[39] The

Secretary of State for Defence responded to a question in Parliament regarding this matter: 'Some reductions in planned expenditure have been made in order to contain the overspend … to protect current operational capability.'[40] The cuts were announced as efficiency drives, but were financially driven. As Sir John Nott later noted, '… that was at the heart of the defence review: money, money.'[41] Manufacturing of weapon systems and ammunition is an area of foreign sales which was and is extremely valuable to the British economy. A balance must be struck between providing for the Armed Forces and foreign sales, such that both are satisfied, but which tends to work for the dissatisfaction of both. The MoD cautioned, for example, 'The balance between output [of Skyflash missiles], RAF requirements and any export orders will have need careful review before any sales commitments are undertaken.'[42] Even major weapon systems earmarked for the Services were not immune. RAF Tornados were sold to Saudi Arabia in 1985 as part of an arms deal with British Aerospace, their Director of Sales commenting, 'The Chief of the Air Staff learnt that we had nicked

ten of his aircraft. No one told him.'[43] Once approval for the purchase of new or updated systems for the Armed Forces had been received, there was a necessary compromise between purchasing weapons and ammunition, making it, according to the MoD, '… necessary to review outfits and reserves in this context to ensure the correct balance between expenditure on … their weapon systems and on the weapons themselves.'[44] Each Service urged more spending on its own needs, even if that was at the expense of the others.

Following the end of the Cold War, the 'Peace Dividend' identified in *Options For Change* was at the forefront of decision making. 'The Government has a clear strategy for future defence policy … based on the ability to adapt to change … the maintenance of force structures … and the continuing pursuit of value for money.'[45] The Services ability to adapt to change was predicated on a very long, uninterrupted run-up to a potential conflict. Very few seemed to take heed of the advice that '… the post-Cold War world would be less stable and predictable.'[46]

# 2
# THREAT ASSESSMENT FROM 1967

Between 1945 and 1991 NATO assessed the threat from the Soviet Union, and later the WTO, in three broad categories. Immediately post-war, the threat was based on conventional numerical superiority. Following the Soviet detonation of its atomic, and then thermonuclear devices, the threat became parity or superiority in nuclear weapons. Once near-parity became a reality, the threat moved to a progressive qualitative improvement in conventional

arms, with updated tactics, to complement the continued numerical superiority.

The strategy, doctrine and policy for conventional deterrence had developed throughout the life of NATO, along with the nuclear deterrent. NATO strategy had to find a balance that did not destabilise deterrence, whilst also managing potential crises. The conventional aspect of collective European defence was central from

US M110A2 203mm howitzers offload as part of REFORGER '84 (variously REinFORce GERmany or REturn of FORces to GERmany). This plan was regularly exercised throughout the 1970s and 80s. (US DoD)

the very first days of the North Atlantic Council (NAC).

With the collapse of Détente in the late 1970s, the build-up of WTO forces, and the apparent disparity between East and West in military terms, the complacency brought about by the earlier thaw in international relations was replaced by urgent demands to strengthen the Western European defences.

Although MC 14/3 placed much greater emphasis on the provision of conventional forces, their combat endurance, their capabilities and the deterrent effect they might have, at approximately the same time the US Government withdrew several divisions of troops from the Central Front in West Germany. Subsequently Britain moved some regular forces back to the UK. NATO strategy and associated plans assumed that before any war there would be a progressive deterioration of international relations. Although there were plans to reinforce the Central

The threat. The T-64 had been developed in great secrecy by the Soviet Union during the 1960s and included advanced armour and an automatic loader for the powerful 125mm 2A46 gun. While it had great potential it was also plagued with development problems and slowly entered service with the Group of Soviet Ground Forces in the late 1970s into the 1980s. The T-64, T-72 and T-80 had many similar features and initially were often confused by NATO observers. (Open source)

Front from the US, known as REFORGER,[1] and from the UK, the delay inherent in the mobilisation and transport of these troops increased the time needed to attain full conventional readiness.

Between 1968 and 1977, the Joint Intelligence Committee (JIC) assessed the threat from the WTO included an additional 100 nuclear-powered submarines, 260 new major warships, the equivalent of a further six infantry divisions and 2,000 tanks, and some 250 new aircraft.[2] Despite the alarm caused by reports such as this in NATO, little determined action had been taken to correct the developing imbalance.

A UK assessment reassuringly concluded that NATO would receive 20 days' firm warning of WTO conventional force mobilisation. Other sources expressed an increasing concern that a limited attack could be launched with no more than 48 hours' warning. The US Government concluded that the WTO force structure was designed for an intensive war in Europe, and the UK MoD agreed with this assessment. But the assumption used by the UK Government in official plans reflected the official NATO line that there would be a steady deterioration of international relations over a period of several weeks before the outbreak of any hostilities. This appeared to be the politicians' 'fall-back' position when discussing the Defence Estimates. The intelligence analysis was not so comforting, however. The JIC produced an assessment that stated only two weeks would be necessary for the WTO to prepare for war, or only two days in some cases. Given the probable caution on the part of NATO countries to mobilise fully, the very real fear was the WTO could achieve mobilisation before the NATO forces were even partially prepared. The Soviet military preparations for the invasion of Czechoslovakia in 1968 brought this into sharp focus, with an apparent disconnection in Western Government circles between the developing political situation and understanding the ultimate

Soviet military objective. This highlighted the problem NATO Governments had identifying WTO intentions, and activating political will in enough time to act. Even with two weeks' warning, it was unlikely that all of the United Kingdom Armed Forces could be brought to full readiness in their correct locations. NATO put in place projects, such as the Long Term Defence Programme (LTDP), to address the evident deficiencies.

In parallel with the military urgings to improve defence, much Labour Government time was spent during the years of détente pressing for multilateral force reductions and negotiating the Mutual and Balanced Force Reductions (MBFR). The Soviet Government had declared a readiness to talk about force reductions in 1972, but despite continuing negotiations, little progress was made. In 1973 the MoD viewpoint of these talks was largely pessimistic:

In general terms, even if land force reductions in the Central Region were negotiated on a mutual basis as favourable to NATO as could reasonably be envisaged, our studies indicate that there would still be a grave risk that a major conventional WP aggression could result in defeat for the Alliance before the enemy's reserve divisions had been committed. In these circumstances the possibility of a quick win might induce the Soviet Union to take risks which the possibility of more protracted operations will probably always deter them from taking.[3]

A cooling of relations began towards the end of the 1970s, and the increasing conventional military build-up by the WTO gave momentum to NATO to reassess the threat posed by the WTO. Dr Joseph Luns, Secretary General of NATO, in his Ministerial Guidance for 1977, wrote;

It is in the conventional field … where the growth of the Warsaw Pact capability has been most pronounced. In particular, the Warsaw Pact ground forces have the capabilities to stage a major offensive in Europe without reinforcement. The improved offensive and deep penetration capabilities of the Warsaw Pact tactical air forces now permit the Warsaw Pact to conduct the initial stages of an air attack to a greater extent than hitherto, with in-place forces. The capabilities of the Soviet Union to exercise sea power all around the world have been enhanced by the introduction of new and improved ships, submarines and aircraft.[4]

Détente ended following the Soviet invasion of Afghanistan and the election of Ronald Reagan as US President.

The JIC warned that, 'The Marxist-Leninist philosophy of the Soviet leadership assumes that some form of conflict between communism and capitalism is inevitable.'[5] Although WTO 'Opportunism' featured in MC 14/3, the broad threat, as assessed by NATO and the British Government, was of an attack by the WTO on the flanks of NATO with not less than 48 hours' warning: directly across the IGB by large armoured conventional thrusts, including at least two tank armies in the 1(BR) Corps sector: air attacks on all NATO members; and denial by the Soviet Navy of NATO maritime freedoms. The Chiefs of Staff Committee acknowledged in 1980 that the improving Soviet navy and air forces particularly were, '… better equipped and more adventurous now than they have ever been; their capability representing a formidable instrument for the exploitation of air power.'[6] The scale of the changes in equipment levels was illustrated by the intelligence evaluation of WTO aircraft production, which every six months was supposed to exceed the entire front-line strength of the RAF. Improvements in tank development – for example the deployment of the T-64 and T-80 – and anti-aircraft defence – the new range of Surface-to-Air Missiles (SAM) and anti-aircraft artillery (AAA) – meant that the forces deployed in Eastern Europe were not only quantitatively superior to NATO but approaching qualitative parity as well. The defence spending of the Soviet Union continued to take up an estimated 12-13 percent of GDP, with their technological capability demonstrably narrowing the gap with the West. The Soviet Union had extended its reach into space, threatening communication and intelligence gathering satellites when they conducted a successful orbital interception of a satellite in March 1981.

Early warning in a crisis allowing reinforcement of the Central Front would be decisive for NATO. It had a direct impact on the ability to reinforce the standing forces in Europe, which was vital to the success of any defence. From a previously firm warning period of two weeks, the possibility was now down to one week's warning of the WTO achieving full war posture. The Secretary of State for Defence was concerned that:

Short-warning aggression … is far more attractive to the Soviet Union and more dangerous to NATO … and in such circumstances seaborne Transatlantic reinforcement might simply become irrelevant.[7]

A 1981 JIC assessment could be no more precise than saying that, '… Warning times are … assessed as remaining at "not less than 48 hours".'[8] The Government War Book (GWB) indicated that the most likely period of warning would be one to two weeks, but contemporary and subsequent exercises used three weeks' or more warning time.

As the WTO looked to new operational and tactical developments, the threat assessment by NATO altered to one of purely conventional operations without reliance on the initial use of nuclear weapons. Leonid Brezhnev, General Secretary of the Central Committee of the Communist Party of the Soviet Union, had looked for agreement with the USA in the 1970s regarding 'strategic sufficiency' of nuclear weapons. This position was reinforced by Brezhnev's announcement in 1982 that the Soviet Union unilaterally, '… assumes an obligation not to be the first to use nuclear weapons.'[9] Utilising doctrinal, positional and political differences within the NATO Alliance, it was feared the WTO planners would seek to exploit speed and numbers to achieve victory. A NATO report from 1984 stated that the WTO forces are, '… organised and equipped to take the offensive right from the beginning of a conflict.'[10] Soviet doctrine had always espoused speed and mass, and the latest iteration of this was the Operational Manoeuvre Group. Intended to break into the rear areas of NATOs defences, this was of deep concern to NATO commanders. The direct threat to the forces in Europe is summed up in the Battle Notes for 1(BR) Corps: 'Soviet military doctrine requires that offensive operations are mounted by a superiority of tanks, infantry and artillery … The primary aim of such operations will be the destruction of NATO's defensive capability …'[11] The doctrine relied on an attack making a quick breakthrough of the 'crust' of NATO's 'Forward Defence'. General Bagnall, Commander-in-Chief of the British Army of the Rhine and Commander of NATO's Northern Army Group, experienced the potential effects during a wargame with a Soviet trained Afghan officer, Colonel Wardak, in 1983. Colonel Wardak had escaped from Afghanistan after the Soviet invasion. General Bagnall invited him to a wargame at 1(BR) corps HQ where Wardak employed the training he had received at the Voroshilov General Staff Academy in Moscow. By using an attack on the British sector, he fixed the British forces with frontal attacks and forced them to commit their reserves. On doing so, his WTO forces surrounded 1(BR) and 1(GE) by breaking through the Corps on the flanks, achieving total victory.

A variety of reports and assessments were prepared covering not only the direct threat in West Germany and Scandinavia, but the maritime and air threat in Europe and against the Home Islands. These highlighted changes in the WTO's dispositions and capabilities. As the WTO forces expanded and the range and capabilities of their aircraft and weapons improved, the air threat to the UK would increase. In the conventional phase of war, attacks on vital infrastructure and installations could be expected. In the latter half of the 1970s, the direct threat to the UK was assessed in detail as being from sea and air launched conventional weapons. The threat of chemical attacks was also considered to be very real. Invasion from the sea or air was considered extremely unlikely. During the conventional phase of war:

… a considerable Soviet air effort will be allocated to attacking targets in the United Kingdom with conventional weapons. The targets selected could include our nuclear installations, air bases, air defence facilities, fuel and ammunition dumps, dockyards and transportation facilities associated with the movement of Allied reinforcements to Europe.[12]

The Chiefs of Staff Committee (COS) recognised that conventional attack would cause problems: 'Neutralisation of ports and airfields which were to receive reinforcements could be more effective militarily in the early stages of a conflict – and perhaps less escalatory – than attempts to neutralise theatre nuclear assets.'[13]

Originally misidentified as the Tu-26, the Tu-22M 'Backfire' was a variable geometry bomber used in significant numbers by the Soviet Long Range and Naval Aviation. While capable of conventional bombing it would have been much more effective in its role as a stand-off weapon platform to launch long-range missiles (Kh-22/AS-4 Kitchen or KSR-5/AS-6 Kingfish) for land or naval strike, with conventional or nuclear warheads. (US DoD)

The Su-24 'Fencer' was a highly capable variable geometry strike aircraft able to employ a wide range of advanced free-fall and guided weapons. It would have potentially posed a great threat to NATO installations. (US DoD)

Though aging, the Tu-16 'Badger' was still employed in a variety of roles by the Soviet Long Range and Naval Aviation, including reconnaissance, electronic warfare and conventional and nuclear stand-off attack with KSR-5/AS-6 Kingfish missiles. (US DoD)

This struck directly at the choke points for defence of the Home Islands, British reinforcements to Europe, and for US and Canadian reinforcements transiting through the UK. It also raised the question of Britain's capability to resist such attacks, and to maintain its mobilisation and reinforcement plans.

The United Kingdom Commanders-In-Chief Committee (Home) (UKCICC(H)) considered the air threat to be primarily against the conventional and nuclear war fighting capabilities of the UK, followed by air defence and transportation facilities. In part of the study on the maritime force structure for 1987, the air threat is identified as being against the UK Air Defence System, notably an attack on the shore-based early warning installations, with follow up attacks on the fighter, Airborne Early Warning and tanker bases. This was considered potentially to have a dramatic effect on the UK's ability to defend the airspace and waters adjacent to the islands, particularly the Channel and North Sea. An attack such as this would make further penetration raids less costly for the WTO, allowing them to attack transport facilities and infrastructure, headquarters, and other installations. Another assessment identifies the nuclear strike forces as being the highest priority. This assessment considers that the operational level of defence in Europe had a direct effect on the weight of attack that the UK could expect to receive. 'Should the battle in the Central Region go badly for NATO ... assuming the nuclear threshold had not been passed ... more of [the WTO] aircraft would be able to reach the UK ...'[14] The implication is that even with the expected attrition of the long-range WTO bombers, the UK would be subject to increasing aerial attack as the war progressed. If airfields nearer to the UK were captured, the WTO Tactical Air Force had several ground attack aircraft available in large numbers which would be able to reach the UK islands.

The WTO's air forces had changed in character from short-range, low-payload aircraft intended for close air support and interception to longer range, heavier payload capable aircraft designed to penetrate NATO airspace. The WTO objectives would be to degrade the UK Air Defence, attack reinforcement bases and airfields. The threat to the UK would be mainly from the Soviet Long Range Air Force (LRAF) and the Naval Air Force (NAF) and that approximately one third of the available force in the West would be used against the UK. In 1979, the Soviet LRAF comprised 756 aircraft, most of which were capable of carrying stand-off ASMs. Approximately 75 percent were based in Europe and the Western USSR. The NAF comprised 770 aircraft, whilst the Air Force comprised approximately 4,650 combat aircraft. Most of the aircraft of latter two would not be available, or indeed able, to reach the UK, except for the medium and long-range bombers of the Naval Air Force.

The threat was evaluated as being equivalent to 229 sorties on the first day of hostilities attacking 12 targets. In another report from around the same time the capability analysis was slightly different. This report read, 'It is estimated that the threat to UK will consist of about 120 sorties per day by the Long Range Air Force, mostly Backfire, and 120 Fencer sorties per day by the tactical force. In addition a number of reconnaissance sorties by Foxbat should be expected.'[15] In yet another assessment of the same time, the threat was expected to be, '... one-third of the [Long Range Air] force [of approximately 550] ... available for operations against the UK base.'[16] This meant estimates ranged between approximately 180 and 240

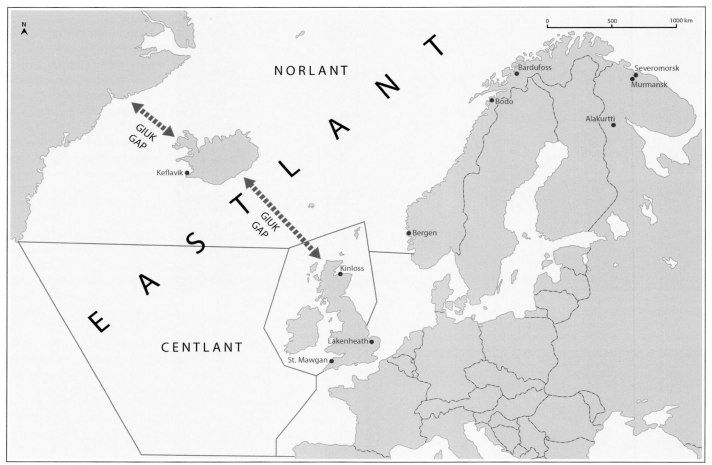

EASTLANT and the Greenland–Iceland–United Kingdom Gap. It was believed that one of the key indicators of pending war would be the sortieing of Soviet submarines from their bases at Severomorsk and Murmansk on the Kola Peninsula. In order to reach the North Atlantic and intercept shipping from North America to Europe the Soviet forces would have to transit the GIUK Gap. This thus became the focus of much of NATO's naval attention. (Map by George Anderson)

sorties against the UK base at the beginning of hostilities. Identified within these reports were key targets which were airfields, Early Warning radar systems, naval bases and operational HQs.

The main air threat was identified as four key aircraft. The Sukhoi Su-24 (FENCER) was an interdiction/strike aircraft capable of reaching the UK from airbases in Eastern Europe. This did not have the weapon carrying capability of some other Soviet aircraft but was available in large numbers. The Tupolev Tu-16 (BADGER) was a medium bomber: The Tupolev Tu-22 (BLINDER) was a high altitude, fast bomber; The Tupolev Tu-26 (BACKFIRE) was a long-range bomber capable of reaching the whole of the UK from East Germany.[17] This aircraft also posed a threat to NATO and allied shipping in the north-eastern Atlantic. In 1978 the Secretary of State for Defence had told the Prime Minister:

The new Soviet 'Backfire' bomber was the main problem … The Backfire bombers … would probably fly very low en route to the UK, thereby beating our radar warning system. Against this, we were improving our radar coverage through the Nimrod flying radar system; and we were also developing the capacity to refuel fighter aircraft in the air. The Nimrods would be operational in 1982.[18]

Older aircraft, such as the Tupolev Tu-20 (BEAR) and Myasishchev M-4 (BISON) were still available but were expected to be phased out of the WTO arsenal by the early-to-mid 1980s. The MiG-23 (FLOGGER) is not mentioned in the main assessments as it is not a strategic bomber, but it would be a threat in substantial

numbers if flown from East German, or captured NATO, airfields. Low-flying penetrating aircraft such as the MiG-23 were a clearly identified threat that resulted in the AWACS development, aimed at preventing mass attacks which could overwhelm the anti-aircraft defence. As most MoD plans indicate that things would definitely 'go badly' in the Central Region, air defence of the UK would become more difficult over time, especially as the forces and supplies available for defence were limited both in number and sustainability. Attacks by large numbers of aircraft were also a serious threat to the naval forces in Allied Command Channel (ACCHAN) and the Eastern Atlantic Area (EASTLANT).

In addition to the air threat, the maritime threat was closely analysed with reports about Soviet merchant fleet operations, amphibious capabilities and anti-ship missiles amongst others. The WTO navies, primarily that of the Soviet Union, showed an increase in numbers of various types of significant vessel, such as submarines, cruisers and aircraft carriers, as well as improvements in technology, turning it from a coastal force to a true blue-water navy. The UK served as a base for NATO maritime reconnaissance and attack covering the Greenland-Iceland-UK (GIUK) gap against Soviet naval forces trying to break out into the Atlantic. Because of this, maritime operations against the UK coastal facilities increasingly offered the WTO an attractive option, especially mining ports and anchorages, direct missile attack on shore based or near-inland facilities, and interference with shipping and access routes to and around the islands. Britain relied heavily on imports of food and fuel for everyday life, and the threat was outlined in a report from the Defence Operational Planning Staff (DOP) thus:

This British infantryman taking part in Exercise Crusader '80 may have been playing the role of opposition forces, as indicated by the soft DPM cap with a band of coloured tape. In a real conflict British forces at home and abroad could have expected WTO Special Forces to disguise themselves in NATO uniforms and operate in rear areas. (US DoD)

The maintenance of food and other supplies to the United Kingdom in the face of this maritime threat will be vital should the period of conventional hostilities be prolonged. Surface launched conventional missiles, primarily intended for use against surface shipping, could be used against prominent coastal targets.[19]

This posed a threat to the reinforcement and resupply by sea, especially if mining of ports was effected clandestinely before the outbreak of hostilities. A crisis would require large numbers of ships to be docked and unloaded as military personnel and supplies were received from Canada and the USA. These would need clear, quick access to major ports and anchorages along the south and west coasts of Britain. The Royal Navy considered that protection against the mining of ports and harbours would be difficult to achieve. A Royal Navy Captain commented in a letter to his Member of Parliament (MP), '… when all the 'Ton' class [minesweepers] have gone in the near future, we may have enough of the costly 'Brecons' to keep one port clear at any one time …'[20]

A direct invasion of the UK by air or sea during a general war in Europe was discounted by the MoD, with the main land-based threat considered to be subversion, industrial action, sabotage, and terrorist activity. The MoD anticipated the WTO would introduce Special Forces into the UK for these purposes. Naval forces would be used to land Special Forces units on the British coast for sabotage attack but were not expected to make serious attempts to attack or land large numbers of troops. Britain's Army was very experienced in counter-insurgency tasks, with their expertise honed in Northern Ireland and other low-level conflicts. Many of the troops with this experience had rotated from BAOR, and in the event of war would have been deployed in West Germany. This left the TA and reservists, who constituted the bulk of United Kingdom Land Forces (UKLF). The reservists would be inexperienced handling sabotage and subversion.

The Government expected the WTO to provide support for dissident and terrorist groups, as well as political organisations that were deemed a threat. Military Aid to the Civil Authority (MACA) was supposed to be available to counter any danger from sabotage, but the number of potential targets for sabotage was large. The defence of installations on land relied on enough time to mobilise in the event of war, otherwise those installations would be vulnerable. The establishment of Key Point defence and Ground Defence Areas would necessarily have to happen very early in any crisis. This was problematic as the Army, '… would, until mobilisation is complete, have insufficient forces to meet its commitments.'[21]

The defensive strategy of NATO did not exclude, once a war had begun, strikes at the enemy forces in their rear areas or homelands, or counter-attacks against enemy penetrations. Indeed, part of the doctrine for the air force was to attack enemy forces deep within Eastern countries with the intention of stopping their progress into the West. This was known as 'Follow-on Forces Attack' (FOFA) was adopted and incorporated as part of NATO's overall strategic doctrine. In the event of war, FOFA sought to attack the Warsaw Pact second-echelon units relying on the technological advantage of NATO targeting and delivery of munitions. FOFA was not new. Large scale attacks on lines of communication from the air has been exploited in almost all conventional conflicts from the beginning of the Second World War onwards. FOFA was meant to exploit the accuracy of new, guided munitions to make the impact of interdiction much more effective. Despite the increased accuracy, collateral damage was to be expected in the chaos of war. This argument follows the course that striking a location where an enemy unit is transiting will ultimately save the lives of one's own armed forces or population. Always a controversial area of military operations, it requires an aggressive use of force aimed at reducing the war-fighting capability of the enemy and accepting that collateral damage in terms of civilian deaths and destruction of property will occur. The intention of this action is that, by waging this type of war, the enemy's ability to wage its war against you is diminished, and the losses to your armed forces and civilians are equally reduced. The utility is a shorter war, with ultimately fewer casualties. NATO, being a democratically based organisation of freely joined members, has always been careful to phrase such thinking in terms considered the least alarming for the civilian populations of countries where fighting might take place. This would inevitably have been West Germany, at least initially. The West Germans were fully aware of this, and their response was Forward Defence in conjunction with FOFA: defence would be employed as close to the IGB as possible, with minimum loss of ground to the invading forces. That way damage to the country would be minimised.

Between 1967 and 1991 the official NATO strategy remained Flexible Response, with minor operational adjustments to NATO and national doctrine as described above. The policy making in NATO was based on the assessment of the threat made by the Military Committee in NATO and the Defence Ministries of the member nations. An estimate of the forces required to counter it was made from these assessments. What NATO defined as 'adequate' forces was the subject of the Force Proposals and Force Goals, presented by the Military Committee of NATO to the member nations for their consideration. Whether those forces were adequate or not would depend very much on their size, strength and endurance.

# 3
# PLANNING

## Force Proposals and Force Goals

Force Proposals were presented to NATO by the Major NATO Commanders, based on their individual assessments, and examined by the Military Committee and the Defence Review Committee. A procedure, adopted in 1977 meant that the International Military Staffs, along with national staff officers and Major NATO Commanders' (MNC) representatives carried out a review of the Proposals. Further reviews by the Military Committee and Risk Assessments followed. The Proposals then returned to the Defence Planning Committee for further consideration. The Military Committee, along with the Major NATO Commanders, then decided which of the Proposals were amended, deleted or deferred, based on the constraints identified by the Defence Review Committee. National Governments could seek to change the Proposals or oppose them in both the Defence Planning Committee and Military Committee. Following this process, the Proposals were adopted as NATO Force Goals by the Defence Planning Committee.

The Force Goals laid out each category that was to be implemented and the NATO requirement in terms of numbers and capability. These Force Goals were then turned in to Force Plans. These plans were an attempt to reconcile national Force Plans with the NATO Goals. The Government representatives identified the best match between their own plans and the Goals in the Defence Planning Questionnaire. This then developed into the Five Year Force Plan where forces were formally committed to NATO.

It was crucial for the strategy of NATO that the conventional forces and facilities under Flexible Response should be able to provide a defence against the WTO, giving time for reinforcements and resupply to arrive. If it was not possible to maintain these conventional forces in action, then the nuclear threshold would have been reached very much sooner. Because of the change in strategic outlook within NATO, greater emphasis was to be placed on providing fully capable conventional forces, ready to move into their warfighting positions. In the early 1980s the proposed increase in conventional forces, in response to the expansion of WTO forces, and the invasion of Afghanistan, had been accepted, '… by national commitments to the biennially agreed NATO Force Goals.'[1]

The limitations of the Force Planning cycle were clear: no Government was duty bound to implement the plans. Each could, and did, plan for their own national security, sometimes to the exclusion of NATO requirements. In the UK, no cost/low cost aspects of the Plans were prioritised. In 1981, only 57 percent of the UK Force Goals were to be fully implemented.

## NATO Initiatives

Throughout the 1960s and 1970 NATO members sought to make budget cuts in defence, some by moving troops to their home country to improve balance-of-payments deficits, others by simply reducing the force numbers. To try and reverse the deficiencies these cuts left, NATO instituted several corrective initiatives. These focussed on readiness, planning, reserves and sustainability and the improvement in the use of technology over different areas of the force structure. These initiatives were meant to be outside of the normal planning process but were eventually subsumed into it.

## AD-70

Improvements in NATO's conventional forces were required following the adoption of MC14/3. Alliance Defence in the Seventies (AD-70) was a detailed analysis of the expected problems to be faced in the 1970s by NATO. The proposals addressed specific areas of improvement to NATO's conventional defence forces. There were eight areas which required attention: armour and anti-armour; air defence (hardened aircraft shelters); ASW and maritime surveillance; maldeployment of forces in the Central Region; the flanks; mobilisation; communications; and war reserves. However, as the areas of defence requiring attention re-emerged in the Long Term Defence Programme, AD-70 was not wholly successful.

## Long Term Defence Programme (LTDP)

As NATO became increasingly uneasy about the military build-up of the WTO, concern was voiced at several NAC meetings that, '… the sustained growth in the Warsaw Pact countries' military power, on land, at sea and in the air [is] beyond levels apparently justified for defensive purposes.'[2] The US put forward a series of initiatives to strengthen NATO's conventional defences. These initiatives were aimed at improving the military capability of NATO member countries from the low point of the mid/late-1960s, and to solve particular problems still associated with moving away from the trip-wire to the flexible response strategy. At the 1977 NATO London Summit meeting the decision was taken to adopt the initiatives. This became the Long Term Defence Programme (LTDP).[3] The priorities in the LTDP for Britain were sustainability, improving readiness and communications, and enhancing the speed of mobilisation and deployment. In the view of the MoD, the LTDP was intended '… to arrest and if possible reverse the drop [in comparison to the WTO] …'[4] Plans were also proposed to increase defence spending by 3 percent in real terms from 1979 until 1984.

Initially the ten task forces were to consider 123 measures, but these had increased to more than 150 by 1981. As an example of the classification of responsibilities within the task forces, 'Task Force 1 – Readiness' dealt with measures related to speed of response to a crisis, and the cost associated with improvements. The, '… Main Action Areas addressed were:

- Armour and Anti-armour weapons
- Nuclear, Biological, Chemical (protection and weaponry)
- Ammunition Uploading
- Air-to-surface munitions
- Operational Readiness Test Programme [ORTP]
- Malstationing and malpositioning
- Commitment of force to NATO
- The Alert System[5]

Task Force 2 looked at the reinforcement of Europe, which required the earmarking of civilian transportation facilities for use in a crisis. Reserve Mobilisation, addressed by Task Force 3, was more problematic. The UK was also not prepared to accept the need to increase training, and certainly did not accept the automatic triggering of mobilisation. Maritime commitments were hit hardest from the list of Task Force 4 goals, especially after the 1981 SDE. A shortage of ships and maritime reconnaissance aircraft was the most pressing concern from NATO, and the UK responded by suggesting that qualitative improvements and survivability would offset the reduction in numbers. Likewise, Task Force 5, Air Defence, would be subject to, '… studies in greater depth …' because of the cost. Task Forces 6, 7 and 8 looked at Communications, Electronic Warfare and Rationalisation, and were all generally welcomed, although subject to further study by the MoD. LTDP Task Force 9, '… concluded that NATO has not the logistic support required for the strategy of flexible response …'[6] and thus would rely on early use of nuclear weapons, or the hope of a short war. The situation had not improved by 1989, with the British Government still unable, or unwilling, to invest in a War Maintenance Reserve that would last more than a few days.

There was a distinct divide between the US and the UK regarding the commitment to the LTDP. In many cases Britain was prepared to endorse the overall programme rather than endorse the objectives themselves.

## Short Term Initiatives

The increase in WTO numbers and capabilities worried the NATO ministers sufficiently to prompt the development of measures to correct quickly some obvious problems with conventional defence in Europe, rather than wait for the LTDP to take effect. The apparent capability of the WTO to attack at short notice was a direct threat to the mobilisation plans of the NATO members. In the past, NATO expected a warning period of several weeks, but now reports suggested that any warning would be very limited. Small modifications to the provision of guided weapons and readiness of troops for deployment were also identified. A third troop of Striker vehicles was to be provided for reinforcement to BAOR,[7] and alterations to the deployment of troops to Northern Ireland meant that fewer troops would be withdrawn from BAOR. An increase in Harrier availability, the purchase of 10,000 additional 'Jezebel' sonobuoys and additional at-sea refuelling capability were included in the short-term measures. Field exercises were undertaken to ascertain and, if necessary, redefine the turn-around times for aircraft operations. As part of the improvement measures, two River-class BP tankers were to be fitted out to refuel combatant ships at sea.

The LTDP died away in the early 1980s. The programme had been resisted by the NATO bureaucracy, as it attempted to work outside of the force planning cycle. The final LTDP report was issued in 1983.

## Conventional Defence Improvement Initiative (CDI(I))

This is a little known, and little studied, initiative which began in 1985 with the intention of, '… achieving our objective of improving our conventional defences.'[8] It sought to deal with the deficiencies still present in NATO's conventional defence posture following the LTDP. The (CDI)I was introduced by General Bernard Rogers, SACEUR from 1979 to 1987, and became part of NATO's defence framework. Rogers expressed his opinion that NATO conventional defences were inadequate when compared to the conceptual requirements. Although the CDI(I) was a US initiative, the US Government attempted to avoid appearing to impose its own agenda. The West German Government sponsored the initiative, which was adopted by the NATO defence ministers in December 1984.

The CDI(I) identified military deficiencies, such as improving munitions supplies and planning. The initiative sought to modernise equipment in the Armed Forces, increase convergence of national and Alliance planning, exploit emerging technologies, as well as to,

Striker was the dedicated ATGW variant of the CVR(T) family of light vehicles. Each carried five ready to fire SWINGFIRE ATGW and a further five reloads. The missile operator could dismount and fire the missiles while separated, allowing the vehicle to remain behind a crestline while still able to fire. SWINGFIRE was a large, heavy missile with a range of 4,000m and capable of defeating most Warsaw Pact armour. The system would be upgraded with a thermal imaging sight in the mid-1980s. (US DoD)

… acquire more ammunition stocks for selected battle decisive systems. The results are promising particularly in the Central Region. Most nations plan more rapid progress towards achieving the 30-day objective in the selected high priority items and there have also been improvements in plans for other ammunition items …[9]

It was telling that, after fifteen years of Flexible Response, and six years of the Long Term Defence Programme, ammunition supply, readiness and planning were still problematic.

## NATO Alert System

Preparation for war depended on how soon NATO could identify an impending assault, how long it would then take to mobilise the forces, and how long it would need to position those forces where they were needed. The timeline for transition to war can be compiled from the exercises undertaken during the late 70s and early 80s.

NATO had three States to the overall alert system; Military Vigilance; Counter Surprise Military System; and Formal Alert. The Formal Alert System measures have a two-stage process for their implementation. Firstly, the request by an MNC must be approved unanimously by the member states. Secondly, the measure is declared, and the separate nations must implement it as soon as possible. This process could be bypassed in an emergency by the MNC making the declaration of Simple or Reinforced alert themselves.

## State of Military Vigilance

Military Vigilance covered periods of delicate relations or rising tensions and required low scale preparation to facilitate a faster transition to higher readiness later. The measures could be implemented unobtrusively and in a very short time.

## Counter-Surprise Military System

These were defensive military actions that needed to be taken quickly in response to, or the threat of, attack with little or no warning, and were not dealt with by the Formal Alert System. These were broken down into ORANGE, which was an indication of possible attack, and SCARLET that required immediate action. The Counter-

Surprise system was meant to deal with rapid or surprise attacks and involved defensive military actions to enable NATO forces to survive such an attack.

### Formal Alert System

These were a series of actions required to complete an orderly transition from peace to war. This has three stages – SIMPLE was the first step which initiated full deployment of all forces assigned to NATO and should be completed as discreetly as possible. Some of the Measures this required would be impossible to implement discreetly; for example, calling-out the reserves and the Ulster Defence Regiment, and ceasing public duties for military units in London and Scotland. REINFORCED was the second stage and should have resulted in the highest level of readiness for NATO forces. Finally, GENERAL marked the transition from peace to war, and would be declared on or immediately after hostilities commence.

## BRITISH PLANNING – TRANSITION TO WAR

### The British Government War Book

The United Kingdom's plans for preparation and prosecution of a war needed to be co-ordinated with those of NATO, as the Government position was that the country would not be engaged in a general war except in support of NATO. According to the British Government, the NATO Alert System, '… is primarily concerned with arrangement for those military forces which will come under the Major NATO Commanders' (MNC) operational command…'[10] but does include some civil actions required to support those military arrangements. The national system, and in particular the United Kingdom's Government War Book (GWB), covers a multitude of military and civil actions. The civil actions had time dependencies on, '… constitutional, political, economic and administrative considerations rather than on international military requirements or assessments.'[11] However, a close analysis of the Government War Book shows that some of the military actions, especially those involving transport, were dependent on these matters as well.

The Government War Book catalogues and describes the actions necessary in a crisis to prepare the civil authorities and mobilise the Armed Forces. It outlined the measures, plans, and groups of plans, to be implemented with the intention of ensuring a smooth transition from peace to war. Each measure was broken down into three steps, or paragraphs. The first paragraph of each measure contains preparatory actions. The second paragraph contains additional preparatory actions, or in some cases partial implementation. The third paragraph fully implements the measure. Each measure could be implemented paragraph by paragraph, or all together, depending on the situation at the time. The GWB measures are categorised A, B, or C. 'A' means a measure that could not be implemented within five days. 'B' is a measure that could be implemented in five days without materially affecting day-to-day life or being provocative. 'C' is a measure that could be implemented within five days, which would materially affect the population and was potentially provocative.[12] In any crisis, the measures in the GWB would be reviewed to ensure they were relevant and up-to-date.

The GWB measures were collected together into 'Group Decisions' (GD). These were collections of measures required to permit the mobilisation of the Armed Forces, the call-up of reservists, the protection of Key Points within the UK and the mobilisation of civilian transport, for example. Several of the GDs dealt with gaining control of transportation, implementing preparations for Energy,

Health Services and the Emergency Services, as well as arranging for the administration of justice to be moved to Regional Government.

The GWBs were, '…unwieldy and complex … from a user viewpoint.'[13] The broader system was complicated by the lack of direct relation to the NATO measures. This was demonstrated by a table which cross-references the NATO State/Stage with the GWB measure. It is a five-page long table which breaks down the NATO alert by the three letter NATO measure, defines the category against which the three NATO commands are to react, and finally shows which GWB measure, and the relevant section, it related to. Despite attempts to align the NATO and UK alert system, the MoD Transition to War Team cautioned that, 'There are a number of national Measures that have no NATO counterpart and a number of NATO Measures that have no national counterpart.'[14]

### The Transition to War Committee

This committee was responsible for coordinating departmental actions and was made up of Permanent Secretaries and a military advisor under the chairmanship of a senior minister. Recommendations were made to the Cabinet to be authorised, or authorised by the Committee directly, depending on the circumstances obtaining at the time.

### The Process

Prior to 1967, the Transition to War plans moved directly from a 'Warning Period' in a 'Pre-Strike Phase' to the 'Strike Phase' of strategic nuclear exchange. After Flexible Response was adopted, the planning for Transition to War included a Conventional Period within the Pre-Strike Phase – a nuclear attack was still part of the expected scenario. Once a crisis was identified, and aggression against NATO might be the result, the first codeword would be issued by the Prime Minister. This would have initiated an urgent review of all departmental War Plans: at this stage political control was exercised by the Cabinet, advised in turn by the Transition to War Committee. This would have equated to the State of Military Vigilance in the NATO Alert System. Unobtrusive preparations would have begun at this stage.

If the crisis were to deepen, and indications of WTO forces moving to a war footing were identified, the second codeword would be issued. The Cabinet Office and Transition to War Committee would seek approval from the Cabinet to instruct all departments and services to implement all preparatory stages for putting the country onto a war footing. NATO would have been at the Formal Alert Stage. More obvious measures, visible to the public, would have made an appearance. The full timescales would vary depending on the crisis and the political will, but as an approximate guide, to implement all UK National Transition to War measures would have taken some three to four weeks. Vital to the functioning of many of the GWB Measures were the Emergency Powers. Many feared the enacting of the Emergency Powers Bill would be the beginning of the implementation of a dictatorial state, but there was practical thinking behind the need for it. The MoD presented it thus: 'Until [Emergency Powers have been enacted] the Serviceman will, with minor exceptions, have no more powers than the ordinary citizen.'[15] But if the Emergency Powers were not enacted until a late stage due to political delay, the vital preparations for troops and equipment movements would not have been completed in time. The speed of mobilisation was crucial for reinforcing the in-place units in Germany.

## Crises, Timescales and Scenarios

The Transition to War process as described in some of the exercises began with a breakdown in international relations. The exercises used a change in Soviet leadership followed by a WTO invasion of Yugoslavia as the beginning of the crisis.[16] Almost all of the NATO exercises used the 'Slow Moving Crisis' as a basis for their scenarios as this allowed the full deployment of forces in the build-up period.

## Crises

There were three outline scenarios for a transition to war and it is worth evaluating them:[17]

- A Slow Moving Crisis
'This scenario is of such a timescale as to allow the Cabinet/ TWC [Transition to War Committee] … to discuss and authorise individual GWB measures and … requests from Major NATO commanders …'

- Intermediate Timescales
'A crisis evolving in the intermediate timescale is intended to be dealt with by a combination of MPDs [Major Policy Decisions], individuall [sic] decisions and, where necessary, GDs.'

- Rapidly Moving Crisis
This was described as a, '… rapid transition from peace to war …' It was in a rapidly moving crisis that timescales for decision making were all important, and as such the 14 Group Decisions would be implemented as rapidly as possible.

There was some confusion in both NATO and the MoD about the likelihood of warning of an attack. The NATO assumption was not that the WTO would launch a surprise attack, but that there would be a steady deterioration of international relations over a period of more than 20 days before, resulting in an outbreak of hostilities. Contrast this with the private comments of the US Secretary of State for Defense in 1979: 'We estimate that the Pact could concentrate ground forces of five 'fronts' – 85 to 90 Divisions – for an attack on NATO's Center [sic] Region within about 15 days … the Pact could also assemble over 4,000 tactical aircraft … within three to five days.'[18] A Joint

Intelligence Committee assessment in 1977 anticipated that only two weeks warning would be available to NATO, perhaps even as little as two days, allowing a surprise attack to be launched.[19] The WTO might have a week of preparation before the signs were noticed by Western Intelligence.

## Relative Timing

Given concern about the speed of mobilisation, the warning time was crucial for raising the nuclear threshold. An indication of just how difficult it was to predict an approaching crisis, or to identify any mobilisation of troops, was shown following the Soviet invasion of Afghanistan in 1979. Little or no warning came from the US Intelligence Agencies such as the CIA. The Soviets prepared an Airborne Division, an independent Airborne Regiment, and five Military Transport Divisions, increased the readiness of two Divisions in the Turkestan Military District, and brought the

Soviet forces parade during Exercise Zapad '81. NATO had difficulty in identifying Soviet and WTO intentions and an exercise such as this could have provided the springboard for a Soviet-led surprise attack. (Open source)

A Soviet MiG-23M photographed over the Baltic in 1989. Western intelligence failed to notice the changes in alert status of such aircraft during the 1983 war scare. (US DoD)

Bridging regiments in the Kiev Military District to full strength for deployment. The Soviets had employed distraction methods to keep the Western countries guessing as to their intentions right up to the point of invasion. Equally, preparations during the war scare in 1983 were missed, with US Intelligence reporting, 'The Soviet air force standdown had been in effect for nearly a week before fully armed MIG-23 aircraft were noted on air defense alert in East Germany.'[20] Western intelligence seemed to have had a problem identifying WTO mobilisations and preparations for war.

Many of the scenarios for simulation were referred to by the respective mobilisation times for the WTO and NATO forces. The initial mobilisation day was referred to as M-day, and the first day of combat as

Nationale Volksarmee T-72M1s on exercise. NATO planning largely assumed advance warning of any Warsaw Pact mobilisation, but an exercise used as cover could have greatly reduced the warning time available to NATO. (Open source)

D-day. There were several scenarios and settings which are used throughout the Government and NATO documentation, referred to in the style 5/3 or 31/24. The first number refers to the number of days the WTO would have to mobilise and prepare, and the second number refers to how much time NATO would have. There was a delay between the WTO mobilising and NATO confirming mobilisation had occurred. The Government War Book states, 'For planning purposes, it is assumed the most likely period of warning of hostilities would be 1-2 weeks …'[21] but plans used by both the Government generally, and MoD in particular, used a longer period of warning thus enabling full mobilisation.

A surprise attack is the basis for the 5/3 setting and would probably equate to the 'rapidly moving crisis', with the WTO mobilisation seen by NATO intelligence five days before hostilities commence. NATO would have begun to mobilise two days after the notification of WTO mobilisation, with NATO therefore having three days' warning before D-day. Because the WTO forces know they will be attacking, unobtrusive preparations for mobilisation can occur up to fourteen days before mobilisation, increasing availability across the spectrum of forces. This would effectively mean the 'rapidly moving crisis' should have been called a 19/3 scenario.

The one- or two-week scenarios, or 'intermediate timescale', involved NATO receiving between seven and fourteen days' warning of the outbreak of hostilities. An extended variant of this was the 25/10 scenario. The 31/24 setting assumes that the WTO was involved in a full-scale deliberate build-up of forces during a period of rising tension and allowed for a full deployment of forces. This could be aligned with a 'slow-moving crisis'. NATO was assumed to mobilise simultaneously with the WTO, but with mobilisation only becoming fully effective seven days after WTO mobilisation. Hostilities begin thirty-one days after the WTO began mobilisation, and therefore 24 days after NATO's full mobilisation started. The 31/24 setting, or minor variations upon it, was used in many NATO scenarios and wargames, as it allowed the largest force

to be mobilised by the NATO countries, and the greatest number of reinforcements to be delivered to the UK and Europe from the USA and Canada. Following from the Israeli example of being subjected to stop-go crises which made mobilisation difficult, even in the face of evidence of the enemy mobilisation, the need for firm political decision making in these scenarios was vital.

## The importance of political decision making

The crucial variable in all the plans for the Transition to War was the speed of decision to initiate those plans. There was, necessarily, a balance to be found, but the longer mobilisation was delayed the more likely it would be that the troops in Germany would have to fight un-reinforced. Unless there was a complete shift from the previous behaviour of Western Governments to reduce the likelihood of 'provocation' to a potential enemy, the prospect for prompt decision making initially looked poor. There would inevitably be a delay inherent in all decision making, as according to the MoD War Book, 'All deployment plans would be subject to the prior agreement of the NATO MC and the concurrence of the British Government as advised by the Chiefs of Staff.'[22]

The timing of mobilisation was crucial to the implementation of NATO plans for defence and reinforcement, and this timing was critically dependent on political will. The need for prompt political decision making was recognised by the Cabinet Office: 'We are … uncomfortably dependent on getting early warning of impending aggression and acting on it boldly.'[23] Provocation of the WTO in a crisis was high on the list of concerns for the political and military leaders of NATO and its member nations. Reinforcement of the forces in West Germany was a highly visible procedure, obvious to the WTO within hours of it starting. For the Armed Forces to achieve their reinforcement and mobilisation timescales, quick decisions were needed from politicians. But in the Western Governments during the Cold War there was a profound fear of acting 'provocatively'. During the Cuban Missile Crisis in 1962

Vulcan B.2 bombers sit on alert in the 1960s. The deterrent value of such aircraft was seen as Britain's main line of defence in the era of 'Massive Retaliation'. (John Fricker Collection)

Prime Minister Macmillan had authorised the Vulcan and Victor nuclear strike force to Alert Condition Three (fifteen minutes' readiness, armed and fuelled) but was reluctant to disperse them to their war locations for fear of provoking Khrushchev. The civil defence organisations were not activated for the same reason. The

WTO seemed less worried about provoking the West. Later prime ministers could not be expected to make quick decisions, either for fear of provocation or internal unrest. Although Margaret Thatcher had taken rapid action against the Argentinians in 1982, the same speed could not be expected against a nuclear-armed enemy.

# 4
# ARMED FORCES' STRUCTURE AND EQUIPMENT

The 1966 Defence Review moved the focus of British defence policy to Europe and the North Atlantic, and the greater part of the forces distributed around the world returned to the UK and Europe or were disbanded. Overall service numbers were to be reduced by 75,000 personnel, but these reductions would not affect forces in Europe. The policy laid out in the 1966 review heralded the adoption of the new NATO strategic concept. The Chiefs of Staff Committee (COS) noted a problem inherent in the connection between policy and strategy;

> There are no criteria which could ever be taken as precise determinants of the total size of the United Kingdom armed forces and therefore our contribution to NATO; nor are there any NATO criteria from which can be deduced in exact and irrefutable terms the correct size of each of the United Kingdom Services, and hence the correct balance between them.[1]

But, in short, the COS stated that;

> Clearly our contribution should be consistent with NATO strategy and NATO force requirements as we interpret them … This is not in itself, however, a sufficient guide to the lines along which our contribution should evolve … The forces contributed by any particular nation … must depend very much upon subjective judgement and national factors.[2]

BAOR was organised into a Corps of three divisions, each comprising two brigades. In 1968 BAOR comprised 1st, 2nd and 4th Divisions in West Germany with one brigade in the UK but under BAOR command. The UK Land Forces also provided troops for home defence. A separate brigade, not under NATO orders, was

based in Berlin. The RAF provided a tactical air force, 2ATAF, as well as the air defence of the UK. The Royal Navy provided the Fleet for the Eastern Atlantic and Channel commands. The old Territorial and Army Reserve forces were replaced by the new Territorial and Army Volunteer Reserve (TAVR), with an anticipated strength of 5,600 officers and 50,000 rank-and-file. The Royal Naval Reserve Forces consisted of some 14,000 officers and 23,000 ratings, whilst the Royal Air Force Reserve Forces totalled 12,300 officers and 71,600 personnel. A Brigade from BAOR and a Squadron from the RAF were redeployed from West Germany to the UK to save money but were still part of the NATO commitment and were expected to train annually in West Germany and be the first to return in the event of a crisis.[3]

Despite the 1966 SDE confirming that the civil defence preparations would be restricted to those which would be likely to contribute significantly to national survival, in 1968 the civil defence establishment was reduced from its previous active status to 'care and maintenance'. The Government would adopt an 'advice-only' approach to Civil Defence in the coming years.

The adoption of Flexible Response gave rise to considerable consternation within the Conservative Government to the extent that in 1973 the then Defence Secretary Lord Carrington asked for a study into the sustainability of the armed forces in the Central Region. The report provided by the CDS noted that any reduction in the current levels would result in losing one- or two-days' resistance to a major attack. Options identified to remedy the problems included redistributing the available forces more evenly, depending more on reserve and reinforcement forces, modifying the concept of Forward Defence to include grater mobility or barrier systems, and greater use of airmobile forces. None of these seemed suitable, and a

The garrison of Britain's Berlin Infantry Brigade included a squadron of 18 Chieftain tanks. From the early 1980s a number of the vehicles in Berlin sported an unusual camouflage scheme of white, blue-grey and brown blocks that worked extremely well in built-up areas, even if not quite so well while on parade. These late examples also have Stillbrew applique armour on the turret front. The composition of this armour remains classified, though it was likely around 100mm of conventional cast armour with a thick layer of rubber (or similar material) between it and the original turret front. This additional armour was developed in part as a result of examining Iranian Chieftains knocked-out in the Iran-Iraq War. (US DoD)

These CVR(W) Fox armoured cars are also on parade in Berlin, though they have the more common British green and black camouflage scheme. The Fox carried a 30mm RARDEN cannon as also carried by the CVR(T) Scimitar and FV510 Warrior, that compensated for its relatively low rate of fire by being very accurate. The Fox had an unfortunate reputation for being top-heavy and prone to overturning and was withdrawn from service in the early 1990s on safety grounds. (US DoD)

possible alternative of early use of tactical nuclear weapons was seen as the only option available, indeed unavoidable.

## Reserves and Reservists

The term 'reserves' covers ammunition, spares and supplies, generally referred to as the War Maintenance Reserve (WMR), Warstocks or War Reserves. The MoD defined War Reserves in three categories:

- Combat supplies. This comprises ammunition, fuel (POL) and rations

- Equipment, vehicles and stores required to bring units up to their war establishment, and to replace losses during operations
- Defence stores and other specialist equipment required for a particular operational or administrative contingency.

Reserves also covers reserves of manpower, embodied in the Regular Reserves and the Territorial and Auxiliary forces, generally referred to as Reserve Forces or Reservists.

## Reservists

Britain had made use of part-time soldiers for much of its history, from the Trained Bands of the Civil War, through to the Fencibles of the French Revolutionary era. Conscription, and a large 'citizen' army, was brought to an end by Duncan Sandys, then Minister of Defence, in 1957. The Sandys reforms had emphasised a move to all-regular armed forces, but deficiencies in the numbers of front-line forces caused by cost-cutting were progressively made up by a reliance on reservist forces.

The Regular Reserves were personnel who had served in the regular forces, and through this had an obligation to serve as a reservist for a fixed period following their discharge from regular service. They would train for several days each year. These were earmarked as Individual Replacements for specialist tasks, or to fill-out particular units. The Territorial Army (TA), or Territorial Army Volunteer Reserve (TAVR), was made up of volunteers who served on a part-time basis, did not necessarily have any previous military experience, trained during evenings and at weekends and attended a two-week annual training exercise. The reservists could be a convenient way to bolster numbers without spending a large amount of money.

The political imperatives for using reserves were clear: it saved money as the reserves were not permanently employed in the same way that regulars were; the numbers looked good when presented for public consumption; politicians could say they were saving money but keeping the armed forces efficient and effective; and with a shortage regular personnel, the reservists were even more valuable.[4] Fighting capability is a function of proficiency and availability amongst other factors, and reservists will not be as proficient in their roles as regular service personnel, as they train for only a small portion of their time, and do not live the military life. The capabilities of the regular forces were maintained by constant training and unbroken exposure to the military system. However capable and committed the volunteer reserves were, or indeed the regular reserves, they would not be as well trained and as capable as the regular units, and to expect anything else would be to put improper expectations upon them. The Government had long seen reservists as a cost-effective option in peacetime but understood that

MILAN was an infantry-portable Franco-German anti-tank missile first adopted by the British Army in the late 1970s. 6th Armoured Brigade was recast as 6th Airmobile Brigade for much of the 1980s to serve in a counter-penetration role, with two infantry battalions each equipped with 42 (some accounts say 48) MILAN firing posts. This example is being used by 4th (Volunteer) Battalion of the Parachute Regiment during White Rhino in 1989; it had been proposed that the three TA battalions of the Parachute Regiment be formed into a similarly MILAN-heavy formation. Note the MIRA thermal imaging sight. (Walter Böhm)

These Territorials of 4th (Volunteer) Battalion of the Parachute Regiment wear the new Kevlar helmet but still carry the 7.62mm L1A1 SLR rifle. The SLR was highly regarded as its 7.62mm round was considered to have much greater stopping power than the 5.56mm NATO round. The 7.62mm round was also much heavier and bulkier and far more 5.56mm rounds (or other items of equipment) could be carried. (Walter Böhm)

The L7 GPMG also remained popular amongst the troops, even though heavy to carry. The belt-fed 7.62mm weapon was felt by the rank and file to offer much better suppressive and killing fire than the LSW that replaced it. These soldiers of 4th (Volunteer) Battalion of the Parachute Regiment have dug-in during White Rhino. The red tape around their helmets helps to identify which side they are on during the exercise. (Walter Böhm)

These men of 4th (Volunteer) Battalion of the Parachute Regiment are seen carrying SLRs in the classic patrol posture as they participate in Exercise White Rhino in 1989. The SLR was gradually replaced by the SA80 from around 1986 onwards, though the SLR would remain with reserve units and supporting arms well into the 1990s. (Walter Böhm)

training would be required to bring them up to the necessary levels of proficiency. The reserves were promoted by the Government as being on a par with their regular counterparts: 'Since many of [their] tasks would put Reservists in the front-line alongside Regular Servicemen, they have to be just as efficient and professional.'[5] Their availability was limited, as they would need to be mobilised by Queen's Order or Cabinet authorisation. They would then take several days more to become deployable. The point made above is significant, that the reserves are *cost-effective in peacetime*, but far less so in a crisis which develops quickly or provides little warning time for mobilisation.

Reservists could be expected to provide mass, and to perform well, but only after several months of training. The military saw the necessity of having a trained reserve of personnel but viewed its development and deployment differently to the politicians. The Army regarded the TAVR as vital to make up the numbers deployed into Europe: '[The TAVR] cannot be regarded as a reserve … which might turn up or might not, for the number of regular battalions allotted to the BAOR divisions is not sufficient to free TAVR

battalions … from a specific role in the Divisional deployment.'[6] It was not just Britain that relied more and more on reservists: for example, by 1985, to provide greater resources for the front-line units the West German Army had cut its supporting forces in favour of reservists.

In the 1983 SDE another reorganisation of BAOR provided three armoured divisions and a new infantry division which was to be based entirely in the UK. The Infantry Division HQ was based in York and comprised three Brigades, two of which were largely reservist in composition (15 and 49). It is instructive to inspect the make-up of particular brigade and divisional level units which were established, and which display the formation's dependence on reserve troops. 15 Brigade comprised six infantry battalions three of which were reservist, and three batteries of artillery, all of which were reservists. 49 Brigade comprised six battalions, four of which were reservists, and three batteries of artillery, all of which were reservists.

The use of large numbers of reservists had an impact on the availability of these formations in a crisis. NATO ACE Force Standards for readiness and the UK measurement were different,

15 Brigade was composed of a mixture of Territorials and Regulars. This radio operator from 15 Brigade, seen on Exercise Northern Foray in 1979, wears an NBC smock and trousers over his regular uniform, a '44 pattern helmet and carries a 9mm L2A3 Sterling submachine gun along with the A41 Larkspur manpack radio. (Private collection)

sometimes deliberately so. The MoD defended their position, noting that NATO standards were aimed more at conscript armies, not volunteer forces. For an Armoured Division for example, ACE required 90 percent manning levels for the regular units. Because the UK forces were mixed regular/TAVR, the overall Divisional manning level would be 74 percent, and so would not reach the required standard. Some units earmarked for the reinforcement of BAOR were at a lower category of readiness than required by NATO because they were either made up almost entirely of reservists or were only cadre strength and would be filled by reservists after mobilisation. The LTDP had tried to address this problem by requesting that Britain comply with the minimum manning levels. The suggestion was accepted 'in principle' but was effectively ignored. As it addressed, '… unit, as opposed to formation, manning levels …'[7] the British Government considered that the inconsistencies would continue.

Reservist units tended to be armed with old or obsolete weapons and transported in soft skinned vehicles. The LTDP specifically moved to reverse this trend, and Task Force 3 – Reserve Mobilisation, prioritised the replacement of obsolete equipment for reserve units by modern equipment. The MoD partially implemented this, with TA infantry battalions receiving MILAN and LAW 80 from 1982 onwards,[8] and the SA80 after its introduction to the regular forces. Additionally, some reserve infantry regiments were to receive the

SAXON APC to replace their lorried transport. Old 5.5" artillery pieces were to be replaced with the 105mm Light Gun, and Clansman radios were to be issued. The Blowpipe Quadruple Towed Launcher was to be issued to the TA Air Defence units, but this was cancelled for financial reasons. The provision to TA battalions of MILAN (6 launchers) and LAW 80 was not in the numbers issued to regular infantry battalions (which was 24 MILAN launchers by 1983). Despite this, the Government proclaimed that, 'The equipping of TA units to the standard of Regular units is progressing well.'[9]

## Personnel – Recruitment and Retention

Retention of experienced personnel within the Armed Forces was a perennial problem, as Forces' pay was poor in comparison to the private sector. Numbers were stabilised by improving pay rates and conditions of service, which led Francis Pym, the Secretary of State for Defence in 1979 to write, '… the signs are now pointing to an improvement in recruitment and retention, although the loss of highly trained and experienced men cannot readily be made good.'[10] Increased pay, and a squeeze on defence spending meant, perversely, some personnel would have to be made redundant. The cuts were to be made, if possible, in the 'tail', as demonstrated when, in July 1981, Sir Frank Cooper, Permanent Under Secretary at the MoD, wrote, '… Service redundancy is to be kept to a minimum. This does not mean you should hold back on measures in the support area …'[11]

The skilled and experienced personnel required were under-represented in regular units. During the 1980s the recruitment reservoir, men and women aged between 16 and 19, shrank. Because of this, some infantry battalions were as much as 10 percent under strength, and the peacetime establishment of the armoured battalions understrength enough to have to put some tanks in 'light preservation'. As measured in 1981, the pool of trained personnel was short by 4,000 in the Navy, 4,000 in the RAF and 10,000 in the Army. In BAOR particularly, some regular infantry battalions had one entire company reduced to cadre strength, to be filled upon mobilisation by reservists. In response to a letter from SACEUR regarding forces in the Central Region which did not meet ACE force manning standards, the MoD replied, '1(BR) Corps units are below strength. On the basis of current forecasts this will be the case until 1983/84.'[12]

In an attempt to overcome the shortfall of regular troops, the TA was planned to expand to 86,000 by the end of the decade, but by 1984 only numbered 64,900 having declined from 72,000 in 1983. The Auxiliary forces of the Royal Navy and Royal Air Force were also to be expanded but suffered the same shortfall in numbers. Several Royal Navy ships were transferred to the standby squadron because of shortages of certain skilled ratings and junior officers which left them inadequately crewed.

To relieve the pressure on the Regular troops, and in the hope of filling the shortfall in the TA, the Home Service Force (HSF) was raised in 1982 and was mainly based with TA units. The HSF was intended to assist regular and TA units in guarding important military and civilian installations during a war. By 1989 the Government expected that, '… 29,000 TA soldiers (including the Home Service Force) and some 45,000 ex-regulars would have home defence roles, guarding installations, undertaking reconnaissance and providing communications.'[13] However, by mid-decade the HSF had only raised 3,000 troops of the anticipated 4,500.

The need for a large pool of trained personnel was indicated by the MoD's estimate of losses. Army attrition rates were expected to be 6.25 percent per day:

The AT-105 Saxon was essentially a lightly armoured Bedford 4-tonne truck armed with an L7 GPMG or L4 LMG (essentially a Bren gun rechambered to 7.62mm NATO). Originally a commercial design, it was bought by the British Army to offer a degree of protection to the non-mechanised reinforcement units travelling from the UK to the 1 (BR) Corps area. Intended to also equip TA battalions, during the Cold War it equipped only the rifle companies in a few Regular battalions in 24th Brigade (2nd Infantry Division) and 1st Infantry Brigade (UKMF – earmarked for Denmark). These became Type A Mechanised Infantry Battalions and all but the rifle companies and recce platoons still used soft-skin vehicles. Documents issued to candidates at the Staff College included dire warnings that the Saxon was not to be exposed to enemy fire under any circumstances. This example is seen participating in Exercise Key Stone '87, before 24th Brigade replace 6th Brigade the airmobile role. (Michael Neumann via Walter Böhm)

When the British infantry were re-equipped with the SA80 they also largely gave up the 7.62mm GPMG in favour of the Light Support Weapon (LSW). The LSW was essentially a heavy barrelled version of the new rifle, firing standard 5.56mm NATO ammunition from a 30-round magazine. New infantry tactics were developed around a section of two similar fire teams of three SA80s and one LSW, as opposed to the older gun group and rife group tactics used previously. (Walter Böhm)

throughout the 6-day period ... The Royal Navy does not assess its war reserves in the same manner ...[14]

But recruitment and retention problems saw the numbers of in-service regular and territorial personnel dwindle throughout the 1980s. The MoD expressed the fear that, 'The reduction from 38 Regular and TA battalions available ... to 35, probably by 1 Apr 83, further accentuates the difficulties of meeting likely commitments, as there are already more tasks than the Army ... is able to undertake.'[15]

## Training

Military training aims to rehearse the practical use of military doctrine to ensure success in its real application. Training works at the individual, team, collective, operational grouping and command levels. If these are not practised during peacetime it will be too late when war occurs. General Wavell wrote in 1933, '... so far as training is concerned I hold that it is a positive advantage to have to train simply 'for war' and that to train 'for a war' is a danger because that particular war never happens ...'[16] It is axiomatic that a reservist who serves a limited number of days per year will be less well trained in any given period of time than a regular, a fact accepted in 1981 by the Directors of Defence Policy:

The TA's lack of expertise, stemming from their limited training and the fact that few have regular Army experience, must cast doubts on their ability to cope effectively with the Regular Army tasks that will eventually be transferred to them. As a result the overall war fighting capability of 1(BR) Corps will be reduced

For the Army, attrition rates of main equipments and manpower are calculated assuming that 50% of the reinforced No 1 (BR) Corps (110,000 men) must be in existence on the eighth day. The RAF assumes that 70% of its front line aircraft will be available and this will lessen its deterrent value.[17]

Training was a soft target for financial savings. For example, in 1980 to find an initial £100 Million savings cuts were made in '...

This close-up view of the LSW shows the heavy barrel, bipod and the SUSAT sight unit. The 'bullpup' design, in which the magazine is inserted behind the pistol grip, necessitated the use of a grip beneath the shoulder stock to steady the weapon when being used in the support role. The SA80 and LSW allowed the average soldier to achieve much improved standards of marksmanship over the previous generation of weapons, but they also suffered enormous reliability and durability problems under field conditions. (Walter Böhm)

in standards of training for the NATO roles. According to the 1979 SDE, the plan to increase the, '... size of the Army by 6,000 ... will improve standards of training and readiness, particularly in BAOR ...'[19] This recruitment target brought its own problems: 6,000 additional troops would take a significant amount of time to recruit and train, leading to a drop in readiness in the short to medium term. Long term cost-cutting and inflation had left the British Armed Forces in a state of neglect which would prove extremely difficult to correct.

## Mobilisation

Readiness of reinforcements presented a consistent shortfall against NATO expectations. Since so many of the reinforcements for BAOR were reservists, the problem

collective Army training in the UK and Germany between 35 and 45%; TA training by 25% and certain other forms of Army training by up to 30%.'[18]

RAF training and flying time had been reduced for financial reasons leading to a serious shortage of pilots for fast jet flying. RAF recruitment in 1977/78 was only 68 percent of that required, with the number of trained pilots 13 percent below target. Because of these economic restrictions, the RAF did not expect to have the required number of pilots until the end of the 1980s.

Standards of training in the Army were cause for concern, with the gunnery standards of tank units and artillery regiments lower than was acceptable. Engineers were also suffering from a lack of coherent training. This was caused partly by the demands of non-NATO postings such as Northern Ireland, by administrative functions and course attendance by only parts of units under training. The specialists such as artillery gunners and tank crews were posted to Northern Ireland as infantry, which led to a deficiency

was acutely felt by the Army. The LTDP had required that reserves were to be re-categorised as C1 (2-day readiness) or C2 (3–4 days) as opposed to the existing C3 (5–15 days) which would enable faster reinforcement. The MoD's response was that 30 percent of reservists would report on day one, 50 percent on day two and 15 percent on day three, which removed the need for recategorisation. Not to be deterred, the 1979–84 NATO Force Proposals included a serial which requested that reserve units earmarked for reinforcement of BAOR were replaced with regular units. This was an unpopular request, and the comment for this proposal reads: 'Accepted in principle. There are currently no firm plans to implement this measure in the Force Proposal period ...'[20] SACEUR introduced the Rapid Reinforcement Plan (RRP) in 1981 to speed up deployment of forces into the NATO Central Region. Part of the problem with the UK contribution was the scale of reservist mobilisation demanded by the RRP. The Individual Reinforcement Plan (IRP) was also introduced in 1981 by the UK Government with the intention of

These troops were taking part in Exercise Brave Defender in 1985, intended to test the ability of Regular and Territorial troops in UKLF to defend Key Points against infiltration and sabotage attacks by WTO special forces. (US DoD)

halving the time needed to mobilise the reservists. However, the use of individual reservists may have had a deleterious effect on unit cohesion due to lack of unit training. The Army conducted research into preparation for Operation Granby in 1991 and found, '… that few commanders deploying to the Gulf [in 1991] considered their units to be battle ready, including those at the peak of their training cycle, not least because reinforcements had to be absorbed and trained …'[21] In a shooting war in Europe, there would not have been time to undergo the intensive training that was available to the troops in the Gulf.

An example of the problem can be demonstrated with the reorganised BAOR structure between 1978 and 1983. The 7th Field Force, which was the direct reinforcement for BAOR, consisted of regular and TA units. Had it needed to take the field quickly, before mobilisation had completed, 7th Field Force would have been approximately 30 percent below its expected field strength. 6th Field Force was the land element of UK Mobile Force, consisting of 13,500 troops, and was the strategic reserve for SACEUR and would have been deployed into Denmark (Baltic Approaches, or BALTAP) as its primary destination. Emergency reinforcement was the responsibility of UKMF, but even after the post-Falklands reforms were implemented, the role and resources of this force were being questioned: 'Some of its tasks are beyond its capabilities … more realistic employment options should be renegotiated …'[22]

Sudden deployment in a crisis would have entailed substantial difficulty, as most of the units within the Logistic Support Group (LSG), 6th Field Force's logistic support, were at cadre strength, and would be filled out by TA reinforcements and individual regular 'Shadow Postings'. Only then would they be fully operational. In a note to the Director of Military Operations the warning was made clear: 'The effect of this situation is that the Regular element of the LSG cannot support the Regular combat element of the 6th Field Force prior to call out of the Reserves.'[23] This meant that a regular force, equivalent to an infantry brigade, would be incapable of supporting itself in a sudden crisis if it were called upon to fight. The same note continues, 'To deploy the Regular element of the 6th Field Force before Callout or at least before a guarantee that Callout will take place, would therefore, involve considerable risk.'[24] This critical situation did not improve throughout the 1980s and into the 1990s. As the 'teeth' to 'tail' ratio was increased for greater 'efficiency', the threat to the operational capability of the Armed Forces intensified.

Nor was the problem of readiness and availability limited to the Army. The Royal Navy kept a squadron permanently available for action in the Eastern Atlantic but suffered from double tasking of some ships. An example is the UK group deployed in the North Sea from mobilisation would lose five of its six ships to provide escort to the 2nd UK carrier group out of the Clyde on M + 10. Ships would also be needed to escort the UKMF and UK/NL Amphibious forces deployment in Europe. The Director of Naval Operations felt, '… unable to say that the service would be fully ready to meet its commitments after the likely warning time …'[25] due to shortages in many major weapon systems, key personnel and inadequate training.

## Logistics

Regular RAF and Army were permanently deployed as front-line units in Germany, with reservists filling out some of those front-line units as well as taking up the rear-area defence. As well as filling combat roles, reservists provided up to 80 percent of the logistic personnel in the British Army during the late 1970s and 1980s. The limitations on recruitment of regular personnel for logistical and rear-area units, along with the policy of cutting the 'tail' to provide for

The UK's Royal Marines enjoyed a very close relationship with the Netherland's *Korps Mariniers*, with a battalion of the latter coming under command of 3 Commando Brigade to form the joint UK/NL Amphibious Group earmarked to support NATO's Northern Flank. This Dutch marine, armed with an 84mm Carl Gustav anti-tank weapon, is taking part in Exercise Northern Wedding '78 in the Shetland Islands off the north coast of Scotland. (US DoD)

the 'teeth', meant that although the regular combat forces – the 'teeth' – could be deployed quickly, they would very soon find themselves without adequate re-supply or reinforcement. Realistically, in anything other than a slow-moving crisis, the front-line units would only have their ready reserve ammunition and stores available, as the logistical chain would not be staffed with enough personnel to enable stores to be moved forward or distributed. This in turn would have presented a problem regarding the timing of the mobilisation of reserves – if the Government was reluctant to mobilise for fear of provocation, as with the Cuban Missile Crisis, but which turned quickly to combat, the reservists who undertook crucial roles in the rear areas would not be mobilised in time to arrive at their designated location.

Timings for mobilisation and deployment of NATO forces had been queried following a 1978 JIC assessment on warning time which indicated as little as 48 hours warning of an attack. The expectation was that regular units would fulfil the ACE Forces Standard time for reaching their defensive positions, which was 24 hours for covering forces and 48 hours for main forces. Thus, they would be gaining their positions as a WTO attack began. Concern was raised regarding the deployment of mobile forces, that the first deployment of Advance and Key parties could only be expected at Mobilisation plus two (M+2) days, with the main force arriving at M+6 meaning they would be transported and deployed during the first few days of hostilities. Further unease was that, '… political pressures could delay the despatch … by SACEUR, or events could move so fast that [they] would not be deployed as such at all.'[26]

Once the troops were ordered to move the act of transporting them, even in peacetime, was the source of logistic problems which would be exacerbated if hostilities had already begun. This was demonstrated by concerns raised by the MoD over sufficient transport for exercises in 1978:

> Increased NATO exercises … and their heavy requirements for movement resources are affecting other exercise programmes. An example is ADVANCE EXPRESS which, when taken with BOLD GUARD, may prevent movement of 5 and 7 Field Forces to BAOR this year because there will be no spare airlift.[27]

The pressure upon transport in a crisis prompted MoD representatives to write that the reinforcement of BAOR under

SACEUR's Rapid Reinforcement Plan, '… will impose considerable demands on movements [sic] resources possibly in competition with other forces …'[28] The number of regular specialist personnel available had fallen due to defence cuts, which meant there were not enough transport drivers for the vehicles in any of the services. A warning note was sounded regarding logistic support, the Rapid Reinforcement Plan (RRP) and mobilisation:

> At present the high percentage of TA in the LSG [Logistic Support Group] and the fact that the force cannot be maintained for more than 72 hours without the LSG, preclude deployment before the signing of QO2 [Queen's Order Number Two].[29]

Overall, the MoD had warned in 1977 that, 'There are serious logistic implications in terms of storage, transport and manpower both in peace and war.'[30] The fighting units, whatever services they belonged to, depended on a logistical tail for supplies of fuel and ammunition and other essentials. The drawback of having so many reservists as support troops was summed up in a memo by the Assistant Chief of the Defence staff in 1978:

> A particular problem is that calculated undermanning of logistic units in order to maintain the strength of combat units is near the point where the combat troops may not be effective because of lack of initial logistic support. In many specialist areas, units are severely undermanned in junior officer and key noncommissioned officer ranks. Among the formations which depend on substantial reserve augmentation, headquarters manning tends to fall below the level required for effective transition to war.[31]

## The War Maintenance Reserve – Stocks and Sustainability

Given the need of the new NATO strategy to maintain conventional forces to resist an attack from the Soviet Union, stocks of ammunition and other equipment and materiel were essential. However, the 1968 Defence Review concluded, 'The level of reserves that we must hold to meet the demands of war and other contingencies has been reviewed and reduced.'[32]

The importance of the War Maintenance Reserve (WMR) is outlined in a Minute to the Secretary of State for Defence in 1977 which asserted, '… our war reserves are absolutely vital … There are therefore several equally critical aspects to this problem – the quantity of war reserves; their deployment and storage; and our ability to resupply forward units at a rate to keep pace with the battle.'[33]

There would be no opportunity to manufacture additional stocks of missiles and equipment in the event of war. Deploying those weapons and equipment that the Armed Forces did have would require pre-positioned stocks of all necessary supplies, vehicles and weapons. In addition, it would be crucial that those supplies which were in place could be moved efficiently to the fighting front, and those reserves held further back could be moved quickly to replenish depleted stocks.

The need for sufficient war reserves was recognised by the British Government, and its importance discussed at Cabinet level. In 1974, the Chiefs of Staff's assumption was that the reserve stocks would need to cover, '… a period of up to eight days at maximum intensity …'[34] In a 1977 report to the Minister of State for Defence concerns over the crucial nature of the reserves for the defence of Europe were expressed explicitly by the Defence Council: 'There will be no time to produce more weaponry in significant quantities and little time to deploy all that we have.'[35]

The UK employed a different approach to NATO in assessing the levels of reserves needed for any anticipated war in Europe, as according to the MoD the, '… Army and RAF plan for 8 days at intensive rates of effort, the Navy 7 days, though they make allowance for a long period of tension and intermittent engagements. NATO plan on the basis of 30 days at lesser rates of effort, which is clearly not in line with the way we and our allies see the battle going.'[36]

Army and RAF war reserves were scaled based on an 8-day war at maximum intensity, the last two days of which were expected to include tactical nuclear exchanges. The Royal Navy assumed a 3-month period of tension, 3 weeks of intermittent action followed by 7 days of operations at intensive rates. The Royal Navy descriptions are illuminating, defining a,

> … period of tension as an increase in the level of operations resulting in an increased consumption of fuel, general stores and detection devices such as sonobuoys, but without the expenditure of weapons.
>
> Intermittent action is defined as increased consumption of fuel and general stores, along with limited expenditure of major weapons. There would be a sustained rate of patrolling by air defence aircraft and Long Range Maritime Reconnaissance involving minor weapons and detection device expenditure.
>
> Intensive operations are defined as involving all categories of weapons and stores.[37]

These assumptions were judged to equate to the war reserves defined by NATO which stipulated 30 days operations at lower rates of intensity. Fuel stocks for the Royal Navy were 60 days at War Usage Rates, although there were recommendations to increase this to 90 days to incorporate 60 days of tension and 30 days of combat.

The need to establish just how long a war might last, when ammunition reserves were limited, was significant. Ammunition production during a conflict with the WTO was regarded as zero, and knowledge that the war would be of limited duration would give the forces confidence that weapons could be used freely. Herein was a source of concern to the Armed Forces regarding the lack of missiles of all types, as only the profligate use of such weapons would be enough to hold back a WTO attack in NORTHAG. Nevertheless, based on experience from the Falklands War, the General War Rates seriously under-estimated ammunition usage. General Thompson noted that in the Falklands usage of larger calibre ammunition was in excess of, '… the rate for the most intense operations envisaged in a war against the Warsaw Pact.'[38] In a war in Europe, this knowledge would result in reluctance to use ammunition for fear of running out at the crucial moment.

To allow military officers to establish what were considered to be the 'correct' levels of reserves, planning scenarios and wargames were used. Once a planning scenario had reached the stage where hostilities break out, the MoD used manual and computer games, or wargames, as well as computer simulations, to assess the likely outcome of the battles. Computer wargame modelling and team wargames contributed to the doctrine of the British Armed Forces in direct, practical ways. Weapon densities were tried out in wargames, with different scenarios representing different approaches to defeating an enemy attack. The stocks of ammunition were assessed through these computer models and wargames, and the requirements for logistical backup and war reserves were derived from these.

The Defence Operational Analysis Establishment (DOAE) used several different models for assessing land, air and sea warfare

A Chieftain taking part in Exercise Key Stone in 1987. The Chieftain had been in service with the British Army for 20 years at this point and whilst it had received a number of upgrades to the fire control, new L26 APFSDS 'fin' ammunition and much work to improve the engine reliability, it was in need of replacement. Note the Simfire device fitted high on the turret front above the gun. (Walter Böhm)

results, and some of the models were severely limited in their range of scenario modelling. For example, the DOAE study on direct fire, '… disregards the expenditure of a proportion of CHIEFTAIN HESH rounds in suppressive and other indirect tasks …'[39] and did not consider attrition of vehicles by air-to-surface attack. In another analysis the use of disposable, one-man LAWs was not attempted, nor the use of chemical weapons by the WTO, despite chemical weapons being specifically mentioned as a threat. In a more comprehensive report analysing the 'Future Battlefield', there was only a limited representation of air defence and logistics. The morale effects of surprise were implemented by a simple reduction in the effectiveness factors of enemy troops, based on the judgement of the players. Fuel and repair facilities to service the warfighting units were almost unrepresented in the modelling.

Factors which were not considered in the calculation of the expenditure of tank ammunition were:

| a. Overkill, | eg, simultaneous engagement of the same target by two or more weapons, or re-engagement of an AFV already put out of action but not outwardly seen as no longer posing a threat. |
|---|---|
| b. False Targets | eg, firing at incorrectly identified targets, such as natural features, as a result of battle fatigue or poor visibility. |
| c. Suppressive Fire | eg, in support of infantry actions. |
| d. Prophylactic or Speculative fire | eg, at possible enemy locations such as copses or farm buildings. |

These omissions meant that a large proportion of combat ammunition expenditure was not calculated. In another report, prophylactic and overkill was assessed purely by 'Military Judgement.' Armoured battles showed that tanks often required more than one hit to put them out of action. Unless there was clear evidence that the tank had been disabled, troops tended to continue to fire at the target until they scored a catastrophic kill.

The NATO usage rates for Chieftain main armament was 7 rounds per gun per day. In contrast, the British Army estimated intensive rates to be equal to a, '… nominal hourly expenditure … per tank …' of approximately 14 rounds during a heavy defensive battle of the sort expected in NORTHAG.[40] The Review of Ammunition Rates and Scales (RARS) allowed for the consumption of 52 rounds per day, and the WMR assessed by the DOAE provided 360 APDS/HESH per tank in BAOR for the 8 day battle scenario (approximately 45 rounds per tank per day). The MoD usage and stock levels were estimated using a combination of military experience and some newly introduced computer simulation systems which progressively replaced manual wargames. Reserves and consumption rates were based on, '… historical evidence from the Korean and Second World Wars modified by various more recent … studies [of the Yom Kippur War] and threat reassessments.'[41]

However, some of the NATO war reserve stock levels had not been reviewed since the 1960s, and few attempts had been made to establish a single definition for the duration of hostilities or the rate of ammunition expenditure and attrition of armed forces. Following analyses of the expenditure of ammunition in the Yom Kippur War standard usage rates were considered out of date. One report published by the DOAE, intended to establish ammunition levels for 1(BR) Corps, concluded, 'It seems inevitable that expenditure in

An L16 81mm mortar of the 2/52 Lowland Volunteers (KOSB) in action in the early 1990s, though most of the equipment and clothing is as it would have been during the later 1980s. The L16 provided invaluable fire support in the Falklands, often being the only weapon available in the indirect fire role, but ammunition expenditure exceeded all expectations. (Thomas Mccafferty)

actual battle will be at a higher level than in simulated trials.'[42] This opinion was reflected in the findings from the Falklands War when the UK rates were once more re-assessed. The Commandos had used five times the Daily Ammunition Expenditure Rate (DAER) for 105mm shells and 81mm mortar ammunition, with the 105s running out of ammunition at one point. This did not bode well for a sustainable supply of stores in an intensive war in Europe.

## War Reserve Levels

Fearing the threat of war with the Soviet Union, as a priority in the 1950s, NATO required a '… complete build-up of ammunition and equipment reserves …'[43] along with Petrol, Oil and Lubricants (POL). Cost-cutting repeatedly hit the stockpiles, and occasional use of war reserves of fuel in times of national shortage meant the levels were never achieved. In 1977, when the Long Term Defence Programme (LTDP) was introduced, Britain's Government was well aware that, '… Our war reserves are not closely aligned to NATO's stated requirements, nor can we demonstrate fully that our holdings meet these requirements.'[44]

As part of the LTDP NATO announced intended improvements in reserves of some ammunition stocks thus: 'Ministers … noted that, for example, the Alliance will increase by end-1978 holdings of anti-armour missiles by about one-third and plan similar improvements in stocks of other critical war reserve munitions.'[45] Although an increase of 30 percent of anti-armour missiles sounds considerable, MoD research suggested that the BAOR holdings should be increased by a factor of 8. There was another two phased programme of short- and medium-term measures adopted at the same time as the LTDP, and accelerated in 1980 following the Soviet invasion of Afghanistan.

According to national policy, stock levels would be improved even before the findings of the LTDP Task Forces were complete: in 1977 an example regarding Army shortfalls anticipates the deficiencies would gradually be made good between 1981 and 1987. The situation

at that time was summed up in a memorandum to the Minister of State for Defence:

Among the most serious shortfalls are Army air defence and anti-tank missiles (Blowpipe, Rapier, Swingfire, Milan, Tow) and [RAF] air-to-air missiles (Sidewinder, Sparrow, MRAAM). [Based on the latest plans] stocks of Blowpipe by 1980 will be sufficient for less than 5 days at intensive rates and stocks of Rapier, only 2 days. [Similarly] 5 days' stocks of Milan will not be accumulated until 1987/88 and of Swingfire until 1984/85. Heavy ammunition is also in short supply, for example Chieftain APDS (3 days' stocks by 1980) [Armour Piercing Discarding Sabot], 155mm shells for FM70 [FH70 Artillery piece] (2½ days' in 1980) and 51mm Mortar ammunition (3½ days by 1980).[46]

The Conservative Government had publicly and repeatedly emphasised its intention to remedy the low levels of ammunition and other stocks, reporting in 1979, '… the United Kingdom is taking positive steps towards implementation and will play a full role in those measures …'[47] After the attempts of AD-70 to improve the situation, and the ongoing LTDP, by 1982 there was recognition by General Rodgers (SACEUR) of, '… NATO's shortcomings … in its ability to sustain its forces in combat with personnel replacements, ready reserve units, stockpiled ammunition and pre-positioned reserve combat equipment.'[48]

Subsequently, in a 1984 pamphlet, the Eurogroup reported the United Kingdom as having, '… earmarked several hundred million dollars over the next few years to increase its stocks.'[49] By the end of the 1980s the words have changed regarding war reserves, asserting that the, '… Army continues to invest heavily in warstocks to improve the sustainability of its operations; its stockholdings generally meet NATO and national requirements.'[50] This phrase of 'generally meeting NATO and national requirements' was also applied to the RAF and Royal Navy, but directly contradicts the memoranda quoted above.

The Royal Navy also had shortfalls in stocks, reporting, 'There are also doubts about the adequacy of new provisioning of some RN missiles and torpedoes, for example Sea Dart [surface-to-air missile], Sea Wolf [point-defence missile] and Mark 24 [Tigerfish] torpedoes.'[51] The Royal Navy assessed the ammunition and fuel quantities required to fulfil its role in the following way:

Each situation is developed to an 'end point' at which the action might logically be supposed to break off i.e. by enemy destruction or withdrawal or by our own disablement or sinking … The resultant figure therefore represents the number of weapons needed for a ship or aircraft to engage in the type of high level

A total of 48 Tracked Rapier fire units were divided evenly between 12th and 22nd Air Defence Regiments of the Royal Artillery (along with a similar number of towed fire units). Originally intended as a commercial project to supply low-level air defence to Iran, the design was adopted by the British Army and entered service in 1983. Sharing the automotive components of the US M548 and M113 family, it was equipped with eight ready-to-fire Rapier missiles. With a range of around 5 miles (8,000 metres) this was the longest-ranged air defence system available to 1 (BR) Corps. (Walter Böhm)

action postulated without running out of ammunition (the criterion adopted is that there should be a 90% probability that the action will end without the weapon stock being exhausted.)[52]

Storage and outloading had less impact on the Royal Navy, as each ship was expected to be able to carry enough stores and supplies for its intended task. In a situation of deteriorating international relations, the Royal Navy would be at sea and using fuel for some time before the situation turned to conflict. This posed the additional problem that refuelling and rearming could be a lengthy process, and would be a time of vulnerability.

Items other than weapons were crucial to the naval war expected in the Eastern Atlantic and were also limited in number. Submarine detection devices – sonobuoys – were required in large numbers. The purchase of 10,000 additional sonobuoys before the end of 1979 had been approved as part of the NATO Short Term Measures, although according to the Royal Navy, until it had more experience in, '… operating passive sonar systems it will not be clear whether or not we are adequately provisioned in this area.'[53]

The financial limitations were manifested as under implementation of second- and third-line war reserves. The exceptions to this were supposed to be POL and rations, but the need to economise led to a £5m cut in fuel holdings in 1980-81, despite resistance from the MoD. Vehicles themselves were the target of cost-cutting and double counting, as the Vice Chief of the General Staff noted in 1977: '… reserves of some vehicles are only maintained at the 80% level by double-earmarking armoured vehicles in the UK Training Organisation and B vehicles from stocks deployed in Northern Ireland.'[54]

Because of this lack of reserve stocks, in the event of a drawn-out war in which nuclear weapons were not used, NATO could suffer defeat through attrition alone. The war reserves of ammunition, fuel, equipment, vehicles and personnel would be used up within the first few days of a war. The concept of a longer war was discussed in NATO, but not given significant weight. This lack of sustainability reached through all the Armed Services; the Vice Chairman of the Defence Staff wrote;

… BAOR does not have the capability to sustain conventional warfare for more than 4 days without resort to nuclear weapons. I am … dismayed to see that … rather than enhancing our logistic posture the Army are proposing a reduction in B vehicles and spares, in order to reach baseline targets. An even more serious prospect is that in order to reach second-line targets both the RN and Army would have to make swingeing cuts in stock levels of key items including Sidewinder missiles, the new tank gun round and rockets for the new multiple launch rocket system. I cannot believe this is right.[55]

Any idea of a sustainable deterrent force in Europe was undermined by these significant deficiencies in ammunition stocks, logistical handling, resupply and reinforcement. In 1981 the Chiefs of the Defence Staff wrote to the Secretary of State for Defence in the following terms:

Present (and past) policies have ... dangerously lowered the nuclear threshold and represent (of necessity) a return to the 'trip-wire philosophy' of the early 1960s at a time when we no longer have strategic nuclear supremacy and possibly not even parity.[56]

The Sterling value of the shortfall of war reserves was not insignificant. The Armed Forces showed nearly a £1,000m deficit (in 1979 prices) in stockpile requirements in 1980 and following the defence review of 1981, if the finances were to be provided as planned, the three services would take up to a decade to rectify the shortfall. The projected cost alone of providing additional SWINGFIRE and missile war reserves was £201M (1978 value).

The need to increase the ammunition reserves and the urgency for it was not always reflected in the planning process, despite the best efforts of the RARS team. With the expected purchase of weapons and ammunition, estimates were that ammunition stocks to sustain usage for six days' fighting on the Central Front would just have been reached by 1991. But simply increasing the stock of ammunition was not sufficient, given the neglect of the past decades: '... the succession of changes in the Defence Programme in recent years has meant that many of the weapons and systems are not of the preferred type. The RAF, in particular, depend to a great extent on older weapons.'[57] According to the Vice Chief of the Defence Staff (Personnel and Logistics) (VCDS(P&L)) the RAF could only work towards reaching stockpile target levels by, '... making do with out-of-date weapons, many of which are an older generation ... In short, our warstocks are seriously low by our own UK standards and they do not measure up to NATO's current minima ...'[58]

War reserves were an area where economies could be achieved without an appreciable effect on the publicly reported capabilities of the Armed Forces. A 1977 report from the VCGS acknowledged that, at national consumption rates, reserves for key equipment and ammunition would be used up between days one and four of the projected eight-day battle.

As a result of an Army Board decision to effect savings ... the majority of the Army's war reserves are temporarily underimplemented to 80 percent of planned scales, exceptions being rations and POL, which have been maintained at 100 percent level, and certain anti-tank and air defence missiles (e.g. SWINGFIRE, RAPIER and BLOWPIPE), the provision of which was already subject to financial constraints.[59]

This meant that those weapons which were needed in quantity, such as anti-tank and air defence, were at a level lower than 80 percent for purely financial reasons, rather than any military considerations. RAPIER stocks were being built up as this was a new item, but, the '... policy of underimplementation has since been, and continues to be, applied to all new service purchases ...'[60] In 1978 there were only two reloads for each Rapier system on the Central Front.

Modernisation programmes, such as the LTDP and (CDI)I, introduced a significant problem for war reserves: as a weapon system was introduced or increased in number, so the reserve stock of ammunition and spare parts needed to be built up. This situation was aggravated by the policy of saving money by retiring older systems before the new systems were available or fully operational, such as Airborne Early Warning capability on the ASW carriers or keeping old and out-dated systems on long beyond their service life, as with the Mark 8 Torpedo.

Rapier was a relatively short-ranged air defence missile system. In addition to an all-weather radar capability, it could also be employed in an optical mode to enable use in an adverse electronic environment. Seen here is the remote missile firing unit with four ready to launch missiles. (US DoD)

Because of production limitations and budgetary restraints, the front-line equipment and ammunition might be bought and introduced, but the build-up of stocks would be spread over several years, leaving the weapons with no true reserve in the event of war, certainly until many years after their initial introduction. Once the production lines closed the possibility of replacement equipment, or additional ammunition, was almost nil. During production, changes to the design or quantities were difficult to implement. The Navy's view was that, 'A lead time of about 3 years is required to change production plans.'[61]

NATO exercises and adherence to SGN rates had the effect of hiding the real lack of sustainability. The Vice Chief of the Naval Staff wrote in 1977, '... There is no doubt that for major weapons overall our provision is barely adequate [but] against current NATO requirements, which are far from satisfactory, we can legitimately claim that we are adequately provisioned.'[62]

## Readiness and Storage of Stocks

At the same time that budget limits were identified as the major stumbling block to successful implementation of policy, the Armed Forces reported that, 'Ammunition readiness ... remains one of the major obstacles to increased readiness and rapid deployment to the GDP positions.'[63] Nevertheless, the LTDP report findings regarding ammunition readiness for the covering and main defence forces in Germany were effectively dismissed: 'The Report ... tends to suggest that the situation is worse than it actually is. Our readiness plans are based on a compromise between the requirements of war, and the constraints of peacetime regulations tempered by financial constraints.'[64] The tension between NATO demands, in the shape of Force Proposals and the LTDP, and Government policy, constrained as it was by severe financial difficulties, was shown up more clearly in the logistical setting than almost anywhere else.

In addition to the need for transport for the stocks, there was also the need for adequate storage. The cost of storage for the reserve stock increases the overall price of any proposed weapon system, changing the budget from a simple one-off purchase to a long-term expenditure. The Private Secretary for the Minister of Defence was moved to justify the parlous state the reserves had got into by saying;

While the policy underlying attrition rates is obviously crucial, it makes little sense to come up with a theoretical war reserves holding which we cannot afford, for which we have no storage

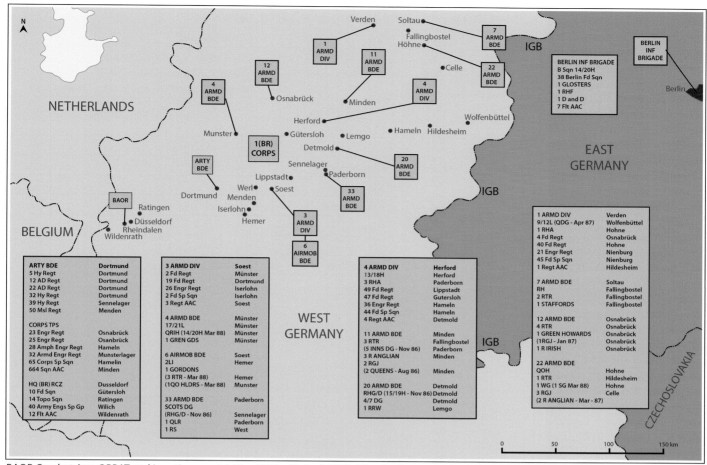

BAOR Combat Arm ORBAT and Locations as at 1 May 1986 – 31 April 1987. (Map by George Anderson)

facilities and which we could not deploy sufficiently quickly after hostilities break out.[65]

Rather than rectifying these drawbacks, the justification was to reduce war stocks as a cost-saving measure because they would never be used.

There were significant deficiencies in logistical handling equipment and the transport chain. In the late 1970s and early 1980s it was evident that the personnel numbers, equipment and transport available to load and move the ammunition reserve was totally inadequate for the task. New ammunition for new weapons cause storage problems in their own right, with the rounds for FH70 and SP70 guns being three times heavier, and twice the volume, of the weapons being replaced. 'The problems of peacetime storage, outloading of depots during a time of reduced warning, and daily resupply are manifold. (Existing war reserve stocks of ammunition weigh over 100,000 tons; a 155mm shell weighs 96lbs [43.5Kg]).'[66] The unspectacular side of defence planning emerged in the need for, '… 1000 additional 8 tonne trucks and 1200 trailers …'[67] Without these and their drivers, the ammunition and supplies would not be delivered to the forward units. The FV431 (a derivative of the FV432 armoured personnel carrier) had been designed as an armoured load carrier for just this type of operation, but only one prototype was built. Vehicles which provided ammunition supply to the armoured units were soft-skinned, such as the amphibious FV620 Stalwart, and vulnerable to small-arms fire. The lorries then available did not have the necessary capabilities for the required readiness levels of the 1980s. An increase in the numbers of forklift trucks, lorries and trailers, as well as 3,000 extra troops, were required to meet the transport needs for an 8-day resupply.

An additional 1,500 support vehicles with a self-lift capability were to be added by 1988. Most of these would be 2nd and 3rd line vehicles, with only a small proportion allocated to the 1st line, or unit, level. Logistic handling systems such as DROPS (Demountable Rack Offload System) and MMLC (Medium Mobility Load Carrier) were developed for the expected combat levels in Germany. By 1989, 827 14-Tonne load carriers and 3,006 8-Tonne load carries of this type had been brought into service. The rail flatbed cars initially bought by the British Government to work with DROPS were not ISO compatible and were eventually replaced. The MMLC and DROPS system was implemented after the fall of the Berlin Wall, but in time for the 1991 Gulf War.

Despite efforts to improve the WMR and ammunition handling and transport problem, the situation would not improve quickly. The planning process had begun in 1971, and as part of the NATO Infrastructure projects, storage and handling depots were planned for BAOR throughout the 1980s. It was estimated that there would be sufficient ammunition storage space by 1986 for only four and a half days of intensive fighting, even though the new Forward Storage Sites were expected to be completed by 1987.

The NATO Defence Planning Programme called for the need to increase holdings of mechanical handling equipment and accelerate the Forward Storage Site Programme. Deciding on the location of main ammunition storage was an operational level problem. The location of main ammunition storage – east or west of the Rhine – was important for two reasons. Firstly, the stores needed to be where they could be quickly outloaded to the necessary units. Secondly, they needed to be far enough back so that they would not be easily overrun by the advancing WTO troops. These demands placed on storage locations seemed to be mutually exclusive, and indeed the final locations were not ideal in terms of proximity to the land forces. Locations towards the IGB, east of major river lines such as the Weser, caused problems for planners because in some scenarios the advancing WTO troops would be at the Weser within 30 hours, negating the utility of having forward located supply dumps.

Unit ammunition was stored within 20km of a unit's barracks, but this would be ready-use ammunition only. The single most difficult problem in providing sufficient storage for reserve stocks of ammunition and POL far enough forward was the FRG Government. It was a, '…difficult and protracted business …'[68] to obtain the land, hence assuming command of existing storage sites was preferred. For example, facilities at Wohle were to be taken over from the FRG as a forward storage site for the BAOR reconnaissance force but was only some 25–30km from the IGB, and thus directly threatened by even a small advance by WTO forces. Loading of ready-use ammunition provided another problem – vehicles could not be left 'bombed-up' and available for use because of the UN Agreement on Ammunition Storage, the FRG Environmental Laws and UK storage regulations. Most British forces were stationed in populated areas, and vehicles carrying ammunition would be vulnerable. As the MoD insisted that all the units could be uploaded in 11 hours, keeping vehicles 'bombed-up' was deemed unnecessary. However, this 11-hour figure is based on full mobilisation of all units, provided only after the reservists are mobilised and moved to West Germany.

| Table 1: Forces committed by Britain to NATO, 1979[72] | | |
|---|---|---|
| Force | Size | Consisting of |
| ACE Mobile Force (AMF) | 1,800 personnel | One infantry Battalion group Logistical Support Battalion Additional combat and support troops |
| | 1 Squadron | Harriers |
| | 1 Squadron | Pumas |
| UKMF | 13,500 personnel | 6th Field Force |
| | 1 Squadron | Jaguars |
| | 1 Squadron | Pumas |
| Strategic Air Reserve | 3 Squadrons | Jaguars |
| | 1 Squadron | Harriers |
| Unit Reinforcements | | SAS Units |
| | 1 Squadron | Buccaneers |
| | 2 Squadrons | Canberra Reconnaissance |
| | 1 Squadron | Vulcan Maritime Recce |
| UK/NL Amphibious Force | | 1 Brigade HQ |
| | | 4 Royal Marine Commandos plus organic logistics, artillery, engineers and special units. |
| EASTLANT and CHAN | 4 | Polaris Submarines |
| | 25+ | Conventional and Nuclear-Powered Submarines |
| | 2 | ASW/Commando Carriers |
| | 1 | Assault Ships |
| | 65 | Destroyers and Frigates |
| | 29 | Royal Fleet Auxiliary ships |
| | 36 | Mine Counter Measure Vessels/Minesweepers |
| | 4 Squadrons | Sea King ASW |
| | 4 Squadrons | Nimrod MR |
| | 2 Squadrons | Phantom Maritime version |
| BAOR | 55,000 – 100,000 personnel | 1(BR) Corps HQ |
| | | 4 Armoured Divisions |
| | | 5th Field Force |
| | | 7th Field Force (from UK) |
| RAF(G) 2nd Tactical Air Force | 2 Squadrons | Buccaneers |
| | 4 Squadrons | Jaguar (strike) |
| | 1 Squadron | Jaguar (rec) |
| | 2 Squadrons | Harrier |
| | 2 Squadrons | AD Phantom |
| | 1 Squadron | Wessex |

## Conclusion

There was a NATO-wide failure to obtain universally agreed stock levels and force requirements. This led to the British Government having to deal with fundamental discrepancies between the MoD and NATO over the War Maintenance Reserve levels. There were disagreements regarding readiness levels and mobilisation of reservists, and their speed of deployment. Whilst publicly declaring conformity with NATO requirements for stocks and reservists, the British Government was secretly very clear about the deficiencies.

The armed forces relied to an increasing extent on reservists to fill-out the fighting units as well as the rear area and logistic units. The levels of the War Maintenance Reserve (WMR) and logistic support were consistently below that required for any sustained combat. These two 'reserve' elements featured in almost all Task Forces of

The Puma HC.1 was the RAF's medium utility helicopter in Germany. There were relatively few available for all the needs that would likely arise. This example, from No. 230 Squadron is taking part in Exercise White Rhino in 1989. (Walter Böhm)

The Chinook HC.1 was the heavy lift helicopter of the RAF's Helicopter Support Force. Rated to carry 44 fully equipped troops during peacetime, this limit was greatly exceeded by the single surviving example used during the Falklands War. It was also frequently used to carry underslung cargo, light vehicles or artillery pieces. Much like the Puma, the Chinook was available to RAF Germany in only limited numbers and demand would have likely greatly exceeded availability. (Walter Böhm)

the Long Term Defence Plan, as well as the Conventional Defence Improvement Initiative (CDI(I)).

The reluctance to accept the LTDP findings regarding the failure of NATO's logistics to support the strategy of flexible response demonstrated a position frequently adopted by the British Government. It did not reflect the deep concern shown by some politicians such as Dr David Owen, and those serving officers who repeatedly warned the Government of the shortcomings of the mobilisation, stocks and supply capabilities of the British Armed Forces.

The Chiefs of the Defence Staff were aware of the deficiencies, and in 1981 warned, 'Decisions taken now to restore stock levels could, for financial, industrial and technological reasons, still take some ten years or more before they have been fully implemented. In the meantime the nuclear threshold will not be far removed from MC14/2.'[69] This meant that, despite NATO adjusting its strategy in 1967 with the full support of the member states, Britain would not be in a position to fulfil the commitment made in the late 1960s until the early 1990s, if all went as planned. John Nott[70] wrote, 'You must never

A flight of four BAe Harrier GR.3s of the RAF operating over Germany. The GR.3 was a versatile platform that could be used in the ground attack or reconnaissance roles and carry a payload of iron bombs, BL755 cluster bombs, or SNEB 68mm rocket pods. Laser guided bombs became available in limited quantities in the very late stages of the Falklands War in 1982. (British Aerospace)

let the ordinary naval rating or soldier down by skimping on his ammunition, his kit, his training and his food …'[71] However, these were the areas which were most prone to financial cuts.

# 5
# THE SERVICES

## Modernisation and reorganisation

Modernisation became a thread that passed through the policy documents of the MOD during the 1970s and into the 1980s. Outdated systems needed to be replaced, and run-down defences strengthened. NATO had, from its inception, relied on improving technology to redress the numerical imbalance between NATO and the WTO. How should an improvement in qualitative terms, such as the NATO modernisation programme, be measured against a qualitative AND quantitative improvement in the expected enemy's capabilities? Against such an improvement by the enemy, a qualitative improvement in one's own forces (in addition to a quantitative reduction such as the British Armed Forces faced), unless it is significant, will not sufficiently level the advantage that the enemy has gained.

As the NATO assessment indicated that the conventional forces were inadequate for the defence of Western Europe against an increasingly numerous, and capable, WTO threat, the Alliance members now had to wrestle with the balance between numbers and new, up-to-date, equipment. Despite the background of economic stagnation and political upheaval, as well as increasing unit costs, the required modernisation was essential, but introduced the problem of 'modernisation inflation'. This suggested that improvements in technology increase the weapon cost per unit and required increased levels of education and training amongst the operators, increasing costs further.

NATO placed great reliance on introducing technology to offset the numerical superiority of the Warsaw Pact. This development included modernised guided weapons for anti-tank, anti-aircraft and anti-ship tasks. Ships, aircraft and armoured vehicles were becoming more complex in their defensive and offensive capability to be able to survive and operate in the expected war-fighting environment. When nuclear weapons were unsuitable extremely accurate weapons were required which could destroy pin-point targets with a high probability. However, those improvements in technology were not universally applied. Communication systems had not been improved in line with

weaponry, which caused the Deputy Commander-in-Chief Allied Forces Central Europe to write: 'Our communications are still abysmal and are still geared to the [MC]14/2 strategy of immediate nuclear response.'[2] The development and implementation of new

The British Army was late to adopt infantry fighting vehicles. The FV510 Warrior only slowly entered service with BAOR from 1988. Forty-five Warriors would displace the equivalent number of FV432s to convert an FV432-mounted mechanised infantry battalion to an armoured infantry battalion, the balance retaining their old vehicles. (US DoD)

An FV4030/4 Challenger of 2 Royal Tank Regiment taking part in Exercise White Rhino in 1989. The Challenger was always viewed as a stop-gap development following the failure of the MBT-80 programme. Adapted at short notice from the Shir 2 destined for Iran, it still shared much technology from the Chieftain, including the L11 120mm gun, though the Chobham armour offered greatly improved protection over the frontal arc against penetration by High Explosive Anti-Tank weapons and the engine was far more reliable. Note the shutter on the right-hand side of the turret is open, exposing the lens of the Thermal Observation Gunnery Sight. (Walter Böhm)

The T-80 was the last of the Cold War Soviet MBTs, entering service with the Group of Soviet Forces in Germany (GSFG) in the 1980s. Well armoured and carrying a 125mm 2A46 gun with an automatic loader, it was further enhanced in the later 80s through the addition of explosive reactive armour (ERA) designed to defeat NATO's prolific anti-tank guided weapons – such as MILAN, SWINGFIRE and TOW – and some were fitted with ATGW of their own (9K112 Kobra/AT-8 Songster or 9M119 Svir/Refleks/AT-11 Sniper) that could be fired through the main gun. The post-Cold War reputation of the T-80 was severely damaged by the excessive and unnecessary losses suffered in the street battles of Grozny in 1994–1995, though in the 1980s it was considered a grave threat to NATO. (US DoD)

equipment or superior tactics and operational mobility to counter the numerical difference. In Britain a new tank and infantry fighting vehicle (IFV) were being developed (Challenger and Warrior) as well as new ships and aircraft (Tornado) and weapons (JP233, LAW80).[4] The developments were the outcome of decades of military demands and technological inventions that enabled those demands to be met. Until these were operational, NATO forces would be entering a battle knowing they had a quantitative disadvantage, relying on the slim qualitative advantage.

New equipment programmes had been cancelled to reduce the defence budget. Notable amongst the cancellations was the CVA-01 Aircraft Carrier and the Tactical Strike and Reconnaissance (TSR-2) aircraft. The TSR-2

technology was a continuous process as were the development of doctrines and plans to exploit it.

In the NATO Central Region, most, if not all the NATO allies were relying on quality to succeed over quantity in a war, but the disparity in the quality of the tanks of each side was not as significant as previously. Indeed, some analysts believed the Soviet T-80 was almost on a par with NATO's Main Battle Tanks (MBT). The Defence Committee noted in 1980 that, 'Intelligence assessments since 1977, accepted in NATO, indicate a much greater advance in the quality of Soviet Tanks … than had previously been thought possible.'[3] Therefore NATO believed it would have been at a quantitative disadvantage which was not levelled by a sufficiently large qualitative superiority. The number of anti-tank weapons available had increased significantly, and so had their effectiveness, but this applied to both sides. NATO could not rely on air superiority, qualitatively superior

These soldiers from the Corps of Drums of the Irish Guards were taking part in Exercise Crusader '80 and had travelled by road and sea from Chelsea Barracks in London. Their role in the exercise was to guard the bridges on the Mittelland Canal against an enemy airborne coup de main, on this occasion the threat being from US forces. (Photo US DoD, with thanks to Tony Trainor, ex-Irish Guards for the additional information)

For those infantry in frontline mechanized battalions that were not yet upgraded with Warrior, the venerable FV432 continued to be their workhorse. A classic 'battle taxi' design dating from the 1960s, troops were still expected to dig-in to fight as their mount had neither the armament nor armour to stay in the battle and would typically be withdrawn to a safe area referred to as a 'Zulu Muster'. (Walter Böhm)

The FV510 was the British Army's first true IFV. It began to enter unit service in 1988 with sufficient numbers to equip one battalion per year with 45 vehicles. This example is being operated by the Staffordshire Regiment in 1989 during Exercise White Rhino. The Staffords would be the first regiment to deploy the Warrior into a war zone when they formed part of 7th Armoured Brigade in Saudi Arabia in 1990/91. (Walter Böhm)

TA battalions. The Field Force structure was found to be unsatisfactory, and BAOR was again restructured in 1983 to provide three divisions in West Germany, with one infantry division mainly consisting of Territorial units in the UK for reinforcement of BAOR in time of war. 1st and 4th Divisions would be stationed on the IGB, with 3rd Division in reserve. 2nd Infantry Division would operate in the rear area protecting lines of communication.

## Royal Navy

A crucial role for the Royal Navy was the free use of the seas by the NATO navies, and the denial of access to, and use of, the Northern and Eastern Atlantic to the mainly Soviet submarines and surface ships intent on intercepting the reinforcement of Western Europe. To achieve this objective the Navy required sufficient vessels armed with adequate numbers of up-to-date weapons. All the major vessels of the Royal Navy were under NATO command or NATO assigned, with the remaining vessels available to support NATO operations. In addition was the Royal Marine Commando (RM) Brigade. The RM were NATO Assigned at high readiness as part of the UK/Netherlands Amphibious force but could also be deployed under National Command.

Originating from the Harmel Report, Standing Naval Force Atlantic (STANAVFORLANT) was a multi-national force established in January 1968.[5] It comprised between four and nine destroyer or frigate-type ships, of with the UK contributed one vessel, operating continuously under the command of the Supreme Allied Commander Atlantic (SACLANT).

had been cancelled in 1965 because of inter-service rivalry and cost-overruns. An order for 50 General Dynamics F-111, which were to replace the TSR-2, was cancelled in 1968.

Reorganisation and restructuring of BAOR persisted through the 1970s and 1980s in various attempts to reduce costs and improve 'efficiency'. In 1975 several brigade HQs were removed and the formation of 'Field Forces' which were stationed in the UK took place. Divisions would have two Task Forces, each of which was equivalent to a large brigade. All BAOR infantry units were intended to be equipped with the FV432 armoured personnel carrier (APC), ultimately to be replaced with Warrior Infantry Fighting Vehicle (IFV). The wheeled SAXON APC would equip the

The Royal Navy was structured for anti-submarine (ASW) and anti-air warfare (AAW), to protect the sea-lanes around the UK and Continent. Assigned to NATO at mobilisation would be two Heli-carriers, two Escort carriers, nine Air Defence/Anti-Submarine Warfare (AD/ASW) Escorts, 17 Anti-Surface/Anti-Submarine Warfare (ASS/ASW) Escorts, four ASW Escorts and 20 submarines. Four Squadrons of Long-Range Maritime Patrol aircraft, originally Shackleton, were dedicated to NATO. The Royal Navy had modern

Ark Royal was the last of three Invincible-class light aircraft carriers to enter service with the Royal Navy. Originally envisaged as a helicopter-only platform, the class actually entered service equipped with a ski-jump, clearly visible here, to enable the Sea Harrier to conduct short rolling take-offs and demonstrated the value of this capability in the 1982 Falklands conflict. (US DoD)

The licence-built Westland Sea King provided the main anti-submarine capability of the Invincible-class carriers, equipped with dipping sonar and armed with lightweight torpedoes. This particular example is seen off the coast of Norway during Exercise Northern Wedding '86 providing ASW support to a US amphibious group, a Newport-class LST of which can be seen in the distance. (US DoD)

The Sea Harrier (SHAR) FRS1 was the Fleet Air Arm's only fixed-wing combat aircraft after the retirement of the last of the conventional carriers in the 1970s. Armed with two, later four, AIM-9L Sidewinder air-to-air missiles when in the air-to-air role, the SHAR was to prove invaluable in the Falklands campaign. (US DoD)

weapon systems, a small pool of highly trained regular personnel, but limited war-stocks of ammunition for its main vessels.

The RN had the Fleet-classes of nuclear-powered hunter-killer submarines and the older diesel electric boats of the Oberon- and Porpoise-classes capable of hunter-killer operations or minelaying. The hunter-killer submarines were intended to sink WTO submarines and hunt the WTO nuclear missile carrying vessels. Accounting for those submarines undergoing refits, in 1979/1980 there was a 20 percent shortfall in war-loads of torpedoes for these submarines.

The 'Anti-Submarine Carriers' such as HMS *Invincible* began sea-trials in 1979. These ships were to provide command and control for ASW operations in the Eastern Atlantic. However, a reduction in the number of ASW helicopters to be carried on them meant that this capability would be at its limit. HMS *Hermes* became the last of the Centaur-class aircraft carriers (HMS *Bulwark* was decommissioned in 1981) and was scheduled for decommissioning in 1982. *Hermes* was saved by the outbreak of the Falklands War, and finally sold to India in 1986. With the cancellation of CVA-01 aircraft carriers in the 1966 Defence Review, and the scheduled disposal of *Hermes*, the 'Through Deck Cruisers' would become the Royal Navy's only fixed wing capable carriers using the Sea Harrier, as well as Sea King helicopters in the anti-submarine and recovery roles. The Sea Harrier was to enter front-line service in 1980, fitted with the Blue Fox radar and Sidewinder AIM-9L. HMS *Invincible* was launched in 1980, HMS *Illustrious* launched in 1982 and HMS *Ark Royal* operational in 1986.

All frigates and larger ships were to be equipped with helicopters, and the anti-submarine role strengthened with the introduction of the Wessex Mk 3. The Sea King anti-submarine helicopter was due for replacement, and a project was under way to identify a successor. It was anticipated that this would be part of a European helicopter package, which turned into the Merlin, or EH101, from what became AgustaWestland. The replacement was urgently required, as there was great reliance placed on the use of helicopters in the Royal Navy anti-submarine role. Notwithstanding the urgent need for replacement of Sea King, the EH101 did not enter service until 1999.

A core part of the force dedicated to NATO was the frigates and destroyers for anti-submarine, carrier and general escort duty. Examples of the ships operated by the Royal Navy for NATO's escort role were the Leander, Type 22 and Type 42 vessels. NATO force goals required the Royal Navy to provide 55 escorts for SACLANT by 1986, with 35 of them being at the highest state of readiness. Because of budget cuts, only 40 would be available, and at a lower overall level of readiness. Equally, 13 escorts were requested for ACCHAN by 1986, but only 10 were offered.

Among the smallest vessels were the Leander-class frigates. These were of an all-purpose type, with a modernisation programme under way. The Ikara anti-submarine weapon system or the Exocet anti-ship missile were to be installed, which meant removing the forward 4.5" gun due to space restrictions. Some Exocet equipped Leanders were assigned to Channel Command, and SACLANT had requested the Leander to be equipped with the Sea Wolf point defence missile for better survivability, but this was not accepted. By 1985 there were 18 Leander-class vessels available.

The Type 22 Frigates were intended to replace the smaller Leanders and complement the Type 42 air defence vessels. These Frigates were to have the Sea Wolf missile, and some were to have Exocet. SACLANT had request six Type 22s by 1984 with five in service in 1984 rising to seven in 1985. Type 22s were criticised for having low cost-effectiveness, and making only a slight, last-ditch, contribution to future anti-submarine warfare as envisaged by the Admiralty.

The Leanders were a prolific class of frigate that first entered service with the Royal Navy in 1963. Built in three distinct batches, they were continually upgraded throughout their life and saw a range of weapon fits. This example is armed with the Seawolf point defence anti-air missile and Exocet surface-to-surface anti-ship missiles. Unusually it does not display a pennant number. (US DoD)

HMS *Liverpool*, seen here, was a Type 42 Destroyer primarily armed with Sea Dart missiles and a 4.5" gun. The Sea Dart was a reasonably effective weapon against medium to high altitude targets in open water, but the Type 42's lack of effective close-in weapon systems led to the loss of HMS *Sheffield* to an Exocet missile and HMS *Coventry* to low level bombing attack during the Falklands conflict. (US DoD)

HMS *Brazen*, a Type 22 frigate, is seen here during the 1991 Gulf War armed with Sea Wolf point defence anti-air missiles and Exocet surface-to-surface anti-ship missiles. It also carries a Lynx HAS.3 anti-submarine helicopter, capable of employing Sea Skua missiles for use against light surface vessels. (US DoD)

The Type 21 frigate, also known as the Amazon-class after its lead ship, seen here, was intended as a cheap general-purpose frigate. It was primarily armed with a 4.5" gun, ASW torpedoes and Sea Cat missiles (though the latter were barely adequate). Some of the class were also fitted with Exocet surface-to-surface anti-ship missiles, as seen here just above and behind the 4.5" gun turret. Two examples were lost to enemy action in the Falklands conflict, HMS *Antelope* and *Ardent*. (US DoD)

The Type 42 Guided Missile Destroyer was proposed as a cheaper replacement for the Type 82 air defence vessels which was intended to escort the new aircraft carriers. It had been cancelled at the same time as the CVA-01 following the 1966 Defence Review. The hull for HMS *Bristol* had already been laid down and was the only example of the Type 82 built.

There were four Type 42s in service in 1979, with two more under construction. The Type 42s were to have been upgraded with a close-in weapons system (CIWS) to improve survivability against missile attack, but this programme was cancelled in 1980 for financial reasons.[6] This was to have dramatic repercussions during the Falklands War, with *Coventry* and *Sheffield* being lost. Twelve Type 42s were in service by 1985, missing SACLANT's Maritime Force Proposal by two vessels.

The Type 42 and the planned Type 23 typified the cost-saving measures demanded by the Government. Keith Speed, who had been sacked as Navy Minister a few days before for criticising the reduction of the fleet, said in the House of Commons on 19 May 1981; '… we cannot continue to have frigates costing £130 million a time, excellent though they are. … They are first-class ships, but, frankly, we cannot afford them in the numbers that we need …'[7]

The Type 42 had been subject to design changes to reduce its cost, and the Type 23 design, approved in 1983, was intended to be a cheap 'complement' for the Type 22. It would end up costing almost as much, with modifications and additional weaponry added, as a consequence of the lessons from the Falklands. Despite these lessons, the Type 23 still was not fitted with an anti-missile close-in weapon system as a result of cost savings. To reduce some of the costs of modernisation there was an effort to replace expensive and sophisticated equipment with simpler, and therefore cheaper, alternatives. The replacement of the Leander and Type 21 Frigates with Type 23 was intended to save money, although with changes following the Falklands War, and other modifications, the Type 23 proved not to be any cheaper than the ship it was replacing.

The Type 23 was designed to be a cheap ASW escort – to provide a helicopter with [nuclear depth bombs] and torpedoes to kill submarines. Cheapness was to be achieved through automation, reducing the crew size, relying on a 30-day patrol cycle (i.e. only staying away from port for 30 days) and presuming that the ships themselves would be provided with protection by other ships.[8] This design proved unsatisfactory, and investment in a significant improvement programme was needed to improve the ship's capabilities.

Improvements in some areas were complicated by a policy which was known to the Royal Navy as 'short-lifing', in which vessels would be disposed of before their scheduled service life ended. This policy was implemented in all the services as a means of saving money in preparation for the introduction of a replacement system. It happened with the Nimrod, and has continued to happen, one recent example being the scrapping of Harriers in 2010 with its replacement, the F-35B, eventually coming into service in 2019.

The naval modernisation programme, which was to be implemented from the beginning of 1980, was hit hardest by the Government moratorium on new defence projects, and the run-up to and presentation of the 1981 Defence Review. Modernisation should have included the addition of several new types of missile to various ship classes, most notably the Sea Dart surface-to-air missile, which had been accepted into service 1978, and was to be fitted to all Type 42 Destroyers. These modernisation plans were abandoned for financial reasons as part of the 1981 review, and a study started to investigate the best method for the upkeep of the vessels.

The emphasis in the 1981 Review was to be on the Army and RAF in continental Europe, with the surface ships of the Navy and the extra-NATO role being the target of cuts. The nuclear deterrent was seen as inviolable, and there remained little to cut in the Continental commitment.[9] This meant the Navy took the brunt of the defence cuts in the 1981 review. The review identified, '… the best balanced operational contribution for our situation – will be one which continues to enhance our maritime-air and submarine effort, but accepts a reduction below current plans in the size of our surface fleet …'[10] This replicated the reduction in destroyers, frigates and mine countermeasures vessels, a reduction in amphibious vessels and conventional submarines, and an increase in nuclear-powered submarines, outlined by the Labour Government in 1975. Forty-nine destroyers and frigates had been previously declared to NATO, but that figure was to be cut to 48, along with a substantial reduction in the RFA and other specialist ships. The Royal Navy provision for the Eastern Atlantic and Channel was lacking by a considerable proportion, and the British Government expected NATO to express concern.

Several shipbuilding plans were either cut or deferred, along with upgrades to some existing ships. Among those cancellations were six Mine Counter Measures vessels and one Type 22. There were some closures of Naval Shore Establishments to save money, but there was the development of Marchwood Military Port, planning for which had begun in June 1978. This was to provide regular shipments to Antwerp for BAOR and featured heavily in its reinforcement plans. Functional, and therefore well protected, ports were essential to all the maritime forces whether combat or transport vessels. Protection of these vital installations required both defensive mining and mine clearance capabilities. Clearing mines in home waters would be a problem, as, according to the Secretary of State for Defence, '… after securing the approaches to the nuclear submarine base at Faslane, we [have] insufficient resources to clear the cross-Channel routes and provide safe access to our major ports.'[11]

The Mine Counter Measure vessels were meant to locate and destroy enemy mines, and the MoD would, '… need to take up ships from trade (on a voluntary basis) in support of these operations.'[12] Great reliance was placed on the taking up of trawlers in periods of tension, but the timing for equipping the vessels would mean that there would need to be a decision early in any crisis. Many of the minesweepers were crewed by the Royal Navy Reserve, and hence would be delayed in becoming operational. In 1979, there were thirty-three Coniston (or Ton) -class Mine Countermeasures Vessels

(MCMV) listed, although three were on standby or undergoing maintenance and sixteen were deployed as either sea training tenders for the RNR, or coastal fisheries protection.

The Ton-class was designed for use in shallow seas and coastal waters or rivers and ports. Being obsolete, with ineffective sensor equipment, they were to be replaced by a new, plastic hulled Hunt-class vessel. Plans were to have 30 new Hunt-class vessels by the early 1990s. The first Hunt-class Mine Countermeasure Vessel, HMS *Brecon*, was due to enter service in 1979. HMS *Ledbury* was to be launched in 1979, with three more ships on order. However, the cuts of 1981 hit the Mine Countermeasure Vessels hard, with six previously planned orders being dropped. By 1985 there were meant to be twelve Hunt-class in service and fifteen Tons, but the actual numbers were ten Hunt and thirteen Ton.

Limited stocks of mines meant that defensive mining, upon which the Navy relied for part of the defence of the home islands, would fall seriously short of requirements, due to some mine development having been cancelled for financial reasons. In planning the defensive mining of the UK, Commander Parry, writing on behalf of the Director of Naval Warfare, listed the number of mines available for protective mining (1,460 in total) and asked that future plans should be based on the number required, rather than those available. Much of the perceived shortfall was due to cost-cutting exercises in the 1970s, and the Director of Naval Plans wrote in reply, 'In noting the numbers of mines available … the suggestion … that plans should be based on numbers required rather than what is actually in stock, DN [Director Naval Warfare] plans … will be guided by the cost restriction … the plan should be limited to involve little or no capital expenditure.'[13]

Supporting all the vessels in the Royal Navy, from Carriers to Minesweepers, were the ships of the Royal Feet Auxiliaries (RFA). They provided everything from fuel supply to sealift capability, and included the stores ships *Stromness*, *Tarbatness* and *Lyness*. *Tarbatness* was to be converted to amphibious tasks in support of the RM Commando Brigade during 1979. This was under review due to costs in 1980, and this vessel shows in the 1981/1982 Defence Estimate working papers as being for sale. All three were sold to the USA to be used as Military Sealift Command vessels but there was no indication of replacement ships from the subsequent Navy lists or the Defence Estimates.

Much of the planning for reinforcement of Europe in time of war relied on the speedy requisitioning of merchant shipping, both for transport of reinforcements and for the maintenance of trade for vital supplies. Ships would need requisitioning early in any crisis as the Royal Fleet Auxiliary had insufficient capacity for all the demands that would be placed upon it. Along with a multitude of other tasks, RORO ferries were to be used to transport troops and equipment to Europe. The need to co-ordinate merchant shipping would be left, according to NATO, until the outbreak of hostilities. The British Government, perhaps conscious of its reliance on maritime supply, had a complex but comprehensive set of controls that could be put in place for the naval control of all shipping of any sort, access to ports and anchorages, restriction of access and departure from British waters, and the requisitioning of foreign ships for national use.

Technological advances in communications and data processing led to several projects throughout the late 1970s and 1980s intended to improve command and control as well as weapon targeting. Improvements for ships and submarines, announced in the 1979 SDE, had contracts awarded in 1984 to Ferranti to develop the 2050 bow mounted sonar, which was subsequently fitted to the Types

42, 23 and 22. A Maritime Navigation System to provide warships with computer assisted navigation was planned, with new satellite and radio communications to be introduced by mid-1980s. The Operational Control Command Control and Information System (OPCON), a new Automatic Data Processing (ADP) system which integrated with the NATO Commands was introduced and updated throughout the decade. The data link between vessels showed its worth during the Falklands War, with various ships sharing data related to threats via dedicated digital links. Other new and emerging technologies were providing the basis for development of radar jamming equipment, new electronic warfare passive surveillance capabilities and radar interception equipment for surface ships. Automated Data Processing systems were extended to cover Royal Navy shore-based establishments, improving data links between sea and land.

## Royal Marines

The role of the Royal Marines (RM) was to support and strengthen the vulnerable flanks of the NATO Central Region, as well as the protection of more vulnerable, but vital, islands of EASTLANT. The Commando units were all lorry mounted and, consequently, significantly less mobile and secure than either the SAXON- or FV432-equipped units. Because of the need to strengthen the anti-armour capability of any units that might have to directly face the WTO troops, the RM Commando were to receive MILAN ATGW, as well as having TOW missiles fitted to their LYNX in early 1980s. The allocation of MILAN was not to be at the same level as in 'heavy' infantry formations (18 MILAN in the RM, 24 in the mechanised Infantry 'A' battalions).

41 Commando had been reformed in 1977 but was to be merged with the other Commandos as a result of the 1981 Defence Review, thus keeping the same number of troops, but reducing the cost of overheads. In a briefing note regarding this, the question was put regarding the effect this will have on Britain's NATO commitments, to which the answer was, '… that we will have one fewer Commando than planned.'[14]

## Royal Air Force

Since the 1950s, the size and capability of the RAF had diminished, especially since the nuclear deterrent role had passed to the Royal Navy. The RAF had a particularly wide-ranging remit under NATO, employed in the Channel, Eastern Atlantic, Central Air Defence Region and the UK Air Defence Region (UKADR). For the Royal Air Force to be credible, it had to counter the threat of large-scale ground and air attack on the Central Front, interdict enemy movement behind the front, and protect the air above and the sea surrounding the home islands. It also had to provide part of the early warning and reconnaissance capability for NATO.

The Nimrod MR1 was a popular and efficient maritime reconnaissance and submarine-hunting aircraft based on the de Havilland Comet of 1950s vintage. Long-ranged, it could carry large numbers of sonar-buoys for use in the ASW role. Its weapons bay could carry free fall bombs or depth charges (nuclear or conventional) or ASW torpedoes. Underwing pylons could carry Harpoon anti-ship missiles and AIM-9 Sidewinder air-to-air missiles, the latter added as an urgent operational requirement during the Falklands conflict. (US DoD)

The RAF was divided into RAF Germany (RAF(G)) and Strike Command. The Commander-in-Chief (CINC) of Strike Command was NATO CINC UK Air Forces responsible for the air defence of the UK and naval units and shipping in the surrounding waters. Strike Command provided offensive aircraft in support of SACEUR and the maritime operations of CINCHAN and SACLANT. No 11 Group provided all-weather fighters for the air defence of the UK base, and one squadron for maritime defence. No 18 Group provided Nimrod maritime reconnaissance aircraft, Sea King, Whirlwind and Wessex helicopters. No 38 Group provided Jaguar and Harrier squadrons for SACEUR's strategic reserve, and also worked with UKMF. The air contribution to the UK Mobile Force (UKMF(A)) was two Phantom ground attack squadrons, one Harrier ground attack squadron, one Andover transport squadron, two Puma and

A pair of RAF Harrier GR.3s are seen here flying in formation. The Harrier's short take-off capability made it useful in support of the UK Mobile Force as it would be able to operate from austere or damaged facilities. (British Aerospace)

Rapier was a short-ranged area defence anti-aircraft guided weapon system employed by the Royal Artillery in support of the Army and the RAF Regiment for the defence of airfields (including some USAF bases in the UK) and Harrier hides. Seen here are the Blindfire radar and target tracking systems. Rapier had a mixed record in the Falklands, with some fire units taking an excessive amount of time to bring online following their voyage south. (US DoD)

one Wessex squadrons. In 1978 it comprised two Jaguar combat squadrons, a Jaguar tactical reconnaissance squadron and a support helicopter force of 22 Pumas and 20 Wessex.

The number of aeroplanes in the RAF was reduced by almost 10 percent in the first few years of the 1980s. In the same way that the other services were subject to severe cuts, the RAF suffered shortages in almost all areas of its operations. Recruitment of the necessary technical and flight personnel was a problem. Two thousand fewer personnel would be recruited in 1981 than had previously been planned. Fast jet pilots and engineering officers were areas of the worst shortage.

The Harrier was under development for introduction into the RAF in 1970, but the introduction of the UK version of the McDonnell Douglas Phantom was delayed because of development problems. The V-bombers were to be transferred from the nuclear role to a tactical role with the launch of the Polaris submarines carrying the nuclear deterrent. Maritime reconnaissance was to be taken up by the new Nimrod aircraft, which was a development of the commercial Comet airliner. This was meant to replace the Shackleton, which was based on the venerable Lancaster bomber from the Second World War.

RAF Germany was to provide close air support for the Northern Army Group (NORTHAG) and air defence for the West German Air Defence Identification Zone. RAF Germany had 11 squadrons in the 2nd Allied Tactical Air Force (2ATAF) to provide close air support for NORTHAG. Some of the air defence and strike aircraft were assigned to the protection of seaborne forces, which included two squadrons of Phantoms and two of Buccaneers. The RAF provided Bloodhound and Rapier missile air defence systems for airfields in Germany and the UK.

Air defence of the UK had suffered considerably during the early Cold War. The expectation had been that any war would turn nuclear very quickly, the provision of expensive air defence systems was considered unnecessary. In 1978 the Secretary of State for Defence warned the Prime Minister;

… there are only enough BLOODHOUNDs, which cover 15 key RAF and US airfields, for a single reload. Air defence relies upon a largely unhardened radar ground environment, supplemented by information from … a single squadron of obsolete airborne early warning aircraft. Much of the command and control system is unhardened, insecure and vulnerable to sabotage and jamming.[15]

By 1981 the Conservative Government saw the air defence of the UK as being, '… at a dangerously low level … The UK is a forward base for SACLANT and a rear base for SACEUR. About 40% of all US aircraft earmarked for use in war in Europe will be based in this country and the UK will be a vital reinforcement platform for Europe.'[16]

The LTDP specified UK Air Defence numbers in 1978 to be 144 fighters, but there were only 98. The Air Defence version of the Tornado, which was supposed to replace the Lightning and Phantom on a one-to-one basis, would not come into service until 1985. This deficit became known as the 'Fighter Gap', a phrase coined to describe both home defence and the capabilities of the RAF on the Central Front. The planned replacement of outdated aircraft on the Central Front by the mid-1980s did not progress smoothly, with a reduction in the number of Tornado F2s ordered. According to the Defence Policy Staff, this meant that, '… the planned declaration of 115 Tornado F2s coupled with the running on of four Phantom squadrons will produce a total declared force of 171 interceptors,

The Phantom was operated by both the RAF and the Fleet Air Arm, until, as with the Buccaneer, the last conventional carrier was retired and the RAF inherited all remaining aircraft. Used by the RAF in a variety of roles, as indicated by the FG.1 and FGR.2 designations, by the 1980s most Phantoms were used for air defence in Germany or the UK, armed with four AIM-9 Sidewinders and four AIM-7 or Skyflash AAMs. (US DoD)

Like many British defence projects, the Tornado air defence variant had a troubled development. The initial F.2s are rumoured to have entered service with a concrete counterweight in the nose, in place of the Foxhunter radar system, jokingly referred to as the 'Blue Circle' – a play on words referencing the former British naming system for radars and a well-known brand of cement. The Tornado F.2 was armed in a similar fashion to the Phantom that it was replacing. (US DoD)

this more than meeting numerically the aim of the Air Defence report's recommendation.'[17]

The Tornado was a superior aircraft to the Phantom but running on four squadrons of Phantoms did not make up qualitatively for the failure to provide the Tornados. Also, basing of the Tornado F2s in the UK, rather than Germany, caused some problems with NATO regarding readiness for a quick response to a surprise attack in Germany. Despite the need for more capable aircraft in both the UK and Germany, the rate of orders for Tornado was reduced in 1984, meaning the intended targets of aeroplane numbers would never be reached.

Two squadrons of English Electric Lightnings and seven squadrons of McDonnell Douglas Phantoms were deployed in the UK for air defence and interception. The Lightning was a UK built interceptor, and the Phantom a US built air defence fighter purchased in place of the cancelled TSR-2. The Lightning was described by Group Captain David Stewart as, '… superb to fly, a bitch to maintain and always short of fuel.'[18] As part of the overall package of improvements for the air defence of the UK the formation of a new Lightning fighter squadron was announced in the 1979 SDE. Subsequently, to save some £5m, the creation of the new squadron was abandoned. Instead, an 'emergency squadron' was to be formed. This was to be done by using the Lightning Training Flight, based at Binbrook, which had four Mk3/Mk6 Lightnings, seven operationally qualified pilots and 62 ground crew. By utilising the 'In Use Reserve' of Mk 6 Lightnings, and recalling pilots and ground crew with Lightning experience, but who are no longer in the front-line, a force equivalent to a full squadron could be created. This 'shadow squadron' would then be declared to NATO at a C3 rating, denoting its lower readiness state. Because of out-dated capabilities and maintenance difficulties the Phantoms and Lightnings were to be replaced in the mid-80s by Tornado aircraft, with the first two squadrons beginning conversion in late 1984.

Hawk trainer aircraft, modified to carry Sidewinder AIM-9L missiles, would be available for UK air defence. The Sidewinder was bought as a replacement for the SKY FLASH MK2, a medium range air-to-air missile, which was announced in 1980 to replace the MK1. It was cancelled the next year for budgetary reasons, prompting the comment from the Assistant Under-Secretary of the Defence Staff that it would result in the '… abandonment of

air defence improvement already announced. Gap until advance weapon available late 80's or early 90's. [sic]'[19] The powerful, but shorter-range AIM-9L was to be bought from the USA, and the SKY FLASH MK1 kept on.

The Canberra first entered service with the RAF in 1951 in the nuclear strike role. This PR.9 reconnaissance variant is seen at a UK airbase in the 1980s. Note the Hardened Aircraft Shelter in the background. (US DoD)

The SEPECAT Jaguar was the result of an Anglo-French project and was originally conceived as a training aircraft. Entering service in the early 1970s it proved a versatile platform. The example seen here is a T.2 trainer variant. (US DoD)

In the Central Region the Harrier, together with the ground attack version of the Tornado, was to be used for close air support (CAS). The Harrier received a considerable boost of confidence following its performance in the Falklands War, and improved variants entered service for both the RAF and the RN during the 1980s. The Harriers were to be upgraded in 1987 to the GR.5 version from the GR.3. Other modernisation plans included fitting chaff and flare dispensers to all front-line aircraft, and this programme was accelerated after the Falklands War, where chaff had been jammed into the airbrakes of Harriers due to the lack of chaff dispensers.

A variety of other aircraft of differing roles were subject to cuts. Photographic reconnaissance, a vital part of the RAF's role, was undertaken by Canberras, which entered service in 1951, and were originally due to be phased out in the mid-1970s for safety reasons. The aircraft were kept on, but then again marked for disposal in 1984 to be replaced by Tornado PR in 1987. The disposal of the Canberras was accelerated to 1981/82 to save money, and the reconnaissance gap was to be filled by a mixture of Jaguar and Harrier aircraft adapted for the purpose. These replacements had only a tactical reconnaissance capability and were not capable of the longer range, comprehensive reconnaissance cover provided by the Canberras. However, as late as 1989 there was a squadron of Canberra PR.9s listed amongst the Photographic Reconnaissance Units, with the last operational Canberra squadron being disbanded in 2006.

The Canberra had started service in the 1950s, at the same time as the Avro Vulcan, and both were due for replacement. The Vulcan squadrons were declared to NATO in both the conventional and nuclear role. A reduction in their number was of considerable concern for SACEUR as they had no immediate replacement with the same capability. Tornado GR.1s were scheduled to replace them from mid-1982, but only entered service in 1983/84. RAF Buccaneers and Jaguars were also declared to NATO in the same roles, but the Buccaneer numbers had to be reduced because of fatigue cracks in the airframes. The Buccaneer had served on the Royal Navy aircraft carriers, but with the last fleet carriers, *Ark Royal*, retiring in 1978, all remaining Buccaneers were transferred to the RAF. To help fill the gap left by the loss of the Buccaneers in the maritime attack role, the Nimrod Maritime Reconnaissance aircraft was upgraded to be able to drop homing torpedoes and carry Sidewinder and Harpoon missiles.

A vital role undertaken by the RAF in times of crisis would be the preparation and operation of the reinforcement airports and airfields, for civil airliners and transports, RAF transports and for incoming

The Blackburn Buccaneer was originally designed as a nuclear-capable strike aircraft for the Fleet Air Arm, entering service in the early 1960s. Following a number of failed projects, the Buccaneer was also adopted by the Royal Air Force, both with new-build aircraft and former FAA aircraft as the RN retired its conventional aircraft carriers. The RAF would also come to inherit the anti-shipping role along with the Buccaneer – first with free-fall bombs and later with Martel and then Sea Eagle missiles. (US DoD)

US and Canadian troops and supplies. Once the reinforcement of NATO had been completed, the RAF Air Transport Force would be transferred to SACEUR's command, however some aircraft would be retained for various national tasks. In terms of reinforcement, the RAF could initially move the majority of its aircraft dedicated to NATO in only a few days. What would take the time, and effort, to move to Germany would be the supporting infrastructure,

The Harrier was above all famous for its short take-off and vertical landing capability. In practice this meant that Harriers could be dispersed away from fixed airfields in order to increase their survivability in a general war scenario. The Royal Engineers were tasked with building such dispersal sites and laying temporary trackways (as seen here), runways and landing areas. The sites had been carefully preselected and surveyed and would have received ground and anti-air protection from the RAF Regiment's Field Squadrons. (British Aerospace)

The Nimrod AEW was another deeply troubled British defence project of the 1970s and 1980s. Intended to replace the aging Shackleton, problems with integrating the two separate radars (one in the nose and another in the tail) and eliminating ground clutter proved insurmountable and the project was eventually cancelled. The Boeing E-3A Sentry was ordered as a replacement but would not enter RAF service before the end of the Cold War. (US DoD)

The Avro Shackleton was a close relative of the Second World War vintage Lancaster bomber and entered service in the early 1950s, serving in the maritime reconnaissance and bomber roles. In the early 1970s a number were adapted to carry the AN/APS-20 radar system, itself already dated, to serve in the AEW role. It would continue to serve until eventually replaced by the E-3 in 1991. (US DoD)

The potential Soviet use of nuclear, biological or chemical weapons (NBC) was of grave concern to NATO. Even if biological or chemical weapons did not cause immediate casualties, the protective measures against them were cumbersome and tiring, both physically and mentally. The cumulative effect could be to severely degrade the efficiency of military personnel and, for example, greatly reduce the sortie rate of aircraft operating from contaminated airfields. RAF ground crew are seen here decontaminating a USAF F-4 Phantom during an exercise in the 1970s. (US DoD)

The Su-24 'Fencer' sat somewhere between the Tornado and F-111 in terms of size and capability. Able to fly at very low altitudes and deliver precision weapons, it may have proven deadly to NATO facilities in rear areas and the UK. (US DoD)

personnel and equipment required to keep the aircraft running, and repair them after operational sorties, and to defend the airfields against air and ground attack.

Bloodhound and Rapier surface-to-air missiles operated by the RAF Regiment provided air defence for RAF airfields in Germany and the UK. Bloodhound, which was originally designed and built in the 1950s and upgraded in the 1960s, was outdated and severely short of missiles. Its replacement, which was planned as a cooperative project between several NATO members, was not expected to be operational until the 1990s. Because of Bloodhound's limitations, air defence of the UK was strengthened by the deployment of three Rapier squadrons by the USAF at West Raynham, Brize Norton and Honington.[20] Rapier was a short-range missile which would not provide the same coverage of UK airspace as had the Bloodhound.

In contrast to the active defence of airfields, the provision of airfield damage repair was slow to develop, partly due to disagreements within NATO on the criteria for particular studies into damage repair and explosive ordnance disposal. Teams for airfield damage repair were required in the UK as well as for RAF(G) as only the Harrier could operate from anything other than a hardened airstrip. Royal Engineer squadrons were allocated to the airfields in Germany for runway repair. They were mentioned in the 1989 SDE: 'The ability of our front-line airfields in RAF Germany has been much improved by the redeployment this year of a Royal Engineers squadron for airfield damage repair …'[21] but during the greater part of the 1980s airfield damage repair had been planned on an ad-hoc basis.

Following the inclusion of the UK airspace as a NATO region, there were several improvements to communications and command and control systems of the UKADGE which enhanced the detection of air threats. These included the deployment of mobile air defence radars, Nimrod AEW aircraft, and later Joint Tactical Information Distribution System (JTIDS). From the late 1970s onwards, there was a realisation that an integrated air defence and early warning system was needed, complete with ground defences for the land bases. This was also partly in response to the WTO development of long-range bombers with stand-off missiles. The UKADGE was developed to integrate into the NATO Air Defence Ground

Centurion formed the backbone of the British armoured regiments of the 1950s and 1960s and enjoyed considerable export success. The first version of the Centurion, the A41 Cruiser, entered service with the British Army in 1945 but just too late to see action. Despite being up-gunned from the 20-pdr to the 105mm L7, it was becoming long in the tooth and was phased out by the British as a Main Battle Tank in the late 1960s, shortly after this photograph was taken. (NATO)

The Chieftain began life on the drawing board in the late 1950s and from the outset was intended to have the best available gun and armour and indeed both were almost certainly the best-in-class in NATO in the 1970s. For most of the Chieftain's life, however, the engine and transmission were an unremitting tale of woe. Designed to meet a NATO requirement to enable to use a wide range of different fuels (that, ironically, was ignored by all other AFV designers) it was underpowered and unreliable. This example is seen crossing a Vehicle Launched Bridge in the 1970s. (NATO)

of the air defence radar and warning installations were sited near to the coast, and several were unhardened, some even in Portacabins on the surface protected by nothing more than a chain-link fence. This vulnerability was caused by delays in implementing the Improved UKADGE system. Air Chief Marshall Sir Peter Harding, CINCUKAF, said, '... of course, I'll be a lot happier when it is all underground ...'[22] Although there were mobile, smaller radars available (90-series), they would not be as capable as the larger, fixed installations, and use by the WTO of attacks with persistent chemical weapons on these vulnerable locations would have quickly rendered them inoperable. Considering the urgent need for the improvements, funding for UKADGE and improved radar proved difficult to progress through the NATO bureaucracy.

One squadron of the venerable Shackleton aircraft, developed from the Lancaster of Second World War vintage by AVRO, provided Airborne Early Warning (AEW). Eleven Shackletons provided radar coverage from Lossiemouth but were expected to be replaced by Nimrod AEW from 1983 onwards (originally the late 1960s). The reduction of the number of Shackletons before the introduction of Nimrod was intended to save approximately £5m, but would, '... permit only one AEW barrier to be mounted in the Faroes-UK gap (against an operational minimum of two) ...'[23] The Nimrod Mk 3 AEW was reported in 1983 to be ready for operational deployment in 1984, but problems with the development of the Mission System Avionics delayed this. The Mk3 project was cancelled in 1986, and E-3A AWACS were ordered to replace the by now obsolete Shackletons in 1987, but by 1989 the Shackletons were still the only aircraft listed as Airborne Early Warning flying with the RAF. One part of the warning system, the Ballistic Missile Early Warning System (BMEWS), had been the only area of major, consistent, investment in the 1960s. It was intended to

Environment (NADGE), with the majority of finance provided from the NATO Infrastructure fund. It replaced the Linesman system, which although planned as part of the 'trip-wire' strategy, had only come into service in 1974.

Some of the installations were upgraded from the original ROTOR installations of the 1950s, and had nuclear, chemical and biological protection added, as well as being buried deep underground. Many

The 155mm M109A2 self-propelled howitzer was in widespread use with the Royal Artillery in 1 (BR) Corps, alongside the aging 105mm Abbot. Common to many NATO armies, the M109 could fire a variety of ammunition types including the M483 Dual Purpose Improved Conventional Munition 'bomblet', though one battery officer described never having seen such a round until in Saudi Arabia in 1990/91. More common ammunition types included L15 HE, and White Phosphorous smoke rounds. (Walter Böhm)

would be provided by the Army and emergency services.

### Army

BAOR was organised as a corps of three divisions, each comprising two brigades. In 1968 BAOR comprised 1st, 2nd and 4th Divisions in West Germany. There was to be a modernisation of equipment in the services. The armoured regiments in BAOR were being equipped with the new FV4201 Chieftain tank, replacing the Centurion, and front-line infantry units were receiving the FV432 armoured personnel carrier. The FV433 Abbot 105mm self-propelled gun, 105mm L118 Light Gun along with the M109 155mm SP and M107 175mm SP artillery pieces were introduced, replacing the outdated 25-pounder and other artillery pieces. Two armoured car regiments equipped with

give as much warning as possible to get a nuclear retaliation launched. Like all the other early warning locations, BMEWS was classified a Key Point, and even though it was an RAF installation, its protection

Vigilant ATGW were to be introduced as an interim until its successor, Swingfire, arrived.

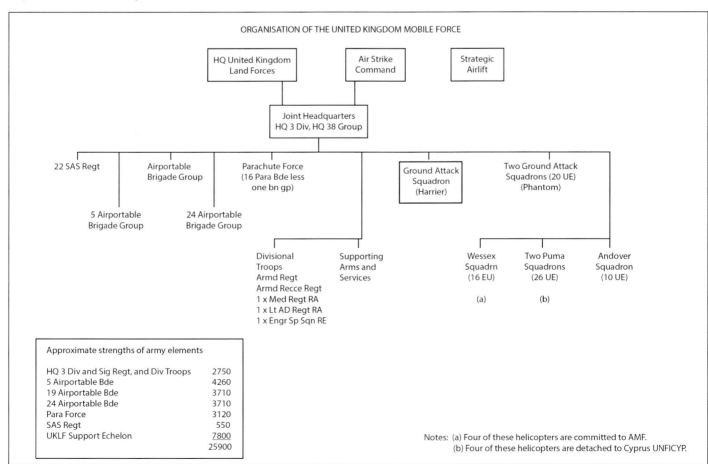

Organisation of the United Kingdom Mobile Force in 1972. (Chart by George Anderson)

The Bedford MK 4-tonne truck, first introduced in 1970, served as the primary transport for non-mechanised Regular and Territorial troops in the British Army. It also performed a wide range of logistics and support roles including a simple cargo truck, fuel bowser, office and communications vehicles, and as the launch vehicle for the Midge Remote Piloted Vehicle. (Artwork by David Bocquelet)

The FV432 armoured personnel carrier entered service with the British Army in the early 1960s. Similar in design and concept to the US M113, it was a classic 'battle taxi' intended to carry infantry into battle where they would dismount to fight. Only offering protection from small arms and shell splinters, the FV432s would usually retire to a safe location. The vehicle served as the basis for a wide range of conversions including 81mm mortar carrier, 120mm WOMBAT carrier, ambulance, fitters' vehicle and for a number of command and communications variants. Attempts to up-arm the FV432 resulted in some examples being fitted with a Peak Engineering turret for a GPMG, and an unsuccessful attempt to produce an IFV by mating the turret from a CVR(W) Fox on the rear hull; the resulting vehicles lacked the capacity to also carry infantry and 12 of the 13 examples were sent to the Berlin Infantry Brigade where they served as fire support vehicles. Camouflage usually consisted of broad black bands covering approximately a third of the vehicle but there were no fixed rules on how this was applied and great variations, including this example, were observed. (Artwork by David Bocquelet)

The AT 105 Saxon was essentially an armoured Bedford MK truck. Originally a commercial venture, the British Army began to introduce it to service in the mid-1980s where it equipped 1st Infantry Brigade, assigned to UKMF, and 24th Brigade of 2nd Infantry Division. It was intended to offer a limited degree of protection to its passengers while they travelled to the battlefield but had poor off-road mobility. Plans to equip Territorial Army units with the Saxon never came to fruition, indeed, even the regular battalions that did receive it only had sufficient for their rifle companies; all support elements remained in soft-skinned vehicles. (Artwork by David Bocquelet)

The CVR(T) Scorpion was the first in a family of light armoured vehicles that was to see widespread service throughout the British Army. The Scorpion was armed with the L23 76mm gun, which fired a useful range of ammunition types including HESH, cannister and white phosphorus. Like many vehicles of all armies, this example carries additional stowage bins added to the original design. This example wears the standard British colour scheme of the 1970s onwards of NATO Green and NATO Black. The latter colour was not applied to a standard pattern, instructions only stated that approximately 1/3rd of the vehicle was to be so covered. (Artwork by David Bocquelet)

The FV438 was the Swingfire-armed member of the FV432 family of vehicles. It carried two ready to launch Swingfire missiles in bins in a turret mounted on the rear hull and a further 14 reloads internally. Swingfire was an early second-generation SACLOS missile system and was able to defeat most then-current Warsaw Pact armour. It appears that some infantry battalions operated FV438s for a brief period in the mid-1970s before control was passed to the Royal Artillery. They then passed to the Royal Armoured Corps with the 1983 reorganisation but were phased out without replacement by around 1986. (Artwork by David Bocquelet)

The Striker was the Swingfire-armed member of the CRV(T) family of light armoured vehicles. This example is shown in the travelling position; when ready to fire the rear deck would be elevated allowing one of five ready to launch missiles to be fired. A further five missiles were carried internally but the crew would have to dismount to reload these; causing problems of contamination if operating in an NBC environment. Striker was initially operated by the Royal Horse Artillery before being transferred to the Armoured Reconnaissance Regiments in the 1983 reorganisation. (Artwork by David Bocquelet)

The Centurion had been the backbone of British post-Second World War armour but by the late 1960s was no longer considered adequate as an MBT and was replaced by the Chieftain. Nevertheless, the Centurion continued to serve on, as an Artillery Observation Post vehicle (still fully armed) through to the end of the 1970s. After a short hiatus these same vehicles were pressed back into service as the 105mm-armed version of the AVRE (Armoured Vehicle Royal Engineers), where they would usually be equipped with the Pearson Mine Plough and could tow a Giant Viper mine clearing trailer or other stores. (Artwork by David Bocquelet)

The Chieftain was the successor to the Centurion as the British Army's MBT. Its L11 120mm gun combined with the .50cal Ranging Gun could accurately engage and destroy most Warsaw Pact armour out to ranges of 1,800m with the L15 APDS 'Sabot' round. When upgraded to the Barr and Stroud Tank Laser Sight this range (terrain permitting) could reach 3,200 metres under ideal conditions. Whilst also very well armoured for its day, the Chieftain became notorious for the extraordinarily unreliable L60 multi-fuel engine and its transmission. Though many of these problems were dealt with later in the Chieftain's service life, it never entirely outgrew this reputation. (Artwork by David Bocquelet)

The British Army maintained a garrison in Berlin throughout the Cold War; the Berlin Infantry Brigade. Following a non-standard organisation, during the 1980s this consisted of three infantry battalions organised and equipped for urban combat. The brigade was supported by a single over-strength squadron of 18 Chieftains. In the mid-1980s the Chieftains, along with some other vehicles of the brigade, adopted an unusual camouflage scheme of brown, white-grey and blue-grey rectangles that proved remarkably effective when stationary in urban areas. Each vehicle had the pattern applied in an identical fashion, in theory making it difficult for observers to identify individual vehicles. (Artwork by David Bocquelet)

The FV433 Abbot was a 105mm self-propelled howitzer sharing many automotive components with the FV432 family. First introduced in the mid-1960s, it was often used to provide close indirect fire support to battlegroups. Normal ammunition loads consisted of high explosive and smoke, but HESH was also carried for direct fire (though this was not the normal modus operandi). Unlike most British armoured vehicles of this era, this Abbot does not wear the usual 1/3rd black camouflage. (Artwork by David Bocquelet)

The US-built M109A2 155mm self-propelled howitzer was longer ranged than the Abbot and threw a much heavier shell; it was therefore more often used in the general support indirect fire role. The M109 was common to most NATO nations and could employ a wide variety of ammunition types – even if not all were standard issue. As well as the common HE and smoke rounds, the DPICM 'bomblet' round could be fired, though this would seem to have been extremely rare in peacetime. In addition, a nuclear round could be fired, though these would have been held by special US units and used under 'dual-control' requiring consent of both the US and the nation owning the firing weapon. (Artwork by David Bocquelet)

The M110A2 203mm self-propelled howitzer was the heaviest artillery piece in use by 1 (BR) Corps in this era. The chassis was common with the 175mm M107, also used by the British Army, and the weapons were interchangeable. Both weapons were primarily intended for the counter-battery role, though the M110A2 was also earmarked for use as nuclear artillery, with ammunition held under the 'dual-control' system mentioned above. (Artwork by David Bocquelet)

The Challenger was a marked improvement over the Chieftain in terms of engine reliability, though was still not without problems. Developed at short notice from the Shir 2 intended for export to Iran, the Challenger was only ever a stop-gap measure intended to replace half of the Chieftain fleet until a better tank could be developed. Challenger and its Improved Fire Control System delivered a notoriously poor performance in the 1987 Canadian Army Trophy – a NATO tank shooting competition. In 1990/91, in preparation for Operation Desert Sabre, the Challenger underwent extensive modifications to enable it to operate in the desert environment, and had improved ammunition stowage and additional armour added to the hull front and sides. Challenger would ultimately perform well and achieve the longest ranged knock-out of an enemy tank ever recorded, at some 4,700 metres, albeit under relatively permissive conditions. (Artwork by David Bocquelet)

The British Army was the last of the major NATO allies to adopt an infantry fighting vehicle. The Warrior only entered service in 1988, with a single battalion to follow each year. By 1991 virtually the entire Warrior fleet had been deployed to the Saudi desert to equip three armoured infantry battalions, with additional vehicles made available to equip the MILAN platoons, mortar fire controllers and to fulfil some artillery command and observation roles. Much like the Challenger, there were concerns as to the suitability of the armour protection for use in an urban environment (it having been envisaged that the British would support the USMC into Kuwait City) and so additional armour for the hull front and sides was designed, manufactured, delivered and fitted in very short order; a quite remarkable feat yet one that may not have been possible in a European crisis. (Artwork by David Bocquelet)

The last outing for British Centurions was as the AVRE. Several 165mm-armed versions deployed to the Gulf, much up-armoured with ERA, where they were affectionately referred to as the 'Antiques Road Show' after a well-known BBC TV programme. Two were lost to engine fires in the build-up to war, but none were lost to enemy action. (Artwork by David Bocquelet)

The British Aerospace Harrier was the primary close air support platform of the Royal Air Force in Germany during the 1980s. This example of a GR.3, from No. 1 Squadron, RAF, is shown with a Matra pod for sixteen 68mm SNEB rockets (which could be equipped with a variety of warhead types) fitted on the outboard pylon and a drop tank on the inboard pylon, and has pods fixed to the lower fuselage carrying two ADEN 30mm cannon and ammunition. The GR.3 had an extended nose equipped with a laser tracker to enable the aircraft to use laser guided bombs, a small number of which were used late in the Falklands conflict. The RAF ordered a total of 118 of the GR.1/GR.3 series of Harriers (with some GR.3s being conversions of earlier GR.1s), the last of which was delivered in 1986. (Artwork by Tom Cooper)

The SEPECAT Jaguar was an Anglo-French project originally intended to deliver an advanced trainer aircraft but developed into a light strike platform, 165 of which were ordered to the Royal Air Force. The example shown here is a GR.1 of No. 2 Squadron based at Larrbruch in 1987. The Jaguar could carry a wide range of stores including Matra pods for 68mm rockets, BL755 cluster bombs, conventional free fall iron bombs or the WE.177 variable yield nuclear bomb. This example is shown carrying a large reconnaissance pod – manufactured by EMI – on the centreline and drop tanks underwing. (Artwork by Tom Cooper)

The Tornado was the result of a very successful joint British-German-Italian collaboration to build a variable geometry strike aircraft that would equip all three air forces in the 1980s. This GR.1 is shown carrying a system unique within NATO to the RAF; the Hunting JP233 runway denial weapon. Designed in a number of configurations to suit different aircraft (though ultimately only deployed on Tornado), Tornadoes carried two large pods in parallel under the fuselage. Each pod carried a mixture of 30 SG-57 runway cratering submunitions and 215 HB-876 anti-personnel mines, the latter intended to hinder repair of the damage caused to the first munition. Whilst effective, it required the Tornado to fly a predictable low altitude path when deploying the system, thus making the aircraft potentially very vulnerable to enemy ground fire during the attack phase. The aircraft shown here is from No. 9 Squadron at RAF Brüggen in 1987 – the first squadron to become operational with the JP233 – and also carries a Skyshadow ECM pod and an AIM-9 Sidewinder AAM for self-defence. The drop tanks almost universally carried have been omitted for clarity of the other stores. (Artwork by Tom Cooper)

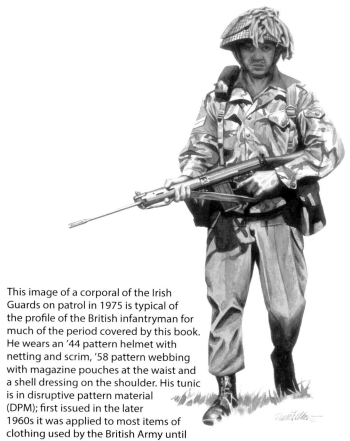

This image of a corporal of the Irish Guards on patrol in 1975 is typical of the profile of the British infantryman for much of the period covered by this book. He wears an '44 pattern helmet with netting and scrim, '58 pattern webbing with magazine pouches at the waist and a shell dressing on the shoulder. His tunic is in disruptive pattern material (DPM); first issued in the later 1960s it was applied to most items of clothing used by the British Army until replaced in the 2000s. Although there were minor variations in colour and pattern (as can be seen in some of the photographs in this book), British DPM remained quite distinctive. The soldier in the original photograph also wears DPM trousers, but we have shown plain light olive green trousers here as were often still worn throughout this period. He is armed with the L1A1 7.62mm SLR, carried left-handed here, a semi-automatic variant of the FN FAL. Though heavy, the 7.62mm round was popular with users. (Artwork by Renato Dalmaso)

From the mid to late 1980s the classic profile of the British soldier began to change. This image is based on one of a series of photographs taken at the School of Infantry demonstrating the new Load Carrying Equipment then under development. The pack was designed so that it could be broken down into a number of separate components and reassembled with zippers to suit a wide range of needs. The large pouch on the right hip carries the soldier's Mk. 6 Respirator and the smaller pouches carry magazines for the SA80 or LSW. The SA80 began to replace the SLR in the later 1980s but suffered from a terrible reputation for unreliability and the fragility of its plastic furniture. (Artwork by Renato Dalmaso)

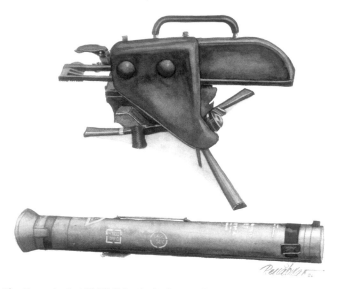

When first introduced to the British Army, MILAN was issued on a scale of 16 per battalion (in four sections of four launchers; later increased to 24 in four sections of five launchers, plus a mobile section of four) for those formations expected to face a significant armour threat, or a single section of six launchers for Light Role battalions (in wartime these may have been reallocated to battalions committed to NATO). This illustration is based on a photograph of a MILAN team from the Prince of Wales Own Regiment of Yorkshire on exercise in Norway with the Allied Command Europe (ACE) Mobile Force in 1980. The launcher is fitted with a spent missile tube for training purposes; a live missile would have had a cap covering the end of the tube. (Artwork by Renato Dalmaso, with thanks to Terry Smith, the No. 2 in the original photograph upon which this artwork is based, for additional information)

The Euromissile MILAN (*Missile d'infanterie léger antichar*) was a second-generation Franco-German semi-automatic command line-of-sight (SACLOS) anti-tank missile. Nominally man-portable, it entered service with the British Army in the late 1970s to replace the 120mm WOMBAT recoilless rifle in all but a very few specialist roles and marked a major increase in infantry anti-tank capability. Though the missile armed after travelling 25 metres, it would not be under positive operator control until it had flown some 400-500 metres, thus marking its effective minimum range. It had a maximum range of 1,950 metres. A new missile, MILAN 2, was issued from 1984 fitted with a larger warhead for use against the newer Warsaw Pact MBTs, and the British Army also adopted the MIRA thermal imaging sight at around the same time. (Artwork by Renato Dalmaso)

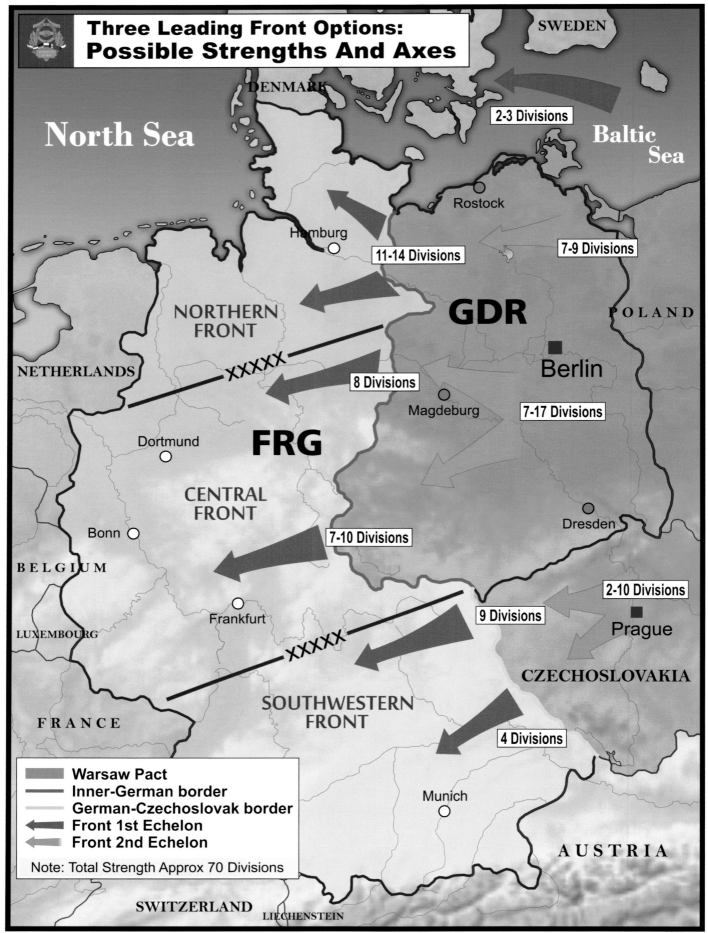

## Three Leading Front Options: Possible Strengths And Axes

SWEDEN

DENMARK

North Sea

Baltic Sea

2-3 Divisions

Rostock

7-9 Divisions

Hamburg

11-14 Divisions

NORTHERN FRONT

GDR

POLAND

NETHERLANDS

XXXXX

8 Divisions

Berlin

Magdeburg

7-17 Divisions

Dortmund

FRG

CENTRAL FRONT

Dresden

Bonn

7-10 Divisions

BELGIUM

Frankfurt

2-10 Divisions

9 Divisions

Prague

LUXEMBOURG

XXXXX

CZECHOSLOVAKIA

FRANCE

SOUTHWESTERN FRONT

4 Divisions

Munich

**Warsaw Pact**
**Inner-German border**
**German-Czechoslovak border**
**Front 1st Echelon**
**Front 2nd Echelon**

Note: Total Strength Approx 70 Divisions

AUSTRIA

SWITZERLAND

LIECHTENSTEIN

This map is closely based on a British document showing expected lines of attack in the event of a conventional war with the Warsaw Pact. The first echelon would consist of Soviet and allied forces based in the GDR, Czechoslovakia and possibly Poland. The second echelon would be drawn from units based deeper in the western USSR. Further echelons could be formed from lower readiness units or those based elsewhere in the USSR. (Map by Anderson Subtil)

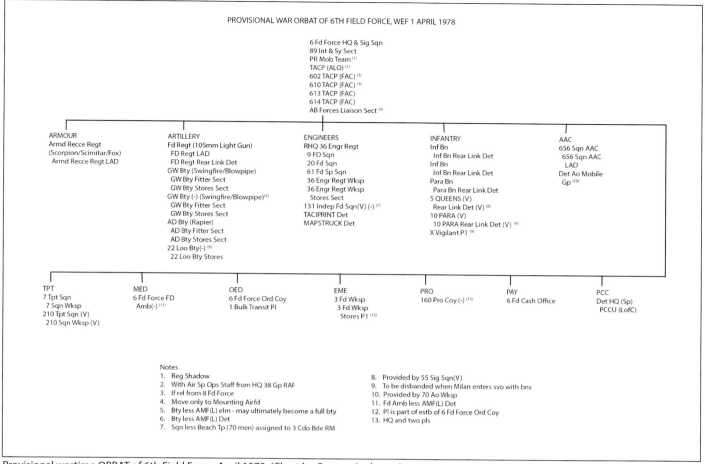

Provisional wartime ORBAT of 6th Field Force, April 1978. (Chart by George Anderson)

In 1966 the Army Strategic Reserve comprised two brigades of air-portable troops, one parachute brigade, along with several close support and transport squadrons of RAF 38 Group. It was intended to fulfil several roles, both in and outside Europe. This became the United Kingdom Mobile Force (UKMF) in 1972.

To further reduce costs another reorganisation and restructuring took place after the 1974 review by Labour Defence Secretary Roy Mason. A major aspect of the reorganisation was the restructuring of BAOR from three divisions into four newly-styled armoured divisions, and the formation of four 'Field Forces', essentially large brigades, three of which were stationed in the UK. The reorganisation removed a level of command within BAOR which was hoped would save money. 5th Field Force was an independent infantry formation directly under BAOR command, with the 7th Field Force in the UK to reinforce BAOR in time of war. 6th Field Force was designated as a strategic reserve for deployment by SACEUR and had limited air-drop capability. 8th Field Force was to remain in the UK as part of the Home Defence forces. There is also a suggestion that 5th Field Force, as an all-infantry unit, was structured in such a way that it could be included as part of the Mutual and Balanced Force Reductions (MBFR) negotiations without too great an impact on BAOR's combat capability. As the main reinforcement for BAOR, 7th Field Force advance and key parties were at 24 hours' notice, with the main units at 72 hours' notice. Its main role was to, '… deploy under command of one of the forward divisions … to conduct blocking operations.'[24] A secondary role was to provide security in the Corps Rear Area. 7th Field Force was described by Lieutenant General Nigel Bagnall as lacking mobility: 'Once deployed and in contact it will be virtually impossible to move it … it moves in soft vehicles and thus is very susceptible to enemy air …'[25]

Project MERCURY initiated in 1978 to examine force structure in BAOR, with the intention of reporting its findings after Exercise CRUSADER 80.[26]

BAOR was again restructured between 1981 and 1983 to provide a total of four Divisions: 1st, 3rd and 4th Armoured Divisions in the FRG, with the 2nd Infantry Division in the UK for reinforcement of BAOR in time of war. 1st and 4th Armoured Divisions comprised three regular brigades, each of at least three battle groups. 3rd Armoured Division comprised two brigades but would be reinforced by 19th Infantry Brigade in wartime. 2nd Infantry Division comprised one regular brigade and two predominantly TA brigades. Armoured regiments were to be reduced to 57 tanks by 1984, with the spare tanks going to form the new tenth and eleventh armoured regiments.

To defend the Home Base and parts of Western Europe, in 1979 the Army had 138,000 regular and 176,000 reservist personnel. The Army consisted of various types of forces, from rapid-response units on permanent high readiness, to large formations of reservists which took weeks to mobilise. Permanently stationed in West Germany was the British Army of the Rhine (BAOR), consisting of 1(BR) Corps, under NATO command. The primary role of 1(BR) Corps was the defence of the British sector of the NATO 'layer cake' in West Germany. 1(BR) Corps was combined with FRG, Netherlands and Belgian forces to form NORTHAG for the defence of the North German Plain, a vital sector of the Central Region. In 1974 the Chiefs of Staff assessed that 50,000 was the minimum strength

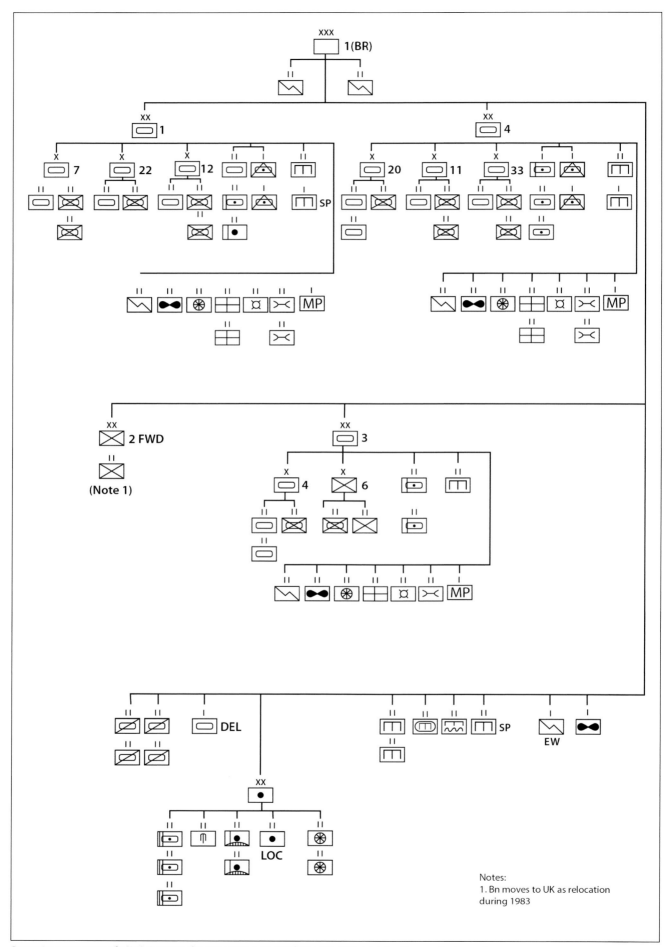

Peacetime structure of 1(BR) Corps in theatre units, 1 December 1981. (Diagram by George Anderson)

Notes:
1. Bn moves to UK as relocation during 1983

for 1(BR) Corps to retain its basic combat capability. Key to the successful defence of 1(BR) Corps area was the mobilisation of the reserves, and the quick reinforcement of troops from the UK. Speed of reinforcement of BAOR had been high on the list of priorities for the LTDP in 1977, but in 1980, the SDE still noted that, 'We need to … speed up the arrangements for the reinforcement of BAOR in an emergency.'[27] Given sufficient time to reinforce, the 1(BR) Corps would exceed 100,000 personnel.

If a crisis arose, the UK Mobile Force (UKMF) was airportable, and intended to deploy rapidly to support the regular forces on continental Europe. This could be a national deployment, or on the orders of SACEUR. UKMF comprised an armoured reconnaissance regiment, three battalions of regular infantry and two of TAVR, and supporting arms including the Logistic Support Group. Because approximately 40 percent of the UKMF were reservists, it might deploy without its reservists if a crisis developed very quickly. Because of the reliance on the reserves to fill-out the numbers, the MoD warned, 'There is a possibility that were SACEUR to request the deployment of the UKMF(L) before the TA was mobilised there might be some delay before the whole force could be deployed.'[28]

There was a need for urgency in deploying forces given that the WTO were thought capable of a quick attack with only 48 hours' warning. BAOR 'Covering Force' units were to be deployed forward of the main defensive positions to delay an enemy advance, and to identify main thrust lines. The covering force was required to be able to reach their combat positions within 24 hours of a warning. All main combat units were expected to be at their General Defence Plan locations within 48 hours of notification, complete with their basic load of ammunition. The main combat units, armour-heavy battlegroups in the Main Defence Area (MDA) were expected to engage and destroy the advancing enemy. There were 16 reinforcing combat battalions (6 Regular and 10 Reserve) which would not be able to achieve this timescale in an emergency because they were based in the UK for cost-saving purposes. In addition, many units permanently stationed in BAOR were kept under-strength, and the cadre companies and units were to be brought up to strength during a crisis by the mobilisation of regular reservists using the Individual Reinforcement Plan. These personnel were for the reinforcement of units categorised as 'A1', the highest state of preparedness. As such, the reinforcements were expected to be with their units no later than 48 hours after being called up. The Individual Reinforcement Plan was introduced in 1981 allowing the reservists to be in their General Defence Plan locations within 48 hours.

From the analysis of the wargames, and the timescales involved in mobilising and transporting the reinforcements to the continent, it was possible that the Armed Forces would face a similar problem to that of the BEF in 1940 during the retreat to Dunkirk. Had a breakthrough of the front-line been created, the rear area troops would have been ill-equipped to stop it. Rear-area troops, such as the 2nd Infantry Division, were poorly equipped to fight a mechanised, fast-moving enemy, having reduced numbers of anti-armour and other heavy weapons, as well as limited mobility. Some units were equipped with SAXON armoured personnel carriers (the armour of which was supposed to be proof against only small calibre weapons), and yet others only had lorries.

## Main Battle Tanks (MBT)

The Army placed a great deal of reliance on the Main Battle Tank as its primary anti-armour weapon. The Main Battle Tank of the British Army had been the Chieftain since the 1960s. The Chieftain was a powerful MBT, deployed in the armoured brigades in BAOR.

Lightly equipped British infantry during Exercise Crusader in 1980. In the event of a breakthrough of the frontlines and into 1 (BR) Corps' rear areas, such troops would have been ill-equipped to resist Soviet Operational Manoeuvre Groups. (US DoD)

Despite initial problems with the power plant and gearbox, it had been improved and updated, but by the early 1980s it was feared the newer WTO tanks would outclass it. A project was undertaken in 1978, called MBT-80, to develop a successor. Due to cost increases and other delays this plan was finally abandoned in 1980, and Challenger tanks purchased. Challenger had been developed for the Iranian army, but the order had been cancelled following the Iranian Revolution. This allowed the Army to purchase the available tanks and those on order. The disadvantage with Challenger was the Army would receive a weapon system that had not been designed specifically for its requirements. In a memorandum to the Cabinet Office, Michael Quinlan stated that the MoD recognised Challenger was, '… not … an adequate long-term substitute for MBT-80 and could not therefore be used to replace the full Chieftain fleet.'[29] There would be a deliberate compromise: Challenger would replace half of the fleet, but the other half would remain Chieftain until a new tank was developed.

NATO wanted BAOR to field 638 of the new Challengers by 1989, to completely replace Chieftain. Financial and developmental constraints meant that the Chieftains would not be replaced on a 1:1 basis. The Force Proposals also requested an additional two tank regiments to be raised. These new regiments were formed by the simple expedient of reducing the number of tanks in existing regiments from 74 to 57 and re-using the spares in the new units. Britain was expected to produce 264 Challengers by 1986, bringing

This Chieftain, photographed in 1985 during Exercise Trutzige Sachsen (Defiant Saxon), shows the original turret profile before the addition of the Stillbrew armour package in the later 1980s. Combat experience in the Iran-Iraq War had shown that even the thickest parts of the turret front could be penetrated by 115mm and 125mm guns at battlefield ranges. (Peter Blume via Walter Böhm)

Even those battalions that did receive the Warrior (referred to as Armoured Infantry as opposed to Mechanised Infantry battalions) still had to use the FV430 series in all roles outside the rifle companies. This FV432 carries a MILAN with MIRA attachment above the rear hatch. The FV432 did not have a mount for the MILAN and so the standard infantry firing post was usually secured in place with sandbags, or similar weights, and bungee cords. This example belongs to the Staffords who had re-equipped their rifle companies with Warrior at this time. A late 1980s Mechanised or Armoured Infantry battalion would have a total of 24 MILAN systems; 20 carried by FV432s and a further four examples carried by Spartans fitted with the Milan Compact Turret. (Walter Böhm)

the Army total of all tanks to 684 plus the WMR. Five Challenger regiments were to be in place in BAOR by the end of the 1980s but by 1986 only enough tanks for two had been ordered. These new weapons were themselves underfunded for maintenance and modifications, and in 1989–90 in Germany, Challenger 1 availability was just 23 percent. A replacement for the remaining Chieftains was expected to be in service by the mid-1990s.

### Anti-armour weapons

Following the success of unguided anti-tank weapons during the Second World War, development of guided weapons saw the introduction of the first true anti-tank guided weapons (ATGW) in the 1950s. The NATO armies recognised the need for heavy attrition on any attacking armour in the first few days of battle, and the maintenance of that capability throughout any war. Only profligate use of anti-armour weapons of whatever sort would act as an equaliser to balance the numerical preponderance in WTO armour.

By the 1970s, the British Army's anti-tank guided weapons included MILAN and Swingfire, with TOW on order from the US. Small, shoulder launched, short range unguided weapons such as the M72 LAW, and the recoilless rifle CARL GUSTAV were also employed, with LAW80 to enter service in the late 1980s. A proliferation of these weapons during the 1980s, enabled by technological improvements, meant individual soldiers and small combat teams were equipped with greater anti-armour capability than ever before. Other improvements in warhead design meant that ATGWs had a high probability of a kill if they hit their target.

One of the key Long Term Defence Programme proposals was to increase the holdings and reserve stocks of these

The Gazelle AH.1 was used as a reconnaissance, observation and liaison helicopter by the Army Air Corps and Royal Marines. It was usually unarmed but could be used to lead TOW-armed Lynx helicopters into action. This example is seen flying over an artillery position during Exercise White Rhino in 1989. (Walter Böhm)

ceased. As a result, the 1981 Force Goals requested that 48 additional STRIKERs were purchased as part of the same programme as the increase in MILAN. Britain had declared 108 FV438 vehicles, and 64 STRIKER vehicles to NATO. The Army responded that the UK intended to meet this by increasing its MBT fleet and the number of MILAN and the redeployment of more STRIKER to BAOR bringing the Reinforced Corps holdings to 48 Striker.

The MoD accepted in 1977 that from 1983 a LAW would be introduced to replace CARL GUSTAV and the M72 on a one-to-one basis. One study suggested each infantry battalion would receive 570 LAW80s, although this was marked as unconfirmed.

anti-armour systems, especially guided weapons. The NATO Force Proposals also leaned heavily towards the modernisation and expansion of the number of weapon systems.

All Long Range ATGW (LRATGW) had been transferred to the Royal Artillery in 1979 and organised into anti-tank batteries.[30] The batteries had individual troops allocated to armoured regiments, reconnaissance regiments and mechanised infantry battalions. The LRATGW were subsequently reassigned to the RAC to coincide with the reorganisation of BAOR.

The British Government publicly recognised the need to improve BAOR's anti-armour capabilities in the 1980 SDE. The NATO Force Proposals for 1979–1984 required that by the end of 1982, 630 MILAN systems would be in place. Each infantry battalion would deploy 24 MILAN launchers. The MILAN was a portable anti-tank guided missile used by the British Army and Marines, deployed in teams in FV432 armoured tracked vehicles, or housed in dedicated turrets on the FV120 SPARTAN armoured tracked vehicle. The LTDP proposed that 20,500 additional MILAN anti-armour missiles be added to the UK's inventory between 1979 and 1984. Declared planning indicated that there would be 11,000 MILAN missiles in the war reserve by the end of 1982. A Review of Ammunition Rates and Scales (RARS) study of about the same time recommended an additional 28,000 missiles. The study indicated that almost 40,000 anti-armour missiles would be required for a variety of combat situations over the expected war fighting period of 6 days. 647 MILAN systems were planned to be deployed by mid-1983, and an additional twelve systems, with wheeled vehicles, were required for UK AMF(L). No increase was included in national planning, so this was not accepted. An additional 180 MILAN systems were to be deployed to BAOR in 1984. Because of the alterations in the number of launchers deployed, the war reserves of MILAN were expected to drop from 58 percent in 1981 to only 36 percent in 1986: the reserve was not expected to reach 100 percent until 1989.

The LTDP proposed purchasing an additional 48 Swingfire systems. These plans were unacceptable due to the cost, as well as the fact that the production of the FV430 base vehicle had

However, by 1981, this had been altered to an unspecified number of LAW80, which, '… will not replace [the M72 and CARL GUSTAV] on an exact one for one basis, but the recommended scales will be an improvement.'[31] How the reduction of the number of LAWs would be an improvement was unspecified. The LAW80 finally entered service in 1988.

It is worth noting here that the type of anti-armour weapon used by the soldiers dictated their tactics. For example, none of the man-portable anti-armour weapons with which BAOR was equipped were capable of being fired from within a confined space due to the severity of the back-blast. This severely limited the flexibility of small-unit tactics when applied to large West German urban sprawl or village 'sponge-tactics'. (The original LTDP requirement had specified that the capability to fire LAW80 from within buildings was desirable. The West German *Heer* developed the ARMBRUST in the 1980s specifically to overcome this limitation and allow their troops to fight from within buildings.)

To keep the anti-tank helicopter force up-to-date, NATO required that by mid-1983 the LYNX be fitted with a replacement ATGW. TOW had been chosen by the British Government as part of its national plans to update the anti-armour helicopters earmarked for NATO. An additional 108 anti-armour helicopters were requested by NATO in 1981, but the same answer was given to support the partial implementation of this proposal as was given for the STRIKER system; more MBTs and MILANs would take up the slack.

In recognition of the increased tempo of war of which the WTO was capable, including night-fighting, the LTDP required night sights to be fitted to all ATGW by 1982. The response of the UK Government was that standardisation could not be implemented immediately because, '… each missile system requires its own tailored night sight.'[32] A Swingfire sight was under test in 1981, fitted to the STRIKER vehicle, and was due to be issued to units beginning in October 1981. 775 MILAN night sights were in operation by 1986, with a further 375 ordered.

The Army Air Corps and Royal Marines used the Lynx AH.1 to carry US-made BGM-71C or D TOW anti-tank missiles with a range of 3,750 metres and capable of destroying all Warsaw Pact tanks. Those assigned to 1 (BR) Corps were primarily intended to be used en masse in the counter-penetration role. Documents issued to Staff College candidates stress that they were a precious asset to be husbanded. A Gazelle AH.1 can be seen in the background, in a typical tactical grouping with the two Lynxes. (Walter Böhm)

## Air Defence

During the 1960s and 1970s small calibre anti-aircraft weapons such as the 40mm Bofors had been replaced by missile systems. The Army used Blowpipe and Rapier anti-aircraft missiles. Provision of a towed quadruple Blowpipe launcher for Territorial Air Defence units was reported in the 1979 SDE but cancelled in 1980/81 for financial reasons.

Despite initial concerns about reliability, and problems establishing firing posts, Rapier was reported to have performed well in the Falklands. Blowpipe performed poorly, achieving approximately a 15 percent hit rate[33] (although Freedman relates that only two hits were achieved from more than 100 launches[34]). Even though improvements were clearly identified from the Falklands, such as the ability to engage crossing targets, some of these were delayed or cancelled, and additional production of Blowpipe deferred. Javelin, a more advanced variant of Blowpipe, began to replace it from 1985 in BAOR.

## Other equipment examples

Other equipment necessary for the defence of the 1(BR) sector of NATO was deferred or cancelled. The introduction of BATES, the Army's new computerised artillery target engagement system, was intended to allow a greater concentration of firepower through improved communication. It would integrate several different communication systems, with improved data processing, and feed target data to differing artillery systems, including the new Multiple Launch Rocket System (MLRS). Part of the 1981–1986 Force proposals, its introduction was delayed to 1987. According to the SDE in 1984, BATES was, '... in full development ...'[35] and one system had been ordered by 1986. Intended for introduction in the mid-1980s, it was delayed by financial cuts until it was described as being introduced, '... in the early 1990s.'[36]

More crucially, the Barmine, necessary for blocking routes of enemy attack and funnelling the enemy into killing zones, was delayed for cost reasons. This weapon was vital not only to defence, but also for flank protection of the 'Counterstroke' attacks and was explicitly mentioned as part of the 'Battle Group Tactics'. It was lighter, provided greater coverage and could be laid more quickly than conventional mines.

The 'Counterstroke' doctrine relied on good communications for the attacking forces to coordinate the advance with their respective blocking forces. Communications had been a problem for the armed forces, famously failing the airborne troops at Arnhem in 1944. The importance of good, secure, communications had not slipped the MoD's notice. Clansman was the Army's new tactical battlefield radio system, which replaced Larkspur. The Ptarmigan system, a communications and data network backbone, replaced the obsolete Bruin system. The Wavell system introduced networked computers into the communications chain, and the overall system improved communications up and down the chain of command. These systems connected higher levels of command with the units and provided data processing capabilities. However, Clansman suffered from a reduction in purchase scale, and the supply was delayed by 'cheese-paring', especially to those units allocated to rear-area or home defence.

## Home Defence

The defence of the Home Base was divided into two distinct but mutually dependent parts: military defence and civil defence. Military defence was divided into two main types: defence against any direct attack on the United Kingdom from external forces and defence to secure the United Kingdom against internal threat.

The defence of the UK home base was undertaken by troops of the regional commands. Army Strategic Command (STRATCO) was set up in 1968 to take command of most units and headquarters stationed in the UK. It comprised 3rd and 5th divisions. 3rd Division comprised 5th, 19th and 24th Brigades and 16th Parachute Brigade. 5th Division existed in cadre form, except for 39th Brigade which had operational duties in Northern Ireland. In 1972 STRATCO was absorbed, along with other regional commands, into United Kingdom Land Forces (UKLF). UKLF was restructured again in 1975 along with BAOR and provided troops for Home Defence roles as well as for SACEUR's strategic reserve. 8th Field Force (later known as 5 Brigade), made up of regulars and TAVR personnel, was assigned specifically for home defence. According to the UK Commander-in-Chief, the primary purpose of the defence of the UK as a whole was to retain, '... the United Kingdom's ability to launch a nuclear counter offensive ...'[37] as well as maintaining the capability of the Armed Forces to carry out their mobilisation and deployment plans. The Chiefs of Staff Committee stated that, 'The Home Defence plan ... must be consistent with NATO doctrine and with the criteria ... for the reinforcement of NATO.'[38]

The Home Defence forces would provide troops for the defence of Key Points, air defence aircraft and SAMs, and other troops deployed for protection of troop and equipment movements. The need to protect the UK home base was explained in MC48/3, which stated; 'Security of Rear Areas. The NATO nations have the responsibility to establish adequate civil defence and internal security organisations within their own resources and to enable NATO forces to have maximum freedom of action and secure lines of communications.'[39]

The United Kingdom Home Base was defined by the MoD as, '… the main-land areas of the UK, its offshore islands, coastal waters out to the 100 fathom line and the airspace within the UK Air Defence Region.'[40] The 100 fathom line (approximately 200 metres) coincides generally with the continental shelf. Defining this region of sea as the home base had operational implications as a naval officer questioned about the definition above remarked; 'It is better to keep enemy submarines out of shallow coastal waters where merchant shipping and naval vessels concentrate at harbour entrances or other anchorages, and under certain circumstances it is easier to conduct anti-submarine warfare in deeper water.'[41]

In 1969 NATO described the importance of the UK home base and the surrounding maritime area in the following way:

Strategic Importance of the British Isles

19. The British Isles, by virtue of their location, industrial capability, ports and airfields, provide a valuable base for early warning and the operation of ASW forces, strategic counter-offensive forces and support of NATO forces in Europe.

Strategic Importance of the English Channel and the North Sea

20. The English Channel and North Sea cover the approaches to the coasts of the United Kingdom, Northern France, Belgium, The Netherlands, Germany, Denmark and Southern Norway, with the major ports therein, several of which rank among the largest in the world. The intensive shipping activity in these areas constitutes the life blood of the economy and prosperity of the countries concerned.[42]

The British Isles were not a part of NATO Allied Command Europe (ACE), but the air over it and sea around it were. Thus, troops which were earmarked for home defence were not part of the NATO contribution, although the defence of some ground installations and infrastructure, vital for any continued operations in Europe in the event of a war, was a grey area within NATO policy. Britain had plans for 35 battalions of troops, plus logistics and communications, to be mobilised to defend the home islands in time of war.

There was no formal link between HQ UKLF and the NATO chain of command. There had been suggestions, which were never implemented, of making the Commander-in-Chief UK Land Forces (CINCUKLF) a NATO Major Subordinate Commander similar to Commander-in-Chief United Kingdom Air Forces (CINCUKAIR). The UK Home Defence plans did not include an equivalent to the NATO 'Counter-Surprise' plan, and as such left the UK Home Base vulnerable in a sudden crisis. Between 1971 and 1985 parts of the Government and MoD War Books were being updated to include new procedural arrangements between HQUKLF and NATO, including the co-ordination of the movement of troops to designated ports for reinforcement into Europe. As far as co-ordination and communications went between NATO,

the Government departments and Armed Services operationally responsible for Home Defence, there was room for improvement.

In order to fulfil part of its obligation, NATO asked the UK to re-categorise some of its forces in order to, '… present a true picture of current status of categorised forces against war authorised strength.'[43] The LTDP had 'invited' the British Government to re-categorise some 33 battalions from 'National Command' to 'Other Forces for NATO', which was accepted. Not accepted was the requirement to re-categorise 11 battalions from 'Other Forces for NATO' to 'NATO Earmarked'.[44] There was debate within the MoD about assigning UK Home Defence ground troops to NATO, which the MoD felt might provide, '… a NATO shield over the UK based forces … which otherwise might be vulnerable to defence cuts.'[45] But this could be a double-edged sword. The Government was concerned, '… whether there is any political advantage to be gained in drawing NATO's attention to forces which exist … and of which otherwise NATO would take no official cognizance.'[46] It might be expected that, in the event of war, SACEUR would be calling for any and all reserves to be shipped to Europe to help defeat an attack. In this case, the British Government would be in a situation like that of 1940 when the French called for more RAF fighters to be sent to France, but which Dowding knew would be needed for home defence, and so refused.

## Military Defence

The defence of the Home Base was the responsibility of United Kingdom Commanders-in-Chief Committee (Home) (UKCICC(H)) comprising Commander-in-Chief United Kingdom Land Forces (CINCUKLF), Commander-in-Chief Naval Home Command (CINCNAVHOME) and Air Commander Home Defence Forces (ACHDF). Their responsibilities were:

- The mobilisation of manpower and material resources
- The reinforcement of NATO
- The defence of the United Kingdom Base
- The reception of casualties and non-combatants from Europe
- The provision of Military Assistance to the Civil Authorities (MACA)

In a period of tension or approaching war, the Armed Forces needed to be free, during the Preparatory Phase, to mobilise and deploy. Their priorities were to protect the nuclear counter-offensive capability, Key Points and transportation routes, and to aid the Civil Authorities and Ministries. This would effectively include all those sites containing nuclear weapons and/or their delivery systems, and the transport network required for war fighting, the carriage of military supplies and dispersal of weapons. In concert with the Civil Authorities, the Transition to War plans would be activated, and MACA implemented.

The Commanders-in-Chief Committee asserted that during mobilisation and Transition to War, '… the security of the United Kingdom base is essential and it is a major task of the Home Defence forces to ensure it is maintained.'[47] There were moves afoot in the late 1970s to have the UK Home Base incorporated as a Land Region of ACE, but these never came to fruition. Therefore, it was entirely in the hands of the UK Government to define the policy and strategy for the defence of the UK home islands. Nonetheless, this policy and strategy had to interconnect with NATO strategy, so there would be the minimum friction in time of war. The two were inextricably linked.

UKLF, CINCNAVHOME and ACHDF HQs would be established at separate locations, with alternate HQs established on land and

Britain's strategic nuclear deterrent was carried by the four Resolution-class SSNBs, each armed with 16 Polaris ballistic missiles. One such submarine would have been on patrol at all times, ready to fire its payload at short notice. Here, a Polaris ballistic missile is test-launched from HMS *Renown*. (US DoD)

US Ground Launched Cruise Missiles (GLCM) were based at RAF Greenham Common (seen here under construction), amongst other locations in the UK and across Europe. Greenham would have been a Key Point requiring protection by UK home defence forces. Greenham Common became the focus of the anti-nuclear campaign in Britain, led by CND, in the 1980s. (US DoD)

at sea:[48] there was no airborne command centre for the Services or Government. Liaison offices from all military services, as well as from the Police, would be established at both central and regional civilian HQs. The country was divided into several Home Defence Regions. Regional Seats of Government (RSGs) headed by a Cabinet Minister with Military Liaison were established with modern communications equipment, some in completely new bunkers.

As part of the Home Defence establishment, United Kingdom Land Forces (UKLF) had specific responsibility for protection of vital NATO and national installations, especially those involved in mobilisation and transport. The MoD mobilisation and reinforcement plans, as well as plans for the staging of US and Canadian reinforcements, required billeting, transport, supply and shipping. Many of the US and Canadian forces would arrive in Europe via the UK, through its ports and airports. The pressure on the Armed Forces for protection duties would be added to by the need to guard such facilities as telecommunications centres and networks, food stores and utilities. The use of Naval and Air Force personnel under Army control was an option available to the ground commander in time of crisis. A microwave communications network covered the country by the 1980s, and was complemented by the older, wired communications provided by the General Post Office, later British Telecom. All of this needed protection from sabotage and direct attack.

The military commanders were uncertain about their ability to fulfil the demands of Home Defence. To relieve the pressure on the Regular troops, and because of poor recruitment numbers for the Territorial units, the Home Service Force was to be raised in 1982.

## Defending the Nuclear Deterrent

According to the Defence Operational Planning Staff, 'The primary aim of the Armed forces in the United Kingdom … is to safeguard

the nuclear counter-offensive capability.'[49] Only once this job had been completed would the subsidiary aims, such as completing deployment of forces to war stations and to support active naval and air operations, be addressed. The defence of locations containing nuclear weapons had a high priority for Home Defence units. It was anticipated that it would also require a large Police presence to counter civilian demonstrations in any approaching crisis. The stationing of US Ground Launched Cruise Missiles (GLCM) meant that active deployment required local protection to enable them to leave the base, and national protection of the road network for operational deployment at their launch locations. Each squadron deployed six transporters for the missiles and control centres, and another sixteen vehicles for the technicians and security personnel. Because these forces were of vital importance their launch sites would be Key Points which would enable the area around them to be designated a Ground Defence Area capable of being defended with deadly force.

## Key Points

Key Points included ammunition stores, communication centres, early warning systems, and as mentioned above, the launch sites for nuclear-armed aircraft. These were locations that could be defended with deadly force, even before the outbreak of a war. Key Points and lines of communication were of great importance not only for the defence of the islands, but for the successful implementation of the reinforcement plans for US, Canadian and British forces in Europe. They were of 4 types:

- Nuclear (Type I). Installations which have at any time a vital role in enabling the country to receive timely warning of an imminent nuclear attack or to carry out a nuclear counter-strike.
- Continuity of Government (Type II). Installations the major disruption of which would seriously affect the maintenance and continuity of government of the country, centrally at any time and, in war, regionally.
- Critical (Type III). Installations which, during specific periods, have a vital role in enabling the country to fulfil its commitments to NATO.
- Survival (Type IV). Installations which would require protection in the survival period.

All Key Points would require protection from the beginning of a crisis, including 'survival' Type IV installations whose function would only begin after a nuclear attack.

## Defence of the Home Base/Islands

Defence of the Home Base required the Armed Forces to provide support for sea and air operations, as well as the protection of locations vital for the reinforcement of Europe. The Chiefs of Staff expected, 'Those personnel of all three Services, including Reserves, who are not assigned or earmarked for assignment to NATO and who are not involved in the mobilisation or support of such forces will be available for Home Defence tasks.'[50] This would have been approximately 100,000 personnel, although given the size of the task, the military commanders were dubious about their ability to fulfil the demands that would have been placed upon them as, '… there are already more tasks than the Army (the other two Services are already fully committed) is able to undertake.'[51]

Locations crucial to the maintenance of order, provision of energy supplies and food stores required protection. The transportation network included Essential Service Routes and the Military Road Route System which were primarily to keep main roads, railways and waterways clear for military traffic, but according to some were also meant as a way to reinforce the 'stay-put' policy. They would have limited civilian access to certain routes, enabling essential traffic a clear path to its destination. Food stores would have required particular attention to ensure the Post Strike Reserve (PSR) rations had been obtained and stored. Food storage facilities had been constructed during and after World War Two for this purpose, located on both the road and rail network to facilitate distribution. The PSR was, '… 30 days food at an austere scale for the mobilised strength of the RN ashore, Army and RAF units remaining in the UK …'[52] Control of food and fuel for civilians post-strike was under the control of Regional Commissioners.

## Civil Defence

Civil defence against conventional or chemical attack was almost non-existent in the UK, being dominated by plans in place for nuclear 'post-strike' continuation of Government, protection of food and fuel supplies, and an attempt to rebuild the nation. There were no professional organisations for Civil Defence other than the emergency services, which would undoubtedly be tied up coping with conventional attacks and protecting vital infrastructure.

The UK Government used two separate definitions for Civil Defence:

- UK Definition. Any measure not amounting to actual combat for affording defence against any form of hostile attack by a foreign power or for depriving any form of attack by a foreign power of the whole or a part of its effect, whether the measures are taken before, at or after the time of the attack.
- NATO Definition. The mobilisation, organisation and direction of the civil population designed to minimise by passive measures the effects of enemy action against all aspects of civil life.[53]

The UK had no national civil defence corps and any response to an emergency was to be organised at a regional and sub-regional level. This was also the level at which any co-operation between military and the civil authorities would operate, including the United Kingdom Warning and Monitoring Organisation (UKWMO). The UKWMO was to identify and report nuclear blasts, allowing the emergency services and military forces to avoid entering areas of high risk following the explosions. In each Region an Armed Forces HQ would be established, with two Sub-Regional HQs. The task of supporting the Civil Authorities would not be easy:

It will be appreciated that should hostilities seem imminent or actually break out, the armed forces are likely to be fully occupied with their primary military roles of deploying troops in support of NATO and securing the UK base. Although some units of the Territorial Army Volunteer Reserve (TAVR) have been earmarked for tasks in this country including protection of certain key installations, it is unlikely that there would be the manpower, surplus equipment or supplies to devote to purely civil purposes.[54]

Continuation of Government was of primary concern for the authorities. Central Government would be housed at the Central Government War Headquarters at Corsham, codenamed 'BURLINGTON', later changed to 'TURNSTILE'. The national organisation was arranged around the Local and County authorities. For emergency planning, local authority organisation was broken down into County Main, County Standby and District Controls. For example, Buckinghamshire had one main, one stand-by and five district HQs in place by 1978 with plans in place for food control, communications and monitoring. Nationwide, there were forty-seven County Mains and three hundred and thirty-three District Controls. The Civil Defence (General Local Authority Functions) Regulations, 1983 (added to in 1986) strengthened the existing legislation, making it compulsory for local authorities to prepare and maintain plans for emergencies, including conventional attack. Civil defence against conventional weapons occupies two sentences in a ten-page Government document detailing the processes for emergency planning. Civilians were not provided with protection against chemical attack, nor had advice been given to the public about chemical weapons.

With the enacting of the Emergency Powers Bill civilians could be conscripted for work to assist the military or civilian authorities, and also gave sweeping powers to the Police. During a transition to war, public opinion would be of great importance to the smooth operation of the Government's plans. If there were strong opposition to the possibility of war, the Defence Operational Planning staff expected it, '… would be exploited by dissident elements. In such circumstances the effect of industrial action upon public life might involve the Armed Forces in safeguarding essential services.'[55]

Pamphlets and radio and television information programmes would provide advice about what to do in the event of a nuclear attack. Most Government advice recommended staying in your home and building a shelter. Critics maintained that the policy of making the population stay-put would result in millions more deaths than if evacuation plans had been put in place. Given the size of the UK and the relative power of the nuclear warheads, it is debatable how successful any evacuation plans would have been, especially at a time when the military needed all the available transport and routes for mobilisation and reinforcement. The priority in a crisis or war was the needs of the military.

NATO defence rested on a slimmer and slimmer technological advantage to offset the increasing numerical superiority of the WTO in almost every aspect of land, air and maritime forces. Quantity does, indeed, have a quality all of its own.

# 6

# MOBILISATION AND COMBAT

```
TOP SECRET

1 (BR) CORPS GENERAL
DEFENCE PLAN 1983

OPO 1/83 — GEN DEF PLAN (GDP 83)

TIME ZONE USED THROUGHOUT THE
ORDER: ZULU
```

### Mobilisation

```
(a) Planning is based on the worst case
assumption that NORTHAG may only receive 48
hrs firm wng of a WP attack.[1]
```

Warning time was crucial to enable timely mobilisation of the Armed Forces. According to the Chiefs of Staff in 1978, mobilisation of the reserves would take, '… between 15-20 days (mobilisation to mainland Europe takes 10 days) …'[2] but this relied on warning time prior to mobilisation. In contrast to this upbeat appraisal, the units required to react most speedily gave a different timescale: 'With no warning time or prior implementation of Transition to War Measures it is clear that it would take up to a fortnight to bring Commando Forces to a full war footing.'[3] The Norway-trained Commandos were supposed to be available to respond rapidly to a sudden crisis.

Herein lay the main problems: firstly, knowledge of how quickly troops can or cannot be deployed was essential to be able to develop plans: secondly, without stores and ammunition they could not fight; without logistic support they would not have ammunition. When so much of the planning involved the use of non-regular troops, timing and warning were crucial. According to the GWB, the plans to provide logistic support to British forces in continental Europe would take nearly four weeks to complete, '… dependent on mobilisation and requisitioning powers …'[4]

Exercises to test mobilisation became more media focussed to garner public support for NATO and British defence policy. For Exercise Lionheart in 1984 the 8,500 men of 1st Infantry Brigade, a regular formation, embarked at Marchwood military port, near Southampton, and arrived 36 hours later at Esbjerg, Jutland. An exercise such as this was good publicity, showing the troops streaming onto and from RORO ferries at ports in England and Denmark. No mention was made of either the lack of enemy interdiction, or the reliance on civilian equipment, especially port facilities. This coverage also conveniently avoided mentioning the missing logistical troops, all reservists, without which this regular formation could only fight with what it could carry.

Transport for the mobilisation of some units might have proved troublesome, depending on the timing. According to Colonel Hellberg, in 1982, when the Commando Brigade was mobilised for the Falklands, '… British Rail were unable to reposition their rolling stock in time to meet any of the deadlines …'[5] The Brigade had to rely instead on hastily arranged road transport to move its supplies. In a full mobilisation, the movement of ammunition by road and rail would be made easier by a relaxation of the laws preventing explosives being transported, but there would have

been an increased demand for that rolling stock which could not have been met.

### Doctrine

```
'Corps preps for war in accordance with Ref C
and, on orders, deploy to locs in Annex A …'
```

Because in peace-time weapon systems take years, even decades, to design and develop, doctrine must develop in tandem with these systems. Doctrine, or 'that which is taught' is the guide by which military forces guide their actions in support of their objectives. It ranges from high level military doctrine to battlefield, tactical doctrine.[6] Doctrine is dependent on the tools available to remain relevant and credible. Guided weapons are an example of how technical development alters tactical doctrine. This can be seen in the improvement and use of all types of guided systems since the Second World War. The Royal Navy relies extensively on the use of guided weaponry and developed tactics to make the best use of these weapons, but their initially unreliable nature and delays in development left hugely expensive platforms relying on out-dated weapons and tactics. HMS *Conqueror*'s use of the old but reliable Mark 8 torpedo, rather than the new but unreliable Tigerfish, to sink the ARA *Belgrano* demonstrated this.

The doctrine for the RAF in NATO ranged from close air support (CAS) for BAOR, and attacks against enemy forces deep within the Eastern Bloc with the intention of stopping their progress into the West. The concept, known as 'Follow-on Forces Attack' or FOFA became an intrinsic part of NATO's Flexible Response strategy. Utilising highly accurate air-to-surface weaponry it sought to create a void between the first and second echelons of the enemy attack. Relying on the technological advantage of NATO in delivering precision munitions the hope was that Warsaw Pact second and rear-echelon units would be decimated before they had the opportunity to use their superior numbers. Sufficient numbers of ground attack aircraft, cover from fighters and air-to-surface munitions were necessary to implement the policy successfully. Buccaneers and

The RAF adopted the Blackburn Buccaneer S.2 after the failure of a number of other aircraft projects and it would continue in frontline service until the Gulf War of 1991. The example seen here is in typical RAF markings and carries a Phimat ECM pod under its left wing. (US DoD)

The Tornado GR.1 was a highly capable variable geometry strike aircraft. Jointly developed with West Germany and Italy, it was designed to penetrate enemy air defences at extremely low altitudes, day or night and in all weathers. The RAF was slow to adopt guided munitions however and despite being a very advanced platform would have had to overfly targets to deliver free-fall ordnance. (US DoD)

Jaguars, and later Tornados, would implement interdiction attacks to disrupt follow-on formations and the infrastructure they require, such as fuel depots and bridges. The decline in aircraft numbers and a reliance on obsolescent weapons and older types of aircraft such as the Phantom meant the capabilities of the RAF were below those demanded by NATO for this role.

As a continuing and credible deterrent to the growing Soviet Navy, the Royal Navy's capabilities were diminishing. Anti-submarine warfare was the *raison d'être* of the Royal Navy's contribution to the Eastern Atlantic and Channel commands within NATO. The role of the ASW carriers and commando carriers was central to the Navy's role, but the fleet only reached near full complement with *Ark Royal* commissioned in 1985; however, HMS *Hermes* had been put into standby in 1984 and was sold in 1986. The cuts to the Royal Navy surface fleet announced in the 1980 and 1981 SDEs meant its capabilities were not up to the level required by NATO. A paper by the Directors of Defence Policy described the situation as, '… an increasing inability … to contain Soviet maritime forces in an area of NATO's choosing or to safeguard transatlantic reinforcement and replenishment, upon both of which NATO strategy depends.'[7] The reprieve from this situation offered by the Falklands War was temporary, with some ships continuing to be 'short-lifed', and others put into reserve in the years following the war.

The British Army's new doctrine of mobile defence and 'Counterstroke' converged with a heightening of East-West tensions, improvements in weapons technology and communications technology. The doctrinal changes improved the morale of the units in Germany and showed the way ahead for the British Army. Yet, despite the increase in provision of transport for the rear echelons, there were not enough troops to crew them unless there was fully fledged mobilisation of the reserve: nor was there sufficient ammunition or weapon systems for the fighting troops. The Counterstroke demanded large quantities of MBTs, and helicopter borne ATGWs, but the British Government had opted for more STRIKER vehicles. The strictures of strategy – ends, ways and means – were not fulfilled for the counterstroke to work in the European Theatre even during a slow-moving crisis.

## Defending the West

(b)  NORThAG, together with TWOATAF, will fight a jt land/air battle as close to the IGB as possible …

A central theme of NATO defence of Federal Republic of Germany (FRG) was Forward Defence. NATO planning had initially based its defence on the Rhine-Ijssel line, to the west of most of the FRG. This was unacceptable to the FRG, eventually moving the defence Eastwards to the Weser-Lech line, then to the IGB. The FRG wanted, naturally, to defend as much of their country as possible. In their view this was as close to the IGB as possible. Their outlook was demonstrated in their choice of language, the subtlety of which is perhaps lost on non-German speakers, and, '… was one of the reasons why the West Germans preferred *Vorneverteidigung* (at-the-front-defence) to *Vorwärtsverteidigung* (forward defence).'[8] The problem with Forward Defence, certainly as seen by the British, was that it tended to restrict flexibility of action. As the WTO threat in the Central Region increased, so NATO had to think of new ways to respond.

By the early 1980s the WTO Operational Manoeuvre Group concept had matured under the guidance of Soviet Chief of the General Staff Marshal Ogarkov. WTO ground force structure and strength conformed to these warfighting theories. In 1985 the WTO had grown to approximately 200 divisions. Army formations and individual units had grown. The WTO armies were tank-heavy, but its order-of-battle was increasingly adapted to the combined-arms structure vital for victory in conventional operations in the new environment. The ratio of tanks to infantry increased in tank armies, and the mobility of divisions was enhanced with improved transport and logistical support troops.

NATO commanders sought new concepts to counter this, and General Sir Nigel Bagnall's developments in the British Army doctrine in the 1970s and 1980s promoted the use of mobile defence and manoeuvre rather than the previous static, attritional defence. This became known as the 'Counterstroke'. The desire to use mobile defence in 1(BR) Corps sector had military and political repercussions with 1(GE) Corps to the immediate north in the 'Layer Cake'. General von Senger und Etterlin, Commander-in-Chief of Allied Forces Central Europe, expressed concern that not only were the BAOR resources insufficient for the proposed type of counterattack, but that the idea of mobile defence would expose the flank of 1(GE) Corps and force it into an early withdrawal, undermining the concept of Forward Defence. Minor modifications were made, and reassurances given to the commander of 1(GE) Corps, General Dr Wachter. Following Bagnall's appointment to Commander of the Northern Army Group (NORTHAG), which included 1(GE) Corps, the doctrine was extended as the 'NORTHAG Concept'.

General Gow, Commander-in-Chief BAOR, wrote to General Bagnall in 1982 supporting Bagnall's new doctrine, but emphasising the need to maintain, at least partially, the '… stiff linear deployments …' associated with Forward Defence.[9] The British Army was planning to use 'Counterstroke' forces in a very different way from the doctrine that had gone before: '… the main defensive phase of the new concept is radically different from the current concept, since it involves the intermingling of RED and BLUE forces …'[10] This reduced the possibility of employing tactical nuclear weapons with the troops of both sides in close proximity. This new doctrine, the Counterstroke, '… is a counter attack with the specific aim of destroying enemy forces which are on the move …',[11] an approach which relied upon mobile forces identifying and attacking weaknesses in the enemy advance, at short notice and using reserves specifically kept for this purpose. The credibility of this doctrine relied on the reinforcements arriving in a timely fashion and being supplied with resources sufficient for their role. It depended on upon mobility in a fluid battle, highly trained troops, good communications between the units involved, and flexible command. It saw positional battles as the precursor to counter-attacks. The positional battles were intended to keep the WTO forces' penetrations as shallow as possible, in keeping with the idea of 'Forward Defence' which would then be attacked in the flank by mobile reserves. A heavy reliance was placed on ATGW-armed helicopters for mobile attack, armed reconnaissance, and flank defence.

ATGW-armed helicopters had not been provided in the quantities required either by NATO or by the MoD's own 'Counterstroke' planning. A DOAE study indicated the attrition rate for helicopter anti-tank sorties was expected to be 50 percent per sortie. This would mean that, flying five sorties a day per helicopter, as assumed in the study, the 75 LYNX/TOW available would be down to fewer than five helicopters by the end of the first day of fighting. The small number of LYNX/TOW available would have imposed serious limitations on any 'Counterstroke' counterattack. Thirty were required for a brigade level counter-attack – 40 percent of the entire LYNX/TOW available to BAOR. An additional 108 anti-armour helicopters were requested by NATO; by 1989 only an additional 25 LYNX/TOW systems had been ordered. It is clear that an MBT or vehicle mounted MILAN system would not have the flexibility of a helicopter mounted system, in tactical manoeuvrability or speed of deployment. The helicopters were vulnerable to small calibre anti-aircraft fire, and the WTO was well equipped with prodigious numbers of hand-held and mobile anti-aircraft missiles and guns, such as the ZSU 23-4 'Shilka', deployed at a rate of 16 systems per Motor Rifle Division, or various anti-aircraft missile launchers, deployed at a rate of 156 per Motor Rifle Division. Evidence from the Soviet equipped Syrian attack on the Golan Heights in 1973 suggested that the Israelis lost three out of every five aircraft sent in to attack the Syrian tanks to anti-aircraft fire.

The plans for the Counterstroke were inconsistent with the availability of ammunition, fuel and spares to prepare for, and execute, the attack. Existing WMR ammunition levels for the Chieftain main gun were 360 APDS/HESH rounds per tank. The limitation unstated in the Counterstroke papers is that each tank could only carry up to 64 rounds and providing replenishment in a highly mobile combat environment had not been accounted for.

The Counterstroke was expected to begin on day three of a war, but ammunition was expected to begin to run out through lack of reserves by day two, which would have left any planned attack short of ammunition, fuel and other supplies. The fighting troops and weapons may have looked formidable, but there was no depth to the forces, and no sustainability. The misconception that the Armed

Forces could become more 'efficient' would have proved disastrous during war.

The ground forces required air cover, as well as the need generally to interdict the enemy in their rear-areas. 2ATAF had this task in the NORTHAG area. The Warsaw Pact had an advantage in aircraft of around 2:1. A serious limitation 2ATAF faced was described by Air Marshal Sir Paddy Hine, Commander 2ATAF between 1983 and 1985;

… we have to keep our own airbases open. Since NATO is a defensive alliance it is inconceivable that we would be allowed to attack the Warsaw Pact airfields before their forces attacked us. So I work on the basis that I would have to absorb the first intensive air attacks by the enemy against us.[12]

A quick response would be essential. Safety for aircraft rested in being either in hardened shelters or airborne;

Unsheltered aircraft if caught on the ground during an air attack are extremely vulnerable. Recent MoD studies have suggested that depending on the size of an aircraft and the degree of dispersal provided, between half and two-thirds could be destroyed in a single raid.[13]

Problems with aircraft identification (Identification, friend or foe, or IFF) meant that the automated system of identification could not be used, and there was a serious risk of shooting down friendly aircraft, especially in the confusion of the early battle. Problems with IFF were to continue to cause concern during Operation GRANBY.[14]

## BAOR Sector Defence
MISSION. To destroy en as far to the east as possible

The CVR(T) Spartan served as a light armoured utility vehicle in a wide range of roles within the British Army, including carrying Blowpipe or Javelin AAGW, engineer reconnaissance, the support or surveillance troop in medium reconnaissance squadrons and with the RAF Regiment field squadrons. This example is with the Staffords in Exercise White Rhino in 1989 where the usual role of the Spartan was as the mount for the mortar fire controllers. Note the poles and tarpaulin that would likely be used to erect a shelter. (Walter Böhm)

The CVR(T) Scimitar was broadly similar to the Scorpion but carried a 30mm RARDEN cannon in place of a 76mm gun. The RARDEN was reputed to be an extremely accurate weapon, deadly against light armoured vehicles, which experienced users describe 'sniping' with out to 2,000 metres. Although it had a nominal rate of fire of 90 rounds per minute this was not possible to realise in practice as it had to be fed from four-round clips. The Scimitar was widely used in the armoured reconnaissance regiments and in the reconnaissance platoons of armoured and mechanised infantry battalions. (Michael Neumann via Walter Böhm)

The following description is based on the Ground Defence Plan for 1983 and contains the newly reorganised divisional structure for BAOR. The style of defence had been progressively adapted from less mobile, linear defence to a more mobile concept based in some respects on the actions of General Manstein in the Second World War. The emphasis of the defence was that it would be conducted using conventional means for as long as possible. However, if the use of nuclear weapons became necessary, the request for release should be made early, so that their effects could be exploited by the existing conventional forces before defensive cohesion is lost. NORTHAG's commander's intention was to fight the enemy as close to the inner German border (IGB) as possible, supported by the Second Allied Tactical Air Force (2ATAF), using three main phases of combat; a covering battle, the main defensive battle, and subsequent operations. A worst-case scenario was of 48 hours firm warning of an attack by the WTO. Approximate timings from the time a warning of an attack was given to Allied Command Europe (ACE) show that Military Vigilance (MV) would be notified 12 hours after initial warning. This was known as VOD, indicating an operational MV warning. A General Alert (GA) coincided with the enemy crossing the IGB approximately 48 hours after the initial warning.

During peacetime, all combat and supporting units were meant to be able to deploy within six hours of warning and should tension increase they would be deployed to their fighting locations. There would be three main phases of operations.

## Phase 1 – Covering Force Action

The principle task of the CF is to delay the en for at least 24 hrs between IGB and the NORTHAG FEBA …

During Phase 1, the Covering Force, consisting of the Corps Screen provided by the Covering Force Brigades (CF) from 1st and 4th Armoured Divisions, would deploy along the IGB. The role of the CF was to delay the enemy's advance and identify the main axis of attack.

Brigadier Royal Armoured Corps (BRAC) would command the CF. In the NATO 'Layer Cake' 1st Armoured was deployed to the north and 4th Armoured to the south of BAOR's defence sector. Each divisional CF would consist of a reconnaissance regiment and an armoured brigade of three battle groups. The *Bundesgrenzschutz* (BGS, or Federal Border Guard) were to patrol the IGB until ordered to withdraw, when they would be relieved by the Corps reconnaissance regiments (although the likelihood was that the reconnaissance forces would be deployed before the withdrawal of the BGS). At notification of a Simple Alert the Royal Engineers attached to the CF would deploy to begin defensive works. Roads would be cratered; bridges would be demolished and booby traps laid to canalise the enemy advance as much as possible. The intention of the CF would be to inflict as much damage as possible on the advancing WTO forces and impede the enemy for at least 24 hours. This would provide time to identify the main axes of enemy advance and to prepare the main defence positions. The CF would comprise three elements: a screen; delaying forces; and local reserves. The screen would consist of Scimitar, Spartan and Striker-equipped units which would not be expected to engage in heavy fighting. Their role would be to maintain contact with the enemy, as well as destroying enemy reconnaissance forces without revealing the CF defensive positions.

The delaying forces, made up of heavy armoured units, mechanised infantry and artillery would be the fighting elements of the CF, engaging the enemy at long range from several prepared positions. The local reserves would be expected to support the delaying forces and intercept any enemy that may have penetrated the delaying force's defences. Ideally the CF would compel the main enemy units to deploy into battle formation for deliberate attacks on their positions. Any need to deploy into regular battle formations would delay the enemy's advance. Artillery and air support would be brought into action to support the delaying forces. NATO commanders hoped this combination would impose a significant interruption to the enemy's movements, providing more time for the preparation of the main defence area.

The Covering Force might be called upon to thin out its defences to provide additional Divisional or Corps reserves, but this would only take place following explicit orders from Commander, Northern Army Group (COMNORTHAG). In this case, HQ BRAC and one armoured brigade would be withdrawn, and the CF adjusted to compensate.

The Scorpion was used in the reconnaissance troop of armoured regiments, and in some armoured reconnaissance regiments. The L23 76mm gun fired a useful HESH (High Explosive Squash Head), cannister (sometimes improvised with spent MG cases) or smoke round. Lacking the accuracy of the RARDEN, the L23 also had high recoil and filled the fighting compartment with fumes, described by one former gunner as 'like being on the deck of the *Victory* at Trafalgar'. Note the additional equipment bins along the hull side and the crew gear festooned around the turret sides. (Michael Neumann via Walter Böhm)

The CVR(W) Fox was mainly used by the Territorial Army's Yeomanry regiments but also served in the reconnaissance platoons of Regular mechanized battalions equipped with AT-105 Saxon APCs and some non-mechanised truck-borne infantry. In addition to a reconnaissance role, they were often detailed in a counter-airborne/heliborne landing role in rear areas. Fox carried the same 30mm RARDEN gun as the Scimitar. This example taking part in Exercise Key Stone '87 has much natural foliage added to enhance its camouflage, a practice that would soon be ended due to concerns about damage to the environment. (Michael Neumann via Walter Böhm)

## Phase 2 – Main Defence Battle

```
Destroy en east of Line ALPHA; this may be
in conjunction with offensive ops by res of 1
(BR) Corps
```

Once the CF had withdrawn, the Main Defence Area (MDA) would be defended to stop further advance of the enemy. The objective of the Main Defence Battle (MDB) would be to stop the enemy advance

as far East as possible whilst ensuring the cohesion of the Army group was maintained. This was a compromise in NORTHAG between the BAOR concept of flexible, mobile defence and counterattack, with the German Army's more rigid adherence to 'Forward Defence'. 1st and 4th Armoured Divisions were expected to provide the backbone of the MDB utilising the mechanised infantry battalions and the Chieftain, and later Challenger, armoured regiments. 3rd Armoured Division acted as the main reserve, with BAOR Corps Rear Area under the command of 2nd Infantry Division HQ. Their reserve was to be the German Home Defence Brigade 52 or 53, but these would need to be released for this role by the *Bundesministerium der Verteidigung* (Federal Ministry of Defence, shortened to BMVg).

Topographical features were identified which would be vital to the defence of a particular area, loss of which would make any local defence untenable. If lost, significant effort would be made to regain these positions. The municipality of Ilsede, consisting of a group of villages running along the river Fuhse, south of Peine, was identified as the ideal location of a firm defence. It was 10km behind the FEBA of the Saltzgitter canal, and consisted of woods, boggy ground and villages which could be used as defensive outposts.

1(BR) Corps commanders expected the battle in the MDA to begin with hasty attacks against the prepared positions of BAOR, intended to quickly dislodge the defenders and maintain the momentum of the attack. If these succeeded penetrations of the defence would be exploited before the defenders could reorganise. Battle Group commanders would deploy the combat teams in depth in order to deny the enemy the opportunity for reconnaissance and to absorb as much momentum from the enemy advance as possible. Mutually supporting positions would be established in depth, making the most of the topography. The intention was to force the enemy to deploy and make deliberate

This Ferret Mk 2/3 belonging to 4/7 Dragoon Guards is seen during Exercise Potent Gauntlet in 1989. By this time the Ferret was mainly used as a liaison or radio relay vehicle. This example has a large storage rack added above the rear engine deck and racks for additional fuel cans on the hull rear; conversions like this were common as the vehicle lacked internal space for crew kit, and even with these modifications extra gear can be seen crammed between the turret rear and the rack. It also has an empty pintle mount for an MG, probably an L3A4 .30 Browning. (Michael Neumann via Walter Böhm)

The Mi-24 Hind was a Soviet-made heavy attack helicopter with no direct NATO equivalent. Large, armoured, and armed with cannon or heavy machineguns and anti-tank missiles and unguided rockets in various combinations according to the precise model, it would have posed a problem for BAOR, with its limited integral anti-air capability, to deal with. (US DoD)

The Su-25 'Frogfoot', known to the Soviets as the *Grach* (Rook), was designed to provide close air support to ground forces. It was broadly similar in concept to the USAF's A-10, being armed with a 30mm cannon and able to carry a wide range of free-fall ordnance. (US DoD)

attacks against the BAOR defences. Significant use of artificial obstacles would be made, including mine fields and wire entanglements. An anti-tank mine field 1,000 metres wide using Mark 7 mines was expected to disable up to 70 percent of tanks and 40 percent of APCs crossing it. The later addition of Bar and Ranger mines allowed faster deployment of minefields. Bar mines were anti-armour mines laid using a plough on the back of an FV432. The Ranger system could deliver up to 1,296 mines per load fired from a multiple launch system and was to be used in conjunction with the Bar mines to make mine-clearing additionally hazardous for the enemy.

The air situation over the battlefield was recognised as being 'adverse' for 1(BR) Corps.[15] The introduction of the Soviet Mi-24 Hind attack helicopter added to the problems of defence for NATO. Armoured and heavily armed, it provided close support for attacking formations. Air defence at the tactical level was one area in which BAOR was deficient throughout the period and defending troops would have to rely on Blowpipe and Rapier for local air defence. As a last resort All Arms Air Defence (AAAD) would be employed. AAAD relied on the use of small arms, mainly machine guns, for point defence, and 'When not deployed in a ground role all MGs must be placed in the air defence role.'[16]

## Phase 3 – Subsequent Operations

```
(a)  Hold Corps vital ground …

(b)  Maint  cohesive  def  and  liaison  with
[flank] Corps

(c)  Be prep to sp Corps or Army Gp ops
```

Subsequent Operations (SO) would be to restore the integrity of NATO territory by employing the Army Group reserves for a counterattack to clear enemy forces from West Germany. NORTHAG reserves were a German Panzer Division, in 1983 the 7th, with the possible addition of III (US) Corps if it was released by AFCENT (Allied Forces Central Europe).

BAOR veterans describe being told that their life expectancy was measured in hours, possibly days, at the beginning of an invasion, and that organised resistance was expected to last no more than eight days. It would be likely that NATO commanders would request nuclear release within two or three days of the beginning of hostilities. The initial use of battlefield nuclear weapons would be to break-up concentrated enemy formations. There was an expectation that once these nuclear weapons had been used, escalation to a full exchange would be rapid.

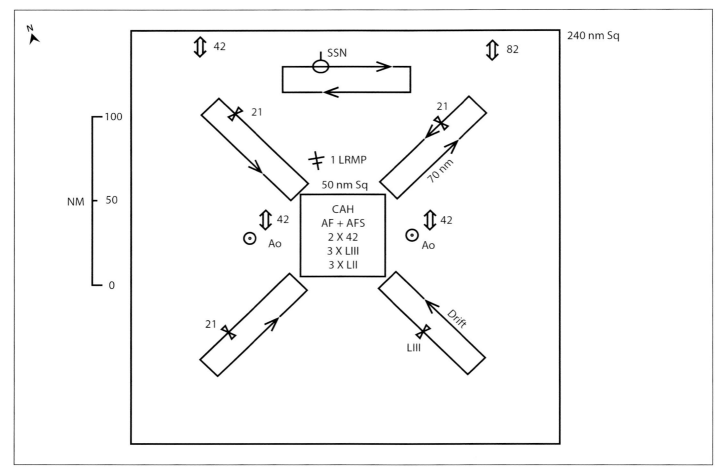

1st UK CAH Group in Transit Area Search, showing: CAH: Invincible-class Anti-Submarine Warfare Carrier; SSN: Nuclear-powered attack submarine; 21: Type 21 Frigate; 42: Type 42 Destroyer; LII, LIII: Leander-class frigate, Batch II and III respectively; AF, AFS and AO: RFA-operated support vessels. (Diagram by Gorge Anderson)

## Other Considerations

NATO saw the Soviet naval priorities as ensuring the deployment of its SSBNs into the Atlantic, whilst denying the freedom of action to NATO's navies. In addition to countering the expected Soviet deployments, destruction of as many enemy naval vessels as quickly as possible was key to NATO success. The Soviet navy was expected to deploy into the Atlantic and North Sea ahead of any war. This would allow the Soviet forces to take up their optimum operational areas before the outbreak of hostilities.

At the core of UK Naval policy the, 'Freedom of movement through [the Eastern Atlantic and Channel] …'[17] was crucial to the success of NATO's overall strategy. Keeping the seaways clear was required for two main purposes; the flow of reinforcements to the continent and from the USA; the supply of food, fuel and raw materials to the UK. Britain needed considerable maritime forces to keep the Greenland-Iceland-UK gap open for shipping, and more importantly close it to exploitation by WTO ships trying to enter

HMS *Invincible* was the lead-ship of its class and saw active service in the Falklands in 1982. Though famous as a platform from which the Sea Harrier performed its duties in that conflict, its role in any NATO-WP war would have been as home to a swarm of anti-submarine helicopters. NATO believed that the Soviet Northern Fleet would attempt a break-out into the North Atlantic with its submarines and the Royal Navy was a key component of NATO's ASW strategy to block the GIUK Gap against such a move. (US DoD)

Another view of a Sea Wolf and Exocet-armed Leander-class frigate. This view clearly shows the stern helicopter deck that enabled the operation of an ASW-capable Lynx helicopter. (US DoD)

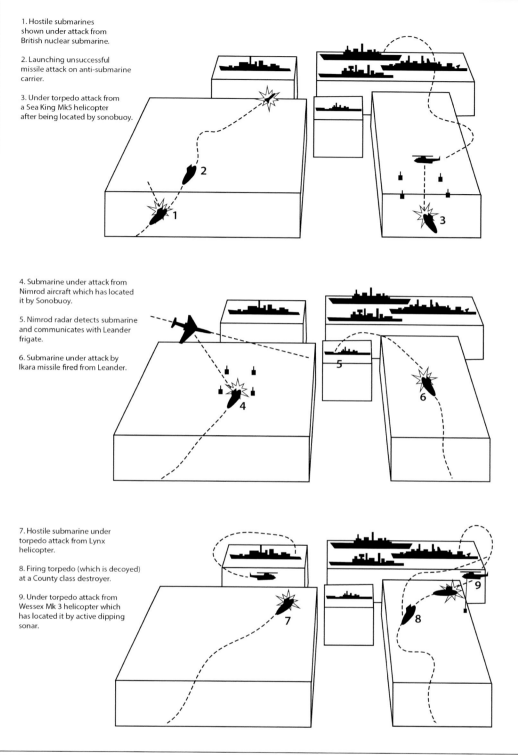

1. Hostile submarines shown under attack from British nuclear submarine.

2. Launching unsuccessful missile attack on anti-submarine carrier.

3. Under torpedo attack from a Sea King Mk5 helicopter after being located by sonobuoy.

4. Submarine under attack from Nimrod aircraft which has located it by Sonobuoy.

5. Nimrod radar detects submarine and communicates with Leander frigate.

6. Submarine under attack by Ikara missile fired from Leander.

7. Hostile submarine under torpedo attack from Lynx helicopter.

8. Firing torpedo (which is decoyed) at a County class destroyer.

9. Under torpedo attack from Wessex Mk 3 helicopter which has located it by active dipping sonar.

Royal Navy surface and helicopter units prosecuting hostile submarine targets with support from shore-based Royal Air Force Nimrod LRMP aircraft. (Diagram by George Anderson)

Western Approaches or other UK waters.

The Carrier Groups from the UK would be deployed to provide ASW support for the 1st and 2nd US Carrier Groups deployed from Norfolk, Virginia on M+1 and M+20 respectively. The 1st UK Carrier Group was expected to comprise one Invincible-class CAH with 11 combat surface vessels and one nuclear-powered submarine in support. Seven Long Range Maritime Patrol aircraft were necessary, with one on task at all times.

The forces deployed in the Eastern Atlantic were focussed on anti-submarine activity, keeping the shipping lanes safe for the reinforcement convoys. Command and control would be exercised from the ASW carriers, and there would be communication and coordination between individual ships and aircraft. Area air defence would be provided by destroyers whilst the frigates would prosecute attacks on submarines and surface ships using their Lynx helicopters. Additionally, dipping sonar from Sea King and Wessex helicopters and sonobuoys from Nimrod long-range maritime patrol aircraft would extend the capability to identify and attack enemy submarines. Whether there would be enough sonobuoys was a serious consideration, one which the Royal Navy could not answer. The additional 10,000 sonobuoys purchased may not have been sufficient for the widespread expenditure expected.

As an integral part of the NATO defences, land air and naval, the Northern Flank of NATO was an area of concern, and relatively weakly defended. The route into the Atlantic for Soviet ships and submarines was monitored from Greenland to the UK and included maritime reconnaissance from Northern Norway. Through bilateral agreements as well as its NATO commitment Britain was to provide support to Norway and, after 1982, to Denmark. These forces comprised the United Kingdom Mobile Force (UKMF) and the UK/NL Amphibious Force. The land forces allocated to Scandinavia by Britain were all lightly armed mobile units. Other NATO forces earmarked for

the Atlantic. The UK Government expected Soviet and Warsaw Pact harassment of merchant shipping in the approach to any war.

Vital to the defence of the Eastern Atlantic were shore-based aircraft for Maritime Reconnaissance and Attack, as there were minimal numbers of aircraft available from carriers after the cancellation of the CVA-01 in 1966. Prior to combat operations the UK Tornado interdictor/strike aircraft allocated to SACLANT would augment surveillance operations. Once hostilities began, they would carry out attacks on any enemy surface ships in the

The Sovremenny-class was a modern Soviet surface combatant, the main armament of which comprised four fully automatic AK-130 130mm guns, eight SS-N-22 heavy anti-ship missiles and 48 SA-N-7 Gadfly anti-air missiles. Several examples of this class were present in the Northern and Baltic Fleets. (US DoD)

Allied Forces Northern Europe (AFNORTH) included a US Marine Expeditionary Force. The 1981 Defence Review would significantly reduce the number of surface ships available to the Royal Navy. The review identified, '... the best balanced operational contribution for our situation – will be one which continues to enhance our maritime-air and submarine effort, but accepts a reduction below current plans in the size of our surface fleet ...'[18] The intended reductions, especially of the 'Through Deck Cruisers', would reduce NATO's ability to control the Norwegian Sea and successfully reinforce Norway.

Denmark and Norway were vital in bottling up the Soviet Baltic fleet by denying them egress through the Baltic Approaches (Skagerrak and Kattegat). Norway was also crucial in the expected battle with the Soviet Northern fleet moving out of the Barents Sea. The Norwegian Sea Campaign was part of NATO's maritime operations concept to defend the Norwegian Sea to allow reinforcements to arrive, and to deny access to the Atlantic through the GIUK gap.

The UK/NL Amphibious Force, an all-regular formation, was to land at Tromsø in Norway if time allowed (such as a 31/24 setting). If the timescales were shorter, for example in a 5/3 setting, it would be directed to land at Esbjerg in Denmark to fight with the UKMF. The UK component was the Royal Marine Commando Brigade including organic logistics, artillery, engineers and special units. The force was to be supported by a variety of anti-submarine and air defence vessels from the Royal Navy, as well as unarmed logistical vessels. Long Range Maritime Patrol and other vessels would be provided by the Netherlands Armed Forces. In discussing their main role, Ewen Southby-Tailyour, a Royal Marine officer, wrote, 'This Amphibious Task Group was expected to sail early in a crisis and certainly early enough to be received by the "host nation" before hostilities began. By reacting so soon, a display of NATO solidarity would be shown that might ... deter an enemy in its actions.'[19]

The Commandos had training in arctic conditions for deployment into Norway, but had they been deployed in Denmark they would have faced armour-heavy enemy forces against which they were not sufficiently well equipped. Despite its vital role, RM winter training was to be cut from 1981 as a cost-saving measure.

The UK Government became increasingly concerned with the limited forces provided by Norway, the Netherlands and Denmark in NORTHAG, and the threat to Norway in AFNORTH. Cuts made by the Danish Defence Ministry included maintaining fewer regular Danish troops and the cancellation of some modernisation plans. The Danish Army amounted to the equivalent of two divisions, spread over Jutland and the islands in the Danish Straits, notably Skælland on which is Copenhagen, the capital. The British Government suggested that the Danish Government was using the NATO reinforcement plans as an excuse to reduce their national defences, although this was denied in Copenhagen.

Two RAF units were to strengthen regional air cover by deploying to airfields on Jutland. The UK Mobile Force (UKMF) was to reinforce the defence of NORTHAG areas, and to reinforce the Baltic Approaches (BALTAP), deploying to Esbjerg in Denmark. If the Warsaw Pact were to focus its attack through West Germany and along the Baltic coast, those forces in Denmark and its islands would be quickly cut-off from the other NATO commands. They might be left to be dealt with later. In the case of extended operations, the Warsaw Pact were expected to attempt to clear the Baltic Approaches and Denmark Straits, occupy Denmark and secure the Kiel Canal, giving them unrestricted access to the North Sea. Whatever the scenario, the UKMF was by now overcommitted through several different reinforcement plans, including the defence of Zealand and Jutland.

The Royal Navy and Royal Air Force had the task of protecting the cross-channel reinforcement effort and the freedom of operation in the North Sea. The UK required as much control over the North Sea as possible, both to protect the oil- and gas-rigs there, and to protect the north-eastern entrance to the English Channel. Channel Command covered the main chokepoint for ship-borne reinforcements to the Continent.

Ensuring the waters around the home islands were kept clear of mines would be difficult. The resources available were insufficient to keep open the approaches to Faslane, maintain access to major ports for reinforcement from the US and Canada, and sweep the shipping lanes in the Channel. One of these tasks could be undertaken, but not all. Priority was given to Faslane.

The air threat to the UK Air Defence System, notably an attack on the shore-based early warning installations, with follow up attacks on the fighter, Airborne Early Warning and tanker bases, was considered to have a potentially dramatic effect on the UK's ability to defend the airspace and waters adjacent to the islands, especially the North Sea. An attack such as this would make further penetration raids less costly for the Warsaw Pact, allowing increased frequency of attacks on transport facilities, infrastructure, headquarters and other installations.

Britain was in an unusual position in that the home islands were not a defined land region of NATO, yet they were a fundamental part of NATO's strategy of defence in depth, allowing air strikes and naval forces to be launched from the home islands. The defence of the UK contributed *directly* to the defence of the Alliance in Europe, and in many ways the defence of Europe would have been much more difficult without it. Large numbers of RAF and USAF aeroplanes were based in the UK and would have provided direct support to any fighting in Europe. The home islands were also to be used as a focal point for reinforcement and resupply of the NATO forces in Europe. As such, Britain was an obvious target for WTO air and naval attacks, as well as sabotage on land.

In Britain were nuclear warhead storage facilities, key communication points, airfields, ports and military locations, all of which needed defending in war. During mobilisation and Transition to War, '... the security of the United Kingdom base is essential and it is a major task of the Home Defence forces to ensure it is maintained.'[20] The MoD mobilisation and reinforcement plans, as well as plans for the USA and Canada, required billeting, transport, supply and shipping of armed forces to Europe. Many of the US and Canadian forces would arrive in Europe via the UK, through its ports and airports. In addition, there were nuclear weapons in Britain which required extra protection during a crisis or war. Britain was a base of attack against the WTO maritime and air threat to shipping in the Eastern Atlantic.

Regional Seats of Government (RSGs) headed by a Cabinet Minister with Military Liaison staff were introduced later. These were located within the Home Defence Regions already in existence. The 'Reading War Room', completed in 1953 for Home Defence Region 6 is the last of its type which survives.[21]

A reorganisation of this structure took place in the late 1970s and early 1980s. Regional Government Headquarters (RGHQ) were established with modern communications equipment.

## Transition to War

As the Third World War never happened, we cannot know the outcome, or the extent of the conflict. What is possible is bringing together this research with the exercises undertaken by the British Government and MoD. It is now possible look at the exercises undertaken in Whitehall and NATO for a more accurate description of what the Government and MoD expected to happen.

The fictional details of a potential Third World War have been described in several works, the most informative of which is *First Clash* by Kenneth Macksey.[23] Other works, most notable *The Third World War* and *Team Yankee*, see the conflict continuing for several weeks.[24] The scenario used in *The Third World War* and the BBC drama *Threads*[25] originated in the Government exercises such as WINTEX (WINter EXercise).[26]

In the exercise from 1983 a confrontation begins with a political breakdown in Yugoslavia and Czechoslovakia during December and January. NATO is concerned that these will prompt a military response from the Soviet Union. Because of increasing Soviet military activity, NATO's Military Vigilance measures are initiated on 31 January.

On 5 February the US/UK Lines Of Communication agreement commences in preparation for the arrival of US reinforcements by sea and air. In Britain, Simple Alert Measures are implemented between 17 and 20 February. Royal Navy ships are positioned in the Norwegian Sea and other peacetime deployment locations. The UK Mobile Force is deployed to Denmark and all land forces exercises are cancelled. UK military installation and Key Points protection is implemented, and regular reserves put on 48 hours' notice to move.

The Government announces the introduction of Emergency Powers and the mobilisation of military reserves on 24 February. Police reserves, special constables and retired officers are put on stand-by prompted by fears of rioting and problems in food shops as panic buying is reported. Many civilians begin to leave large urban areas and head for the countryside in what is euphemistically referred to as 'self-evacuation.'

From 26 February the National Health Service begins the accelerated discharge of patients from hospitals across the country. Increased maritime air reconnaissance identifies four Soviet nuclear submarines sortieing into the North Atlantic. Soviet aircraft are peacefully intercepted around the British Isles by Phantom interceptors, but worryingly demonstrate the Soviet Air Force's ability to attack from the south and south-west. British Airways is now fully engaged in ferrying reinforcements to the continent. On this one day some 37,000 US reinforcement personnel are in the UK in addition to the permanent US garrison. Reinforced Alert is 95 percent complete, according to the UK Government.

The SEPECAT Jaguar became an important attack aircraft for the RAF in the Close Air Support role. This example from No.2 Squadron is seen at RAF Wildenrath in Germany in 1978. (US DoD)

This Harrier GR.3 is seen firing 68mm SNEB rockets. Such rockets offered a degree of stand-off and could be useful against lightly armoured targets. (British Aerospace)

Soviet and Warsaw Pact forces are reported gathering in the Kola Peninsula to threaten Finland and Norway; in the south to threaten Turkey, Italy and Gibraltar; and in the Central Region a build-up of forces is noted. BAOR reports that outloading of supplies is going well, and will be completed by 3 March, however until the TA mobilisation is complete there are insufficient forces to guard all of the Key Points.

Rationing is introduced on 27 February in order to reduce the panic buying of food. Government War Book Measures to prepare the UK for nuclear attack are now being implemented. This threat is made more acute as Russian military aircraft violate British airspace when they overfly Scotland and Northern Ireland. The problems associated with maritime supply are increased as some ports become unavailable, as in the Western Dock at Southampton where a Polish ship sinks, closing it indefinitely. The capacity of the road-freight businesses are all-but monopolised by the needs of reinforcement and supply.

During the increase in tension Supreme Allied Command Atlantic (SACLANT) had requested a maritime exclusion zone be declared around Norway and Denmark, which would allow freer movement of Allied battle groups and amphibious forces in those waters. However, this was declined by the Military Committee of NATO. SACLANT would have to find other ways of protecting the ships.

Yugoslavia is invaded by

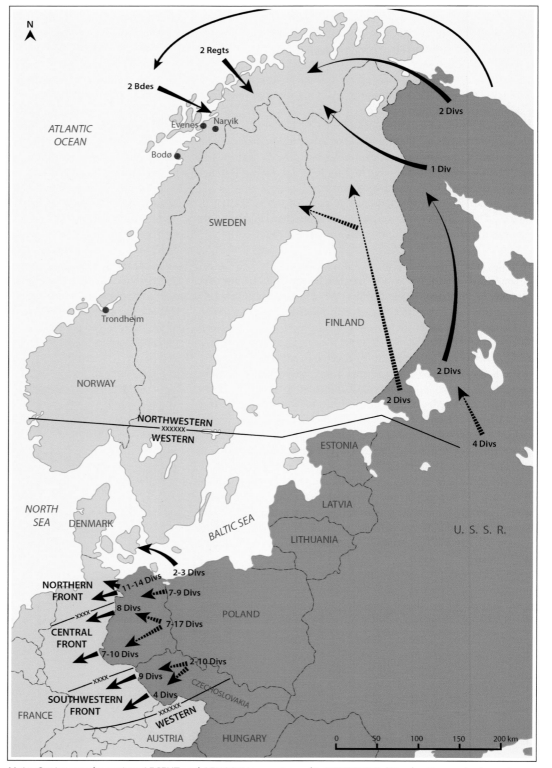

Major Soviet attacks against AFCENT and AFNORTH as envisaged in WINTEX '83. (Map by George Anderson)

Soviet, Bulgarian and Hungarian forces on the 28th. As a result, the danger level increases and the UKWMO is activated as well as the main body of 1(BR) Corps deployed. Command of the national forces in NATO is now transferred to Supreme Allied Command Europe (SACEUR). The NATO Defence Planning Committee met and assessed that the Soviet Union had already taken the decision to attack NATO, and that the warning should be raised to its highest level. The Soviet Union representative at the UN proposed a conference to discuss the current tensions.

Guidelines for the use of nuclear weapons are distributed to War Cabinet members in Whitehall, and the Government begins to issue 'Protect and Survive' advice to the public.[27] At the same time, war breaks out between several Middle Eastern states as some seek to take advantage of the focus of the superpowers concentrates on Europe. Soviet naval forces are continuing to gather in the GIUK Gap and the Norwegian Sea. An amphibious group, supported by the Kirov group, has departed Murmansk.[28] Finland rejects a request from the Soviets for freedom to move troops over its border.

The BMP-2 followed on from the BMP-1 in the early 1980s. Armed with a 2A42 30mm gun and 9K111 Fagot or 9M113 Konkurs (AT-4 Spigot or AT-5 Spandrel) ATGW it was much more capable than the BMP-1 though no better protected. This example is seen in service with the Nationale Volksarmee of the GDR. (Open Source)

The BTR-60PB was an eight-wheeled APC armed with a turret mounted 14.5mm KPVT machine gun. The first versions of the BTR-60 had been open-topped and the design gradually evolved into the PB seen here. One disadvantage of this design was that the infantry section carried could only mount and dismount through hatches on the roof of the hull. This example seen in the US had probably been captured in the Middle East in 1973. (US DoD)

Commandos (battalion-sized units) plus organic logistics, artillery, engineers and special units. Problems with weather and congestion at ports mean that the logistic element is delayed. However, with the assistance of US helicopters the British forces are deployed around Tromsø by 2 March. The RAF has completed the movement of squadrons to West Germany and is now fully mobilised. Jaguar, Harrier and Phantom squadrons have moved to their operational airbases.

Commander-in-Chief Central Region (CINCENT) reports that although all units have been deployed to their main positions, defensive preparations may take another four days to complete. British civilians, mainly families from BAOR, are evacuated to Britain using sea and air routes. Some 100,000 are expected to be evacuated by the end of 3 March.

The British Cabinet authorises Major Policy Decision 39 which aims to prepare Britain for nuclear attack by dispersing vital services and activities and introducing the BBC Wartime Broadcasting Service.

On 2 March Soviet naval activity increases with large naval groups and two amphibious groups at sea threatening Northern Norway, and the Northern Fleet's SSBNs preparing for sea. These are seen as a direct threat to the Carrier Battle Groups in the Norwegian sea. Defensive minefields are laid in many of the main sea approaches to Britain, Ireland and the continent to protect the

As February ends and March begins, several Soviet naval battle groups are seen approaching the Iceland/Faeroes gap, threatening the NATO carrier fleets and the amphibious groups. Fighting is still going on in Yugoslavia, and NATO detects large movements westwards of Soviet and WP units in the Central Region. The fighting elements of the UK/NL Amphibious Force and US Marine Corps (USMC) 4th Marine Amphibious Brigade (MAB) along with the Canadian Air-Sea Transported Brigade Group (CAST) are in Norway preparing for a Soviet invasion. The UK component of the Amphibious Force comprises a Brigade HQ, four Royal Marine

entrances to harbours and ports. In addition, WP transport aircraft are concentrating westwards in apparent preparation for large scale airborne operations.

Early on 3 March some WP reconnaissance forces are reportedly landed on the Norwegian coast in anticipation of an amphibious assault on Namsos. CINCNORTH request additional air support, and two squadrons of Jaguars are transferred to Tirstrup in Denmark with a squadron of Harriers deployed to Tromsø. The UKMF(L) is deployed across the neck of the Danish peninsula between Hamburg and Lübeck.

The Soviet forces in the Kola peninsula begin offensive action against Finland. This is expected to develop into an invasion of Norway. WP troops were also reported moving north-west in Yugoslavia, approaching the Italian border. Fears are that Italy will be invaded soon.

Soviet amphibious forces, supported by paradrops in battalion strength, attack the Namsos and Lyngen Fjord areas early on the morning of 3 March, but suffer significant losses to their ships in the process. Five large warships, five smaller destroyer sized vessels, and numerous diesel submarines are sunk by NATO air and sea forces in the operation. Another divisional-strength amphibious attack goes in against Andøya. There is no news about the fate of the NATO troops defending Norway.

In the Central Region, WP forces cross the IGB north of Hannover in the Dannenburg salient accompanied by heavy air attacks on Oldenburg and Hameln. An attempt to take two bridges over the Salzgitter Canal by desant are fought off successfully. Losses to 1(GE) Corps and BE Corps are heavy. The attack against the 1(GE) Corps is held by a spirited defence, although Corps reserves were already being deployed by the West Germans. 1(BR) Corps deploys a reconnaissance screen but there is little pressure in this area. The fear in 1(BR) Corps is of being surrounded as the two flanking corps come under increasing pressure from the WP.

Britain is now coming under increasing attack, both from the air and from Special Forces, with nearly 3,500 casualties reported. Key Points throughout the country are attacked with varying levels of success. Many of these KPs relate to air defence, and nuclear warning and launch locations. A toll is being taken of enemy aircraft in attacks, but in the first day UK Air Defence loses four aircraft. Only profligate use of air-to-air missiles is minimising Soviet air attacks on Britain. But, the stocks are diminishing rapidly, and the main air defence interceptor, the Lightning, has only 44 percent of pre-war stocks of Red Top missiles left.

Navy losses continue to mount with HMS *Andromeda* and RFA *Austin* sunk, and HMS *Yarmouth*, *Leander* and *Torquay* damaged. The stocks of Sea Dart and Sub-Harpoon missiles are reported as zero. The limited number of minesweepers are fully engaged trying to keep the Clyde clear, but other ports such as Felixstowe, Hull and Immingham are mined and unusable. Air attacks persist, and the Government issues an announcement of the 'stay-put' policy. Transport routes are to be controlled and essential travel only is allowed.

The 4th brings news of WP forces making progress in the 1(GE) and BE Corps areas, with increasingly powerful attacks against 1(BR) Corps. 1st Armoured Division in 1(BR) sector reports penetrations of up to 15km, and counterattacks have been planned for overnight. 1st Armoured Covering Force has suffered serious loss of men and equipment in delaying the Soviet first echelon attacks, however details of casualties from 1(BR) Corps are uncertain.

A battle report from 1st Armoured describes an action conducted by a battlegroup comprising tanks from the 3rd Royal Tank Regiment and infantry from the 2nd Battalion Royal Green Jackets, supported by Royal Horse Artillery Swingfire units and Royal Artillery Abbots. This force was pitted against at least a Motor Rifle and Tank regiment-sized enemy force supported by helicopters and large amounts of artillery. Two enemy tank battalions of T-80s supported by Motor Rifle battalions of BMP-2s and BTRs crossed the river Fuhse and assaulted the British positions placed along the Ballenberg Ridge near Soehlde, and the Messeberg Ridge by Hoheneggelsen. The initial attack by the Soviet forces was against Soehlde with large amounts of artillery preparation. The Soviet

The original BMP-1, armed with a 2A38 Grom 73mm gun and 9M14 Malyutka (AT-3 Sagger) ATGW, came as a rude shock to NATO when first introduced. In addition to carrying an infantry section, its own weapons were easily capable of destroying any NATO tank then in service, however it was only lightly armoured and would suffer grievously in the 1973 Arab-Israeli War. Subsequent NATO MBT designs would pay great attention to defeating the threat posed by HEAT weapons. (US DoD)

Commander then pushed additional forces to the south of the town to outflank the British positions. This manoeuvre ran into two squadrons of the 3rd RTR and lost many tanks. However, tank numbers and overwhelming artillery support forced the 3rd RTR and Green Jackets back onto the Messeberg ridge. The attack was held there while preparations for a full withdrawal were made. Despite heavy losses from Lynx ATGW helicopters the Soviet forces secured the Messeberg ridge and forced back the British battlegroup with considerable casualties.

6 March showed stocks of some naval surface-to-air and surface-to-surface missiles are being reported as zero. The continental reception ports had come under attack, and this was disrupting the outloading of those ships into Europe. Of the Home ports, ten of the twelve were closed until further notice through bombing and mining, and the Clyde was closed for at least 24 hours. Warship losses had reached 35 percent, which would cause serious problems for the defence of convoys and anti-submarine efforts. Norway north of Tromsø was considered lost to the Soviet invasion, and those forces were expected to push south to Namsos. 3 Commando Brigade is moving North towards Tromsø to counter this threat. Amphibious and airborne landings were made in Denmark on Zealand supported by heliborne assault and chemical attacks.

1(BR) Corps mounted a counterattack overnight against the Soviet penetration of 1st Armoured Division, but was unable to hold any ground gained and was forced back. The 1(BR) Corps reserves had been committed to this counterattack, and more generally in NORTHAG all corps level reserves were now fully engaged. More worryingly, WP forces were employing chemical weapons in increasing numbers. Two assaults, one heliborne and the other parachute, now hold the bridges over the Weser at Nienburg and over the Leine at Ahlden. SACEUR is expecting the WP forces to attempt a breakthrough on one of the main axes of advance in the next 24–48 hours.

Shipping losses in the Channel and South West Approaches reach almost 75 percent. Anti-submarine operations are continuing in the Atlantic to ensure the lines of communication between the US and Britain stay open.

By 7 March supplies of anti-tank guided weapons (ATGW) and Chieftain tank 120mm ammunition are reported as very low, and entirely exhausted in some places, and 2nd Allied Tactical Air Force (2ATAF) sortie rate has been reduced by up to 40 percent.

Chemical weapons continue to be used by the WP in Europe and against targets in the UK. The situation is becoming desperate, and SACEUR requests nuclear release. Early on the 8th NATO launches a limited attack using tactical nuclear weapons on WP bloc targets in an attempt to stop the follow-on forces reaching the battle front.

Political efforts are made to inform the Soviet command that the attacks are limited in scope, but whether this is believed or not is unknown.

At this point the exercise ends, presumably to avoid the inevitable nuclear escalation.

# 7
# CASE STUDIES

## Overview

The case studies below give examples from the period which demonstrate the activities of the British Armed Forces. They are drawn from two cases of preparation and deployment for war. But one must be cautious about extrapolating real-world events too far. Some lessons can be drawn from the campaigns which were relevant to NATO, but it must be remembered that they were fought in entirely different conditions to those prepared for in Europe, and under circumstances that make the drawing of some parallels difficult. In the words of General John Jumper, generic lessons should not be drawn from an idiosyncratic campaign.[1]

Applying the MoD's definitions of crisis types to the Falklands War, it would fall under the title of a 'Rapidly Moving Crisis'; The Gulf War 1991 was a mixture of 'Slow Moving Crisis' and 'Rapidly Moving Crisis'. Both Wars showed ingenuity in planning and flexibility in execution by the Armed Forces. The Falklands War was a clear success: Britain had recovered the Falklands against overwhelming logistical and operational problems, and against a numerically superior enemy close to its own homeland. The First Gulf War was another success. With minimal losses the Armed Forces had again demonstrated their capability, and the Government had confirmed the success of their policy.

## The Falklands War

The mobilisation for the Falklands War provides an in-period example of the British Armed Forces preparing for, deploying to and carrying out combat operations. In 1982 Britain sent two enhanced brigades of infantry (5 Brigade and 3 Commando) and more than 100 ships to the South Atlantic. Analysis of the effort to send ships, men and aeroplanes to the South Atlantic provides a measure of the readiness and capability of the armed forces and civilians involved.

The Falklands War can be analysed for the activation of naval units, land units and logistical resources, as well as the resupply in theatre of the combat forces. It offers some fine examples for the preparation and transition to war by the Royal Navy and Army. Although the Falklands War was fought 8,000 miles away, it is the process by which the forces were mobilised, fitted out, supplied and supported that is relevant to this research. The distance between the UK and the Falklands will need to be considered in any analysis.

In EASTLANT and ACCHAN the Royal Navy intended to be used under an umbrella of land-based Airborne Warning and Control System (AWACS) and Maritime Reconnaissance (MR) aircraft. The Royal Navy was prepared for escort duties and anti-submarine work against the WTO Navies, rather than remote outpost protection. The First Sea Lord commented the year before the Argentinian invasion of the Falklands that war, '… seldom takes the expected form and a strong maritime capability provides flexibility for the unforeseen.'[2] The conflict was as far from the Eastern Atlantic/European theatre

as could be imagined, both geographically and militarily, but the mobilisation, materials usage and logistical effort retains relevance. Could lessons be learned for Europe, despite it being in Lawrence Freedman's words, '… precisely the war for which Britain was planning least …'?[3]

The Royal Navy's operations in the Falklands have been described by Dr Geoff Sloan as a 'War without a doctrine.'[4] Some of the more advanced naval weapons, and thus the training for their use and tactics developed around them, were not as successful as anticipated. Missile and torpedo reliability were questionable, which meant that faith in the weapons' abilities was fragile. As a consequence of Cold War planning and cost-cutting, the Royal Navy did not equip its ships with anything other than missiles for air defence and had no close-in point defence missile systems other than Sea Cat, which entered service in 1962, and three vessels of the Task Force equipped with Sea Wolf.[5] The air threat demonstrated the inadequacies of Sea Cat, but also showed the potential of Sea Wolf. These missiles were intended as anti-aircraft defence aboard warships, but Sea Cat only recorded one hit from ten launches; Sea Wolf was claimed to have five hits. Some ships had general purpose machine guns (GPMGs) fixed to the rails around the decks to provide close-in anti-aircraft fire, but this was a temporary expedient. If we translate this into an Eastern Atlantic scenario, considering the WTO air force and navy were heavily equipped with air-to-surface and surface-to-surface missiles, the Navy's vulnerability was marked.[6] Vulnerability to missile attack was the principal lesson taken by the Navy from the Falklands, despite being identified in the LTDP as a vulnerable area which required improvement. This weakness was subsequently addressed by the purchase of Phalanx and Goalkeeper close-in weapon systems (CIWS).[7]

In Tigerfish, the Royal Navy had an unreliable torpedo that had failed its acceptance tests but was still put into operation. The lack of reliability meant that when HMS *Conqueror* attacked the ARA *Belgrano* the decision was taken to use the old, but reliable, unguided Mark 8 torpedo. The Royal Navy may have struggled with some unreliable weapon systems, but the presence of some major vessels was only possible because of the timing of the Argentinian invasion. Had it been delayed by a year or two, several major ships would have been missing from the Navy lists. Two ships essential to the retaking of the Falkland Islands, HMS *Intrepid* and HMS *Fearless*, were to be disposed of prematurely in 1982 and 1984 respectively, as according to the 1981 SDE, '… the likely needs did not warrant replacement …'[8] Indeed, HMS *Intrepid* was in the process of being decommissioned for sale but was quickly brought back into service to go to the Falklands. No provision was to be made to run these ships after 1984. They were to be replaced operationally by using commercially available RORO ferries. If the British Commando Brigade was only to be deployed into Europe, this disposal of ships made financial sense in the short term. However, this would mean that only in a slow-building crisis would the Commando Brigade be capable of being deployed using ferries. In a sudden crisis the great demand for ferries would limit their availability. Also, the use of ferries would provide its own problems if the dock facilities were damaged. Unloading in San Carlos from requisitioned ships was fraught with problems. Kenneth Privratsky wrote that RORO vessels, '… had been designed to pull next to piers and either open side doors and let cargo roll off or use pier-side cranes … now … there were no piers … vessels like Norland could not lower stern doors sufficiently to reach mexefloat lighters … The offload rate for civilian vessels averaged only twenty tons per hour, compared to ninety tons per hour for LSLs.'[9]

Ships such as HMS *Fearless* and *Intrepid*, and the Landing Ships Logistic (LSL) such as RFA *Sir Galahad* were designed specifically for unloading military equipment. This can be bulky and cumbersome, and without the use of purpose-built ports were more than four times faster than the RORO ferries to unload. Speed was essential in the San Carlos landings, limiting the risk to those troops doing the unloading, and also those awaiting the stores and equipment being unloaded.

The vulnerability of the fleet extended to the threat from mines which the Royal Navy suspected the Argentinians had laid in Falkland Sound, against which they initially had no answer. The lack of mine counter-measures (MCMV) and minesweeper vessels with the fleet deployment meant that on at least one occasion a major ship, HMS *Alacrity*, was used to check for mines in Falkland Sound by the simple expedient of sailing through from end to end. This was a serious risk and highlighted the deficiency in mine sweeping capacity for the Task Force. There were several MCMVs and minesweepers available, but they were designed for use in shallow water and could not make the sea voyage. Fishing vessels could be requisitioned, along with other types of vessels, for naval, military and other special purposes, most notably minesweeping and countermeasures. Deep sea minesweepers or MCMVs could be obtained by requisitioning deep sea trawlers and converting them. There were, at the time of the Falklands, two deep sea trawlers chartered by the Royal Navy for deep sweeping and based on their performance and design several new ships were to be added to the Royal Navy's fleet. With the Hunt-class Mine Counter Measure Vessels (MCMV) not yet operational, and existing Ton-class vessels not capable of the long sea voyage to the Falklands, five deep sea trawlers were requisitioned and sent South. They were not available in the area until after the initial landings at San Carlos.

Vessels taken up from commercial trade, such as the trawlers, had serious limitations. The extension of communications capability, as well as data sharing and satellite links, to Ships Taken Up From Trade (STUFT) proved problematic. Without specially trained crew and installed equipment, those ships not designed for use in war took time and effort to bring up to the required standard. Although some vessels could be converted to wartime use, encrypted communications and data handling required specialist equipment and operators. Because of the limited numbers of specialist navy technicians, the flow of signal traffic during the Falklands War exceeded the capacity to handle all the data. Important signals were filtered out and acted upon, but less important signals were left, some unread to the end of the campaign. A similar problem affected the possibility of arming the STUFT vessels with defensive weapons. Without the communications equipment and radar necessary to operate the sophisticated weaponry, they could fire at friendly ships or passing aircraft.

The two Fearless-class LPDs were each capable of lifting a battalion-sized Royal Marine Commando and played a major role in the Falklands War. In the event of a general war in Europe they would almost certainly have been committed to support NATO's Northern Flank. HMS *Fearless* is seen here with US CH-53s and AH-1s overhead during Exercise Northern Wedding '82. (US DoD)

The Royal Navy also included the Royal Marine Commandos, and like many of the ships in the task force, they were on high readiness and could be mobilised quickly. 3 Commando Brigade formed part of the UK/Netherlands Landing Force contribution to the amphibious forces of NATO.[10] It comprised three battalion-sized Commandos (40, 42 and 45 Commando) plus supporting artillery and air troops, besides much else. The Brigade had organic logistical support in the form of the Commando Logistics Regiment. As a high readiness force, the Brigade was permanently on seven days' notice. Following the 1981 Defence review, the Royal Marines were to be retained in their infantry role, but were to lose the specialist shipping which was vital to their amphibious role, vital in retaking the Falkland Islands in 1982.

Before sailing, 3 Commando's establishment was reinforced by the 2nd and 3rd Battalions of the Parachute Regiment and Special Forces. Most of the Brigade's logistics troops were regulars, and immediately available for service. Colonel Hellberg, 3 Commando's Logistic Regiment commander, recorded the personnel of the Logistic Regiment who went to the Falklands consisted of, '… 346 officers and men with only 54 prime movers and nine motor cycles.'[11] One significant omission was the Petroleum Troop. 'The Regiment's Petrol Troop (383 Troop) was TAVR and therefore had not been mobilised.'[12]

There was insufficient transport to move the enlarged 3 Commando Brigade and all its equipment and stores upon mobilisation: Colonel Hellberg wrote, for transporting the WMR of 3 Commando Brigade:

> … at very short notice, HQ United Kingdom Land Forces (UKLF) had to provide a massive fleet of Royal Corps of Transport (RCT) 16-ton vehicles. Additionally we had to requisition many civilian freight vehicles. Although not planned, these additional vehicles (many driven by Territorial Auxiliary and Volunteer Reserve (TAVR) drivers to augment our own Transport Squadron) provided an excellent service …[13]

The War Maintenance Reserve (WMR) for 3 Commando alone weighed 9,000 tons. Colonel Hellberg wrote '… the WMR of 3 Commando Brigade consisted of a total of 30 days' stocks of Combat Supplies at Limited War rates with 60 day's stock of technical and general stores.'[14] It was moved using the ad-hoc formations of RCT and commercial vehicles and voluntary drivers described above, which meant '… the roads to Portsmouth, the Royal Corps of Transport marine base at Marchwood, on Southampton Water, and Devonport were the scenes of activity not seen since the end of the Second World War.'[15]

Supporting 3 Commando was 5 Brigade which had been formed from parts of 6th and 8th Field Force after they were disbanded. Upon mobilisation for the Falklands War, the Parachute battalions normally on its establishment were used to reinforce 3 Commando Brigade. They were replaced by the 1st Welsh Guards and 2nd Scots Guards, which had just finished public duties. Despite a conference covering the subject in Aldershot on 4 May, 5 Brigade went to the Falklands with, '… only two ordnance companies, since its intended logistics unit were reservists …'[16] General Thompson wrote, '5 Infantry Brigade had come south with inadequate logistic support so an ad-hoc logistic support group was cobbled together by the Commando Logistic Regiment …'[17] This failure indicates what would have happened in a rapidly moving crisis had any of the reinforcement units for BAOR been moved before mobilisation of the reserves had taken place. After the Falklands the brigade was converted into 5 Airborne Brigade, and as a direct consequence of the logistic problems faced in the Falklands a dedicated Logistic Battalion was established.

The war highlighted deficiencies not just with mobilisation plans but also with individual items of equipment. Simple items were missing from the Army's inventory; the infantry Bergan was not available for the Guards battalions sent to the Falklands, and civilian replacements had to be bought. The lack of modern night vision equipment, used extensively by the Argentinian forces, would cause serious difficulties in the Falklands, and was rectified in subsequent SDEs. The improvements in simple items like boots and protective equipment could also be attributed to the war. A lesson learned from the Falklands War, and relearned from previous wars, was that anti-aircraft guns, either machine guns or small calibre quick firing artillery, can be invaluable against low-level aircraft attack both at sea and on land. The MoD had moved towards an all-missile defence for ground forces, but this was rethought after the Falklands, with anti-aircraft artillery and machine guns being reintroduced (some of which were captured from the Argentinians). The Argentinian forces were well equipped with anti-aircraft artillery (AAA) as well as surface-to-air missiles and brought down five Harriers with ground fire.

To provide sufficient Sea Harriers for the fleet the initial squadrons (800 and 801), which had only eight aircraft each, had to absorb other aircraft, pilots and maintenance crew to bring them up to strength. By using training aircraft and one trials aircraft twenty Sea Harriers were accumulated. The Sea Harrier was in such short supply that RAF GR.3 Harriers were also pressed into service. Pilots, however, were in short supply. At least two were still being trained on the voyage down to the Falklands.

The RAF used the Falklands war to justify the need for the JP233 runway denial system. The freefall bombs used to attack Stanley Airfield by the Vulcan bomber and Harriers may have caused great damage, but only one hit was registered on the runway. Concern over the AAA meant the Harrier pilots preferred to 'toss' the bombs at the airfield, rather than fly in close. The JP233 was introduced in the 1985 after lengthy lobbying from the RAF as a means of making attacks on enemy airfields more effective. Because of the need for low level attack to use the weapon, it is difficult to assess how effective it would have been in the Falklands, where Argentinian

The SHAR proved both deadly and versatile in the Falklands conflict. It could carry only a limited bomb load however and the combined efforts of the Fleet Air Arm's Sea Harriers and RAF GR.3s and Vulcan B.2s never completely closed Stanley Airfield to Argentine aircraft. The RAF would use this to lobby for the purchase of the Hunting JP233 runway denial system. (US DoD)

radar-controlled anti-aircraft defence had good coverage around Stanley Airport.

For the Commandos, the Falklands Campaign was a testament to the training of the personnel involved, and their determination to succeed. General Thompson wrote, '… that in just over forty-eight hours, without warning and with no contingency plan, they had prepared the staff tables for a greatly expanded Brigade to load into shipping, much of which had only been allocated a matter of hours before …'[18] For the Royal Navy, it was justification for the existence of their service, especially the surface fleet, but left some questions about vessel vulnerability.

## Operation GRANBY – The Gulf War 1991

The British deployment to Saudi Arabia under Operation Granby can be analysed in a similar way to that for the Falklands. Overall, this deployment can be analysed as a slow-moving crisis, but with some elements of a rapidly moving crisis, using some of the plans developed for Western Europe, but modified for special in-theatre requirements. Operation Granby is seen by many as a validation of the 'improvements' and 'efficiencies' of the previous years' defence policies. It is also used as a confirmation that the reforms of doctrine undertaken by Generals Bagnall and Farndale in BAOR were effective.

The First Gulf War of 1991 saw Britain deploy more than 45,000 personnel to Saudi Arabia. The Gulf War demonstrated the plans for the Transition to War short of full mobilisation. The reinforcement plans for Britain's contribution to NATO required large numbers of reservists, both regular and volunteer, to fill-out units deployed or deploying in NORTHAG. Because of the political situation, however, the initial mobilisation for the Gulf War was carried out without the reservists which would fill the gaps in the deployed units. The initial deployment followed the overall plans for a 'Rapidly Moving Crisis', which would allow forces to be deployed quickly without reservist mobilisation.

Initially, to bring 7 Brigade up to warfighting establishment Brigadier Cordingley had to draw on the rest of the army: the Staffordshire Regiment required more than two hundred men; each tank regiment needed additional 12-man tank troops; and the artillery needed to double in strength from five hundred personnel to one thousand.[22] The Staffords were to absorb almost an entire company of the Grenadier Guards to bring them up to

# Cost cutting and the problems with 'Shiny Sheff' and the Type 42

During the Falklands Campaign, Admiral Woodward had set a combination of Type 22 and Type 42 vessels as radar pickets to warn of incoming Argentinian air attack. The need for the Type 22/42 combo was specific to the Falklands, as there was no Airborne Early Warning (AEW) available in the early stages of the war. Exposed and isolated, these ships were a priority target for the Argentinian air force. Without AEW it was inevitable that some of the pickets set by Admiral Woodward would suffer in the same costly manner as those of the US Navy during the invasion of Okinawa in 1945.

Intended as a fleet air defence vessel, with the capability to fly anti-submarine helicopters, the Type 42s were a cheaper replacement for the Type 82 cancelled in the 1966 Defence Review. As a cost-saving measure, the Type 42's hull was shortened which caused poor sea handling. The Treasury view was that the decision must be based on value for money. The shortening of the hull was made against the normal Navy weight, space and stability margins, and caused 'slamming' in bad weather. 'Slamming' is the bottom of the vessel hitting the surface of the sea whilst sailing in high seas. This puts excessive loads onto the structure of the vessel and can cause serious damage. It was also known that this caused 'wetness' (spray and waves breaking over the deck) forward of the bridge. The reduction in length was reversed with a modified design for the eleventh ship and all subsequent orders. As early as 1975 the Type 42 was identified by the Admiralty as having a

reduced capability, but, '... nevertheless it is not unreasonable to retain the unit in the construction programme for the time being. As improved SEADART/radar capability will be needed later, the design can be reviewed when the way ahead on the weapon systems is clearer.'[19]

The performance of the early Type 42 was described by Admiral Woodward as, '... unreasonably slow in a short swell, with their bows slamming into the waves rather than splitting them to each side cleanly.'[20] The deck spray ('wetness' forward of the bridge) had a damaging effect on the Sea Dart launcher system, with the continuous soaking by salt-water causing malfunctions – the flash-doors would not open and sensing equipment failed to recognise that a missile had been loaded, and unnerving experience when under attack. Because of the shortening of the hull, the, '... consequences had not been obvious ... now they were ...'[21] These vulnerabilities were exposed notwithstanding the threat from Argentinian air attack being less than expected from the WTO in a war. The consequences would have been far more serious if the WTO air threat is considered. The overall vulnerability to missile and air attack demonstrated in the Falklands War was a serious concern for the Navy despite having been identified in a report by the Chiefs of the Defence Staff in 1981. The Type 42, intended as it was to be the fleet air defence vessel, was an example of cost-cutting in peacetime severely hampering the military during war.

HMS *Broadsword* was the lead ship of the Type 22-class, armed with Exocet, Sea Wolf and a Lynx ASW helicopter. Sea Wolf was supposed to provide point defence in the Type 22/42 Combo but its performance in the Falklands was patchy and there was no modern gun back-up. (US DoD)

HMS *Liverpool* was a Type 42 destroyer. This photo clearly shows how, even in very modest seas, the design ploughed *into* the water rather than *through* the water, described as *slamming*. Wet decks and sea salt would cause problems with the Type 42s' exposed weapon systems in the Falklands conflict. (US DoD)

war establishment. This may have had a deleterious effect on unit cohesion due to lack of unit training. As previously mentioned, the Army was acknowledged these shortcomings after the war, 'Research has shown that few commanders deploying to the Gulf [in 1991] considered their units to be battle ready, including those at the peak of their training cycle, not least because reinforcements had to be absorbed and trained, equipment modified etc.'[23]

In a war in Europe, even in a slow-moving crisis, there would not have been time to undergo the intensive training that was available to the troops in the Gulf.

When the Army deployment was expanded from a brigade to a division, the problem of finding sufficient troops was exacerbated. Sir Peter De la Billière, Commander-in-Chief of the British forces deployed in Kuwait, commented;

The trouble with Operation Granby was that nobody could tell how long it might last and because many of the British formations had been specially tailored to take part, replacing them was going to be extremely difficult, if not impossible. To create the first wave of formations had been relatively simple, as we simply poached men from other units to make numbers up, but it was obvious that by the time we came round to forming a second wave we would already have done our poaching and would find ourselves in serious difficulties.[24]

The House of Commons Defence Committee commented that the plans for mobilising troops at short notice for an emergency, were, in some cases, found wanting.

In the First Gulf War the entire logistical effort of the Armed Forces was focussed on keeping one enhanced division, comprising five tank regiments and five infantry battalions, in the field.[25] The amount of ammunition shipped to the Gulf was almost half of the WMR held by Britain in Germany for whole of BAOR. Each day a division would use approximately 4,500 tons of supplies in mobile operations. The House of Commons Defence Committee reported that 95 percent of Royal Corps of Transport personnel were, '… deployed on operations in the Gulf or elsewhere … meaning that it was at the limit of Regular availability …'[26] Indeed, according to Lt Col Reehal, responsible for transport and movement in the Gulf, the, '… whole RCT was decimated to provide the necessary personnel and vehicles …'[27] He continues:

Trucks were taken away from units engaged on outloading UK and BAOR depots and the blinding realisation that to support one division, let alone four, required virtually every RCT soldier and vehicle in the British Army, was a salutary one.[28]

Spares for all sorts of

Many of the specialist vehicles used by BAOR, and subsequently deployed with 1st (UK) Armoured Division, were of considerable age. This Centurion AVRE was a specialist engineer assault vehicle armed with a 165mm demolition gun. Its armour has been upgraded through the addition of explosive reactive armour panels. Several AVREs were lost to engine fires but none to enemy action. (Major Phil Watson)

Equipment had to be drawn from far and wide to fully equip 1st (UK) Armoured Division. These CVR(T) Scimitars were used by 9th/12th Lancers, as part of the Armoured Delivery Group. They had been drawn from 3 Light Infantry and are here marked up to be returned to them in Germany. Many of the vehicles supplied were lacking even such basic equipment as radios (note the absence of antennae on the nearest vehicle) and NBC packs. (Major Phil Watson)

equipment were not available and had to be taken from the other formations to equip the forces in Saudi Arabia. The situation was such that, according to General Thompson, 'There were no operational Warrior AIFVs and only about 10 running Challengers left in the whole Rhine Army, not to mention a host of other equipment left useless by cannibalisation.'[29] In the same manner, all

RAF(G) support helicopters were deployed for GRANBY leaving none for operations on the NATO Central Front.

Challenger itself caused some problems. Because of its complexity, a lack of spares and also lack of proper funding, maintenance of the vehicle and its systems had been inadequate. In BAOR, '… at any one time over three quarters of the tanks were under repair or otherwise out of service.'[30] The HCDC considered it, '… scandalous that the

This photograph of an FV510 Warrior shows a number of features at that time unique to those deployed for Operation GRANBY. When deployed to Saudi Arabia in 1990, the British armoured infantry battalions each only had sufficient Warriors to mount their three rifle companies. In early 1991 they received an additional allocation to mount the mortar fire controllers and, as seen here, the MILAN platoon. This example has its turret facing away from the camera but the MILAN firing post is visible above the turret hatches. Storage racks for additional MILAN rounds can be seen beneath the tarpaulin marked with a chevron. This vehicle also has additional armour on the hull front and sides, supplied as a UOR in similar fashion to the armour for Challengers and AVREs. (US DoD)

The LYNX/TOW attack helicopter was a disappointment in the Gulf War. This was a weapon system, like the Challenger, that was relied upon extensively in the doctrine of 'Counterstroke' but had been identified as needing urgent replacement. This system had two vital roles in the Counterstroke doctrine: flank protection and anti-tank attack role. The aim of the attack role was to cause heavy losses on enemy armour as the counterattack commenced, and to provide deception as to the point of attack. Flank support was to protect the counterattack against enemy forces. Survivability in this situation was paramount, considering the weight of anti-aircraft fire that WTO Motor Rifle and Tank regiments possessed. The Counterstroke anticipated facing an enemy of Divisional size. The HCDC complained the helicopter, '... lacked the capabilities, particularly survivability required ...' for such operations.[33]

The deployment of forces from Germany relied heavily on sea-lift capability, which caused

Challenger 1 tank fleet was in such a poor state in BAOR.'[31] The vehicles were also to suffer with sand ingress to the engines, but this was not a problem confined to the desert. The air filtration system had previously been identified as problematic, with dust ingestion causing problems on exercises in Germany. Writing on the problems with Challenger, Lawrence Freedman commented that, 'Engine troubles were embarrassing enough in exercises in Germany: they would be catastrophic in actual war.'[32]

Challenger and Warrior were subject to extensive improvement, including up-armouring, on arrival in Jubail. Some of the additional armour for the Challengers was to improve the protection of the storage bins, and to bring the early Mark versions up to the latest armour specifications. This upgrade process depended on an extended timescale to supply and fit the improvements. This would not have been available to the Armoured Divisions in Europe, even in the 30-day scenario.

The desert provided a perfect environment for long range anti-tank fire, especially as the Challenger out-ranged its opponents by a considerable amount. However, a comparison with what might occur in a European war must be considered carefully. Tanks and anti-tank missiles could hit targets at extreme range in the desert, whereas in Europe the line of sight is much more restricted, with tank-to-tank engagements expected to take place at an average of 500m. An advantage in weapon range would not count for so much in the European theatre as in the desert, which would level the disparity in weapon capabilities between NATO and the WTO.

some problems in obtaining sufficient ships of the right capabilities. This demonstrated the drawbacks inherent in the Government policy of replacing specialist military equipment, in this case

This Challenger Mk 3 of the Royal Scots Dragoon Guards demonstrates the armour package used for Operation GRANBY, consisting of side skirts using conventional and Chobham armour and the explosive reactive 'shoe' armour mounted on the hull front. Additional armour was thought necessary as Challenger had been designed, in accordance with British doctrine, to fight from hull-down positions and the hull was not as heavily armoured as the turret, and it was thought that Challenger may have to engage in close-range fighting in the built-up areas of Kuwait. This armour was designed and built at short notice under an Urgent Operational Requirement (UOR). (US DoD)

shipping, with contracted civilian substitutes. There was also some confusion about the powers to requisition vessels. Concerns over precisely this problem had been expressed by the House of Commons Defence Committee in 1988 in their report '*The Defence Requirement for Merchant Shipping and Civil Aircraft.*'[34] The Committee urged that numbers of merchant vessels available for military use be increased.

The problems with the military use of commercial ships which had already been identified in the Falklands War reappeared in the Gulf War. Initially there was only one berth available, in Jubail, which was capable of taking the British RORO vessels. Had the US ships not been equipped with their own side and rear ramps, the demands for this berth would have exceeded capacity. Indeed, as some problems were experienced with the internal ramps on RORO vessels, ship's cranes had to be used, slowing the unloading process considerably.

There were concerns that the standard L23 APFSDS 'fin' ammunition carried by Challenger would not be able to deal effectively with Iraqi T-72s and so limited quantities of the new L26A1 depleted uranium rounds, codenamed 'Jericho', were issued. British forces did not encounter T-72s on the battlefields of Iraq and Kuwait; this destroyed example is being examined by troopers from 9th/12th Lancers on the Kuwait-Basra highway immediately after the cessation of hostilities. Despite a number of advanced features, the T-72 would prove to be extremely vulnerable to catastrophic ammunition and fuel fires in action. (Major Phil Watson)

Without the establishment of dedicated port facilities at Jubayl in Saudi Arabia, and the unlimited fuel availability, the HCDC considered that, '… the United Kingdom would have been stretched to provide logistic support …'[35] There was more than sufficient time to establish operating bases and rear-area support, and The HCDC noted, 'The six month period of grace in Operation Granby meant … that some deficiencies in our ability to provide intervention forces from a standing start were not fully exposed. Units cannot be deemed to be ready for operations if they rely unduly on mobilisation of Reservists, in particular for support resources.'[36]

General Thompson commented that, 'Operation Desert Shield … was a classic Red Carpet operation, that is a build-up in a friendly country, which provided three key assets: airfields, ports and an enormous bonus, fuel; all without any enemy interference whatsoever …'[37]

The HCDC also identified simple deficiencies which needed immediate rectification. Some 40 percent of stretchers did not fit the stretcher carriers in the Hercules transport allocated for casualty evacuation. There was disappointment in some sections of the Armed Forces that many of the expensively acquired vehicles and weapons worked less than well in the desert environment. Engines failed and weapons jammed due to simple dirt ingress. Although some of the weapon failures was attributed to poor or incorrect maintenance, the HCDC reported, 'Some section and platoon commanders considered that casualties would have been suffered because of weapon stoppages had the enemy put up more resistance in close combat.'[38] This problem was to recur in Iraq and Afghanistan in later years.

Each British armoured regiment in Operation Desert Storm included eight CVR(T) Scorpions, each armed with the L23 76mm gun, this example being from the Royal Scots Dragoon Guards. Further examples were operated by 16th/5th Lancers as the armoured reconnaissance regiment of 1st (UK) Armoured Division. The latter were placed under operational control of the Commander Royal Artillery and tasked with finding deep targets for the guns and MRLS. Note that this example has multiple recognition aids; the large black chevron, a hi-vis panel and a national flag. (US DoD)

The RAF was considered to have fared well in the Gulf overall, but some concern was raised over the medium level attack training. This lack of training had been caused by the 'cheese-paring' of training flights and fuel use over the previous thirty years. Nor could the success of the air war be taken as an indicator of future wars. In the First Gulf War, and subsequent NATO and coalition operations, British and allied aircraft have operated in a permissive environment, almost absent of the threats a major war would entail.

The Handley Page Victor had long-since been retired as a bomber, but many continued to serve as aerial refuelling tankers such as this K.1. Coalition air operations in Operation Desert Storm would have been much restricted without such tankers, and these could only operate in the permissive air environment that prevailed in 1991. (US DoD)

This FV432 ambulance can be seen in a form-up area in the desert on the Iraqi border. Coalition operations would have been much more difficult had the Iraqis been able to employ their air and artillery effectively against such Coalition rear areas. Note also the M548 with Red Cross markings in the background. (US DoD)

Squadron Leader Dick Druitt, a pilot in the Gulf War commented, 'If the opposition had been anything like military people, the first planes they'd have taken out would have been the tankers and the AWACS, because without them the others could never have reached their targets.'[39]

The RAF considered the JP233 was essential to the success of the air superiority campaign. Its use was problematic: the attacking aircraft had to climb to a minimum of 500 feet to release the weapon whilst flying along the target runway, making it extremely vulnerable to anti-aircraft fire.[40] According to the RAF, for the loss of four Tornados, 'Eight Iraqi main operating bases had been closed while the operations of several others had been markedly reduced.'[41] This had been in a battle-space without serious enemy contention in the air. The nature of the allies' air superiority was marked by the fact that the RAF fired no air-to-air missiles during the war. Given the demands placed on air interdiction against WTO air forces in MoD and NATO planning, it is difficult to imagine what the losses would have been when faced with the dense WTO integrated air defence.

Although a great success, GRANBY was fought in an almost entirely permissive environment without enemy interdiction of supply routes or serious competition for air superiority or control of the seas. The coalition rear area logistic areas were not subject to attack by enemy air or land forces. Log Base Alpha, as it was called, was the central logistic base for a large part of the allies' supplies. General Cordingley commented how the logistic area stood out in the desert and would have been an inviting target had the Iraqi forces been capable of an attack.

NATO defence in NORTHAG, and British doctrine, relied on absorbing the first attacks from the WTO and then employing the 'Counterstroke'. Whilst this posed little problem for the troops involved because of their professionalism, it showed the limitations of the equipment, supply and support which would have been provided for any battles in Europe. It is clear from General De la Billière's comments that, once the first attacks had been met, had a similar situation obtained, there would have been serious difficulties in providing for any counterattack. An attempted 'Counterstroke' would have been stillborn.

## Conclusion

Common threads that run between Corporate and Granby are: the shortcomings of vessels provided for shipping; a need to oversupply ammunition and POL when compared to the scales for NATO;

This RAF Puma HC.1 is seen in support of British forces during Operation Granby. Coalition air supremacy enabled such activities to be conducted unmolested. (US DoD)

lack of suitably qualified personnel in essential roles, both combat and support; and insufficient numbers of essential weapons and platforms to perform the required tasks. The HCDC noted, 'During the Cold War, MoD considered it was what the forces had in their 'shop window' which was important: the United Kingdom did not apparently expect to have to use it.'[42]

Margaret Thatcher wrote that the Falklands War, '… had real importance in relations between East and West: years later I was told by a Russian general that the Soviets had been firmly convinced that we would not fight for the Falklands, and that if we did fight we would lose. We proved them wrong on both counts, and they did not forget the fact.'[43]

The Falklands showed some deficiencies where readiness of forces was concerned. Although the Royal Navy was able to mobilise a fleet, some of it was not functioning correctly (HMS *Invincible* requiring a gearbox change soon after departure.) The Army suffered from readiness problems, even with the forces that were supposed to be specifically for emergencies. The Falklands did not have much of an impact on Home Defence thinking but did show up some deficiencies in the AEW and anti-missile defences. What British operations in the Falklands War lacked was a credible doctrine for a non-WTO enemy.

The reliance for the balance of the Armed Forces on reservists had serious implications for their operational capability in anything other than a slow-moving crisis. 3 Commando Brigade went to the Falklands with a reduced logistical tail, and entirely without its fuel handling detachment. This was keenly felt during the build-up of forces at San Carlos when knowledge of the hazards of handling petroleum and aviation fuel in large quantities was essential. The demands placed on fuel handling in the Falklands by Rapier systems alone took up more time and resources than was expected. Maintaining quality control of the fuel was also crucial, as contaminated or poor-quality fuel damage engines and make equipment inoperable. 5 Brigade logistical troops were all reservists and were not called up because of the urgency of the situation.

Both examples of real mobilisation were not on the scale which reinforcement of BAOR would constitute. That would have been a much larger movement of troops and equipment over a timescale similar to the Falklands War, but much shorter than the Gulf War. The British road, rail and air transport infrastructure would have been stretched to or past breaking point.

Because of the defensive nature of NATO, the operational and tactical needs for attack had been neglected in the British Army. The Falklands War was to provide an opportunity to relearn the need for close support weapons such as grenade launchers to help in the attack. In addition to Bagnall's rethink of doctrine this was to prove extremely important. The troops would need to be re-equipped to take into account the different tactical demands this would place on them. Manoeuvre warfare as espoused by Bagnall and Farndale is all very well, but unless it is backed up with a fully functioning logistic tail it will very quickly run out of essential supplies. The tail must be capable of following any attack, thus requiring mobility

and the capacity to withstand enemy interdiction that would inevitably result.

Operation Granby showed what the British Armed Forces were capable of, given time and money. But the deployment highlights the lack of sustainability inherent in the policies and practices adopted over the previous twenty or more years. The Gulf War, because of the Government's reluctance to mobilise the reserves, is a demonstration of what would have been available for a rapidly moving crisis in Europe. The time taken to develop the deployment, however, highlights several worrying deficiencies which would not have been rectified, even in a slow-moving crisis in Europe. The upgrades to vehicles, training of troops and deployment of the logistical tail took longer than would have been available had war come to Europe.

As a demonstration of the fighting capabilities of the 1st (UK) Armoured Division, using the doctrines developed from Bagnall's work in the 70s and 80s, the Gulf War shows their potential. But it also highlights the weaknesses. Without supplies, without sufficient helicopter support, and with an aggressive enemy air force, any 'counterstroke' in a war on the Central Front may well have been abortive.

Both wars were successful in achieving their aims and the Government publicly confirmed the success of their policies. But the reality did not support the Government's position. The Gulf War showed how dependent a British deployment was on a slow logistic build-up and the provision of generous Host Nation support. Both wars revealed problems in providing sufficient support for the fighting troops.

# 8
# CONCLUSIONS

## Overview

In the words of Albert Sorel, the French historian, this book has analysed the '… eternal dispute between those who imagine the world to suit their policy, and those who arrange policy to suit the realities of the world.'[1] The findings suggest that the former dominated the latter. Overall, the link between threat assessment and force provision was almost independent of any perceived threat, and heavily dependent on available financial resources. Probably the most significant finding of this research had been the current political and policy continuities based on a misinterpretation of past events.

The conclusion is that Britain did not meet its commitment to NATO in either the ways or means to achieve the ends. So what? If these policies occurred during the Cold War, are they of any relevance now? Why are they important? The answer to this question lies in the context. In the bipolarity of the Cold War, we know now that no full-scale war took place. However, many of the policy decisions which were taken at the time have trickled down into current policy. We cannot say that those policies were successful. All we can say is that they were never tested. Thus, saving money, cutting the military 'tail' to provide for the 'teeth' are ideas that have been perpetuated.

Henry Kissinger, former US Secretary of State, regarded it as scandalous that British troops in West Germany had supplies of arms for only two weeks. In an exchange of letters concerning Kissinger's statement MoD representatives commented that they

were in no position to deny the suggestion. There is a mixture of surprise and concern expressed in these letters, along with reluctance to discuss in any detail, even with trusted allies, the true situation. This exchange seems to encapsulate the circumstances within the British Government at the time: a few knew the fighting capability of the forces were insufficient and passed that information on; some knew but were evasive or offered ambiguous information; some knew and kept it to themselves; others did not know but were naturally concerned; and yet others never knew. Prime Ministers such as James Callaghan and Margaret Thatcher were both, at least initially, unaware of the deficiencies in Britain's defence.

The analysis of NATO's fighting capability later presented by Mearsheimer and supported by Strachan (and many others) contradicts the opinion expressed by Kissinger. The true levels of materiel reserves available to NATO armies were a relatively well-kept secret, even to those in positions of authority. Kissinger had, however, identified the crucial drawback with NATO's strategy. He may well have known the truth and used this as a pointed reminder to the British Government, but the reactions of British Junior Ministers and civil servants were revealing in its honesty.

## NATO Strategy

Superficially, the policy and strategy of Flexible Response appeared convincing, but was ambiguous. The aim of NATO policy, defined in the strategic concept document MC 14/3, was to prevent aggressive action by the WTO through credible deterrence. But if deterrence failed NATO would seek to restore the *status quo ante* by employing force proportionate to that used by the aggressor, or threatening escalation. It was, essentially, a compromise between the need to maintain US attachment to Europe, and the European fear of war and occupation.

As a compromise between European reluctance to accept the cost of building conventional forces to fight a long war, and US calls for a no-first use policy, MC 14/3 was something of a hollow concept, an attempt to please all the NATO members, but pleasing none. Although all NATO members adopted Flexible Response, none undertook the full expansion of conventional forces required for its successful execution. Because of this failure, whilst seeming a positive attempt to lower the nuclear threshold, MC 14/3 had no such effect. NATO as a whole did little from the late 1960s until the early 1980s to alter its response to a WTO invasion of Western Europe. Inherent in the lack of fighting capability was the near certainty of the choice between capitulation and the use of nuclear weapons if a full-scale war broke out: the uncertainty regarding nuclear use was of how, when and how many. Clarity on this last problem was never achieved.

The assessment of the threat from the WTO – whether it was right or wrong – was the basis for the strategy developed over the years following the end of the Second World War. The assessments, made by such groups as the Joint Intelligence Committee (JIC) and the Chiefs of Staff Committee (COS), were the starting points for the plans and processes put in place to deter and, if necessary counter, aggression from the WTO. Most of the assessments accepted that the WTO had the potential to mobilise with greater speed and secrecy than NATO's various armed forces. NATO's strategy was primarily aimed at deterring the prospect of war if a crisis had reached a tipping point. The early 1980s was a time of deep suspicion between East and West, and any display of weakness or indecision could have been easily misinterpreted. Deterrence at the time was a delicate balance between the two.

Deterrence must work at all levels, as a nuclear war could have been the result of a conventional beginning, with an aggressor failing to obtain a sufficiently speedy victory – what Sir Francis Pym described as, 'Short-warning aggression, and … short-duration war …'[2] – what were referred to as 'salami-tactics'. Since the possibilities for accidentally launching a nuclear attack were remote, as Michael Quinlan had suggested,[3] if the objective of raising the nuclear threshold was to be realised, and to counter to the WTO threat, conventional forces in sufficient numbers and sustainability should have been the rational policy.

As both sides in the Cold War moved away from immediate use of nuclear weapons, the conventional defence of continental Europe, the Channel and the Atlantic was a necessary condition of NATO policy. NATO Strategy and British policy appear to have been publicly positioned to answer the WTO's military capabilities, but secretly the posture responded to the assessment of the WTO's intentions. The British Government repeatedly concluded that the WTO had no intention of deliberately starting a war. In a crisis that might accidentally have turned into war, a short duration conflict allowing political negotiations and a cooling-down period was hoped for.

## British Policy and Strategy

It may be that, in private, politicians and senior military officers believed a low nuclear threshold was inevitable. Fundamental conventional policy, followed quietly in the background, can be

seen to go back to a document from 1968 produced by the Chiefs of Staff Committee (COS), 'In major hostilities … we believe that tactical nuclear weapons would almost certainly become necessary; and since we do not envisage prolonged hostilities thereafter we do not believe that NATO resources should be devoted to those conventional capabilities appropriate only to sustained operations at the higher level, or to a campaign dependent on the attrition of the enemy's forces or war making material.'[4]

This is contrary to the public assertions regarding improvements in the Armed Forces efficiency, increasing the nuclear threshold, getting greater value for money, and cutting the tail to improve the teeth. The Chiefs of Staff Committee believed nuclear weapons would be used relatively quickly, and as such resources should not be committed to providing for a long or attritional conventional war. This appears to have been the unpublicised, but executed, policy Britain pursued throughout the last twenty years of the Cold War, in contrast to the publicly declared policy. It was not unusual for publicly declared policies to be ignored behind the scenes: the contradiction between Labour's emphasis on nuclear disarmament and the Chevaline upgrade to Polaris is a good example.

Britain had been identified as crucial to the defence in depth of NATO, and as a rear-area for the reception of reserves and reservists. Despite this important role, the British Government appeared to circumvent its full commitment to NATO through tergiversation and the use of political rhetoric which did not reflect the practice. The Government reduced defence spending as a percentage of the wealth of the country, even at a time of great threat. Increases in spending, such as after the Falklands War, were maintained only for a short time, and the trend as a percentage of GDP was consistently downward. Economics more than threat assessment influenced strategy, and ploys such as 'cutting the tail to provide for the teeth' and dependence on reservists placed the Armed Forces in an extremely vulnerable position.

Whilst in Government, Dr David Owen, Fred Mulley and Francis Pym were candid in their private comments regarding the paucity of defensive and logistical capabilities with which British defence policy had left the Armed Forces. In the 1960s and 1970s the Labour party had leaned towards effecting détente and devoted greater energies to pursuing disarmament as a means of preventing war – and saving money. The Conservatives moved détente into a secondary role and pursued a policy more akin to warfighting deterrence. The events in Afghanistan and Poland confirmed Western fears of Soviet aggressive intentions, but not sufficiently for an increase in defence spending.

Unseen by most of the public at the time, but sometimes leaking out from the Government, were the differences of opinion robustly shared between politicians, and by some of the military officers. Sir Francis Pym, leader of the Tory 'wets', was famously removed from his position of Defence Secretary because, according to Margaret Thatcher, he had sided with the Ministry of Defence and failed to adhere to the monetarist policy imposed by the Government. Keith Speed, Navy Minister, was sacked in 1981 for disagreeing with the reduction in the numbers of Royal Navy vessels. The 1981 Defence review effectively returned Britain's policy to that of 1952 – national policy was to focus on an intensive war in Europe which was to be of short duration, and the use of nuclear weapons was explicit in the planning. In one naval officer's view, the review '… emasculated the conventional war capability of the Royal Navy and our national commitment to the NATO alliance in favour of a national strategic weapons system.'[5] The Directors of Defence Policy agreed with this conclusion.[6]

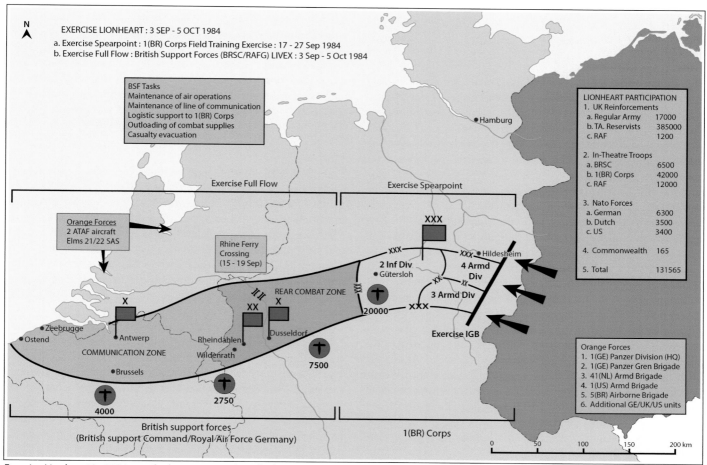

Exercise Lionheart in 1984 was the largest peacetime deployment of British troops post-1945. (Map by George Anderson)

The main policy announcements made by the British Government appeared to be an attempt at public reassurance. The idea of a long warning period was central to almost all overt British planning and was made public to reduce fears and demonstrate preparations for the eventuality of war. The field exercises, for example Exercise Lionheart in 1984, continued for ten days of conventional combat, and had extensive media coverage. Far less public was the assumption that the use of nuclear weapons would, sooner or later, have been inevitable. The probability was, based on even the most minimal expenditure of conventional ammunition, that the use of nuclear weapons would have been necessary within a few days. Nevertheless, both NATO and British policy advocated the need to raise the nuclear threshold, improve conventional defence and increase overall readiness. With the resurgence of CND in the late 1970s and early 1980s support for raising the nuclear threshold was politically expedient. The political rhetoric supported the policy, but the practice did not match the words.

In previous European wars, the British Armed Forces had had the opportunity of using time to recover from any early setbacks, reorganise and re-arm, before returning to the fray to defeat the enemy. This situation occurred in the Napoleonic wars, First World War and Second World War. This time was also available to re-tool industry for the output of weapons and ammunition to continue the war. At the beginning of the Second World War British Bomber Command found some of its expensive investment in aircraft to be of little value. Their withdrawal meant that quantitatively Bomber Command was unable to deliver its promise until the new, heavy four-engine bombers arrived. Night-time area bombing was adopted until the technology became available for accurate target location at night. All of these deficiencies were compensated for by the

development, over time, of new and better equipment. Air Marshal Tedder summed this situation up when he wrote, 'Surely it is the problems of the early stages of the war which we should study. Those are the difficult problems; those are the practical problems which we and every democratic nation have to solve ... It is at the outset of war that time is the supreme factor.'[7] The temporally compensatory buffer was a crucial component that would be missing from the training and development aimed at fighting the next war. In the Cold War, if weapon systems were ineffective, there would have been no time to recover and redesign them. The 'trip-wire' posture of NATO up to 1967 effectively removed all these temporal benefits, and replaced it with one 'wargasm', a phrase used by Herman Kahn to describe the all-out nuclear war that the trip-wire response would elicit. Flexible Response was supposed to remove the 'wargasm' reaction to WTO aggression. This was supposed to apply from the adoption of MC 14/3: in effect it simply gave a few days' more grace before nuclear weapons would be used.

Had a breakthrough been created by a successful WTO attack it is possible that the British Army might face a similar problem to that of the BEF in 1940 during the campaign in the Low Countries and the retreat to Dunkirk. Having limited mobility and reduced numbers or complete absence of anti-armour and other heavy weapons, many rear-area BEF troops were poorly equipped to fight a mechanised, fast-moving enemy. Forty years later, a similar situation obtained in BAOR. The 2nd Infantry Division was equipped with light scales of weaponry, SAXON armoured personnel carriers (the armour of which was supposed to be proof against only small calibre weapons), and soft-skinned vehicles. These, mostly reservist, rear area troops would have been ill-equipped to stop any substantial breakthrough. The superiority in technology which NATO had would have been exhausted within a few days, and those remaining forces left to fight on very unequal terms.

## Ends, Ways and Means

The means provided to the Armed Forces were, on cursory inspection, sufficient to provide for deterrence, and the planned response to aggression. NATO instigated several projects to remedy shortcomings in numerous areas, mostly without success. The main recurring themes in the NATO projects were force levels, reserves, readiness and planning. The means to sustain the forces were, nonetheless, deficient in all essential areas. Weapons dictate tactical doctrine, and the absence of sufficient sustaining stocks of particular weapon types and ammunition stocks meant the 'sponge-tactics' or 'counterstroke', amongst others, were effectively redundant. The RAF was incapable of many of its roles in the Follow-on Forces Attack, as it had to rely on older or obsolete, unguided, weaponry.

One of the UK Government's explicitly stated goals was to maintain Alliance cohesion, effectively bridging the gap between US policy and that of the majority of continental European members. NATO policy was an attempt to balance contradictions within the Alliance whilst also achieving a level of collective defence against the perceived Soviet threat. Attempts to balance the internal political and bureaucratic demands may have led to an imbalance in the military forces available to NATO. Some aspects of Alliance theory seem to hold true, such as smaller countries taking a disproportionately smaller share of the defence burden. That burden enlarged as the cost of technology increased the cost of weapon systems and reserves.

In any crisis of conflict, the plans show a delay for reinforcement from either the UK or the US/Canada. The US was dependent on REFORGER, which would become effective up to 90 days after the beginning of a crisis. In conjunction with the delays in mobilising sufficient forces from the UK, the regular forces deployed on Continental Europe and the seas around it would be stretched beyond breaking point whilst waiting for reinforcement.

The true reason why cost-cutting was feasible, and shortfalls in ammunition and reserves accepted, may be seen in the scenario papers for WINTEX 83 which read, 'Initial release of nuclear weapons by NATO in response to an overwhelming conventional attack could take place when NATO was faced with a militarily untenable position …'[8] Knowing that NATO would never commit the resources needed to achieve the mass required for defence against a conventional WTO attack, it was inevitable that it would quickly face a militarily untenable position, leading inexorably to the first use of nuclear weapons. This enabled those making the policy to have a face-saving position when questioned about the intended use of nuclear weapons, and NATO's dependence on them. Thus, money could safely be saved from the defence budget. Even as the Cold War dissipated after the arrival of Mikhail Gorbachev, the plans and expectations for war still anticipated nuclear release after a few days. With this qualification to any defence policy, limited expenditure on the Armed Forces becomes more understandable.

Analysts and Academics such as Mearsheimer, Chalmers and Unterseher may have had a point when they compared force sizes between the WTO and NATO and found little support for the gross inequality proposed by others. But as with many analysts and academics writing about NATO doctrine and policy at the time, they failed to understand that a 'bean-count' of fighting forces was insufficient to establish a true view of the military balance.

Some 'knowledge' of the period was simply assertions made without reference to the original material, such as the 55,000 man force level minimum for BAOR. These numbers were repeated so often that they became part of lore. Similarly, assertion that NATO's conventional defences were not weak but simply required alternative strategies missed the central problem: the strategy was sound, but the nations which had subscribed to it could not, or would not, spend the money necessary to increase the conventional forces and support materiel which were necessary. For the British Government, not alone in NATO in its thinking, the answer was to fill the gaps in the forces with reservists – the cheaper alternative.

## Logistics

There has been little attempt in studies of defence planning to understand the causes of the lack of endurance of NATO or the national forces. This has shown itself in a disinterest in the logistical limitations of the Armed Forces, and their increased reliance on reservists. None of the published works reviewed for this research make the link between the plans, their timings, and the use of reservists and limited material resources. This research has sought to provide the detail and connection between these important aspects of defence planning, and to identify common themes persisting in current policy.

All logistics within NATO were a national responsibility, and NATO forces, including the British Services, lacked any kind of sustainability for armed combat against the WTO during the Cold War. The inability to distribute materiel in a crisis was a serious concern for the British Armed Forces. However, this concern was confined to a very few of the more obscure academic publications, and within the Armed Forces themselves. Some relevant articles have been published by the Armed Forces, and some academic papers, but they have been few and far between.

In the event of a crisis, there would be two logistical supply problems face by the Armed Forces: the first would be the more mundane equipment in the rear-areas; the second the technologically advanced front-line weaponry. Armoured transport for front-line replenishment of supplies was non-existent. In the rear areas the limited numbers of regular specialist personnel and heavy haulage and lifting equipment, and the reliance on civilian transport, would have severely curtailed the ability to fulfil the logistic demands of the fighting units. Lorries with sufficient load capacity had been in short supply, as was commercial railway rolling stock and engines. Without dedicated shipping for transport, reliance was placed on RORO ferries, and if the dock facilities for these were damaged, the unloading times would have been multiplied several times. NATO expected the WTO would target ports and dock facilities in their planning, but field exercises did not account for this contingency. It is doubtful if the reinforcements for BAOR could have been transported in sufficiently quickly, even in the most benign of circumstances.

The British Government was aware of the insufficient war-stocks and the inadequate supporting infrastructure. A conventional war of any length would require an established industrial base capable of switching to war production within the necessary warning times. No Western Government had such capabilities, nor were they prepared to invest in its creation. NATO and its member states chose to talk about raising the nuclear threshold, strengthening conventional forces, and improving deterrence, whilst certainly at a national level being aware that any war would have been short and have ended in first nuclear use. Had the British Government been serious about providing for a non-nuclear war, the plants used to manufacture essential war material and vehicles would have been mothballed after the initial production run. As it was, the production lines were dismantled, meaning no more 'complex-consumables' such as

FV432s, Warriors or Chieftains could ever be produced. With high attrition levels expected, the supply of fighting vehicles would have been a limiting factor on the prosecution of any counterattack.

Attrition in war would account not just for the transportation but the ammunition and materiel as well. An insufficient War Maintenance Reserve was unquestionably a serious problem. The personnel using those weapons would be left with no recourse: whether at sea, in the air, or on land, the Armed Forces would be rapidly left incapable of carrying out their mission. War is wasteful, and requires a plentiful supply of weapons and ammunition, and sufficient forces to employ them. As was recognised at the time, only the profligate use of ammunition would be sufficient to stop an attack. In this respect, capability, and therefore 'efficiency', must be measured using a different metric to that used outside the military.

'Doing more with less' has been symbolic since before the 1950s. This totem has manifested itself in efficiency drives and demands for more effective Services. The 'efficiency' of the Armed Forces has been 'improved' with each defence review, aiming presumably at a goal of transcendent efficiency at some undisclosed point in the future. There is some confusion between 'efficient' and 'effective' in the policies of successive Governments. The idea promulgated since the 1980s by politicians that business practice can be applied to military organisations is seriously misplaced. The business notions of efficiency of production and operation are narrow concepts for single products/services which rarely put people's lives in jeopardy. The military does not, and cannot, work in the same way. Too much depends on the tools being provided to them working properly in situations not conceived of by anyone. In a combat operation, people's lives depend on the kit, weapons and tools working in extremis, and possibly not in their originally intended role. An office worker taking a delivery of the wrong sort of paperclips does not seem to reach the same level of criticality.[9]

In pursuit of 'efficiency' the Armed Forces had been cut to low levels, yet asked to do more. The concept of moving towards a 'more efficient structure' is relatively meaningless with regards to the Armed Forces. It implies that there is a 'most efficient' structure for the Forces. How can this be, when the roles they are required to fulfil are so disparate?

The plans created by NATO and the MoD were based on threat analyses which were the best guesses of the analysts of the time. They were an attempt to respond to the actions expected of the Soviet Union and WTO in a crisis or time of war. But the plans also show the British Government attempting to deal with what was an intractable problem – providing the ways and means for achieving the strategic ends without the economic resources fully to do so. British defence planning was a case of trying to avoid the worst whilst planning for the best.[10]

Defence planners do not have a crystal ball with which to see the future, but the Cold War was perhaps more predictable than many other situations. Despite this apparent predictability, the politicians and military did not provide sufficient resources to meet the demands of the plans created by the British Government. There may have been a credible nuclear deterrent, but there was certainly little credibility at the conventional level. NATO's overall posture was not a plausible working of Flexible Response, and NATO has been shown to have had concerns over the credibility, both qualitatively and quantitatively, of Britain's contribution.

The situation regarding Britain's home defence was little different. Home Defence was wholly inadequate, made apparent by the insufficient level of forces to protect the seas, airspace and key points of the country. A dependence on unsuitable civilian infrastructure

and equipment, transport and supplies was dangerous. Had Britain been called upon to fulfil its role in a war in Europe, this research suggests that the forces provided were insufficient for their task with no certainty of sustainability beyond the first 48 hours. The plans did not necessarily reflect the military's preferred way to deal with the threat as they assessed it.

The plans made, extensive though they were, appear more for convenience than to deal with either the WTO intentions or capabilities. The whole strategy for deployment and operations of the Armed Forces was predicated on a slow-moving crisis turning to a general war along a predictable timeline. This did not consider NATO's concern that a swift attack launched by the WTO could reach a conclusion in a few days. This would present NATO leaders with an accomplished fact whilst they decided on nuclear release. The WTO intention would be to undermine Alliance cohesion, leading to a break-up of NATO.

The credibility of British defence policy was precarious at best. There were not enough of any supplies, and what was available may never have been capable of being transported to the fighting forces. Greater reliance on non-military equipment for military duties meant delays in offloading, and sometimes unavailability of transportation. Obsolete or obsolescent equipment was retired before its successor was deployed, leaving gaps in the military capability. The most feared, and possibly the most likely scenario was the short warning, but with the WTO mobilised secretly. This would allow no time for REFORGER and only limited mobilisation in the UK. Named 'smash and grab' by some, WTO plans were released in the early 1990s showing the Rhine as a main objective[11] which indicated what the WTO though would be a possible outcome of a war.

NATO has maintained from its inception that it would rely on the development of high technology weapons to provide the edge against the numerically superior WTO forces. This was enshrined in MC 14, published in 1950. The developments, seen as a 'revolution' were the outcome of decades of military demands and technological inventions that enabled those demands to be met. To replace nuclear weapons and their associated risk of escalation if used, extremely accurate weapons were required which could, with a high probability, destroy pin-point targets. The development of these weapons was a continuous process, from Second World War onwards, as was the development of doctrines and tactics to exploit them. Armed forces have always been required to adjust to changing situations, but the relative stability of the political situation of the Cold War should have enabled policy and strategic decisions to have been made that were capable of being implemented in full. Problematically, weapon systems that had been factored into future defence policy and doctrine had been cancelled when nearing completion. Additionally, reductions and alterations in force levels and composition were made, but the purpose and objectives of those forces were not changed.

Industry related to military production in Britain provided many thousands of skilled jobs, but with the reduced defence budget, and greater cost of technology, the loss of jobs was inevitable. Nevertheless, Britain developed a significant technological industrial base with defence roles, especially in aerospace and satellite manufacturing, even as the older heavy industries, such as shipbuilding, declined. Technology developed in Britain, such as TIALD was rushed to the Gulf in 1991 and proved extremely capable.[12] However, the technological lead established by the NATO members has been lost in the last decade. The armed Forces can no longer rely on this superiority to make up for lack of mass.

The victory in the First Gulf War was presented to the public as a clear indicator that the policies and modifications undertaken between 1979 and 1991 were successful. Closer analysis exposes the severe limitations the Armed Forces were working under, and how, in the First Gulf War, almost the entire resources of BAOR – resources meant to sustain a Corps – were only just sufficient to put a reinforced Division into the field.

The British Armed Forces would have been unable to fulfil their commitment to NATO even in a slow build-up to war. Defence spending had been cut to such an extent that, although the Armed Forces had capable weaponry, those weapons were limited in their use by a restricted supply of ammunition. Evidence from the Falklands and Iraq shows that the daily usage rates would have been exceeded, sometimes by large margins. This would have meant an even earlier collapse of any defence than was previously thought. The records from the National Archives have shown that, on many occasions, Armed Forces officers made this point to their Government representatives. On several occasions concerned Ministers did the same, but the results always seem to be unchanged: ammunition stock levels were kept low to save money.

## Conclusion and Final Remarks

Current threats include nuclear, chemical and biological weapons. Pandemics, such as the recent COVID-19, show that preparation for disasters, natural or man-made, is a vital part of national security. The preparations that were made during the Cold War, including stockpiles of vital equipment, protective clothing and supporting infrastructure, were quickly dismantled. We are paying the price for short-sightedness.

When, not if, Britain is involved in another large-scale war, the loss of capability caused by the apparent success of the 'cheese-paring' cuts to the Armed Forces will return to trouble the policymakers of the time. That is, if the war is not over within a few days.

This research has questioned the links between policy, planning and execution for British defence. Overall, many of the links that should have existed – the feedback between policy, strategy, doctrine, tactics and technological development – have been found wanting. Each seems to have remained isolated. Since the end of the Cold War, the NATO strategy of MC 14/3, and British defence policy, have been held as examples of success. They have justified continuation of cuts to defence spending. The justifications derive from two false premises: firstly, the policies employed in the past sixty years have all been successful; secondly that by cutting the Armed Forces, they will become more 'efficient' and, therefore, more 'effective'. The evidence undermines these beliefs: Flexible Response's success is unproven; rather it was not seen to have failed. Politicians demanded cuts in defence spending. Main weapons and projects were costed for up to ten years ahead. The only way to save money was to cut other, 'soft', aspects of the defence budget – fuel, ammunition, spares and training. A problem was created by the demands of the politicians, the limitations of the development and purchasing of major weapon systems, and the 'can-do' attitude of the Armed Forces.

The way in which the WTO and the Soviet Union were dissolved means the cause cannot be identified solely in the strategy and policy adopted by NATO after 1967. Care must be taken lest a *post hoc* analysis is applied to their demise. The fact that a war never happened in Europe during the Cold War is not proof that NATO strategy worked, and we should not be led into current or future vulnerabilities by believing so. The reasons for the end of the Cold War were more complicated than the ability to out-produce the Eastern Bloc in tanks and missiles, and are still debated today.[13]

An authoritarian system dependent on central planning, riven by corruption and inefficiencies could not survive in a socially and technologically developing world. The threat that had existed for more than 40 years, whether real or imagined, disappeared suddenly.

The German philosopher Hegel wrote 'What experience and history teaches us is that people and governments have never learned anything from history, or acted on principles deduced from it.'[14] This holds true today, with short term thinking affecting long term policy outcomes. The conclusion has so far dealt with the effects defence policy had on the Armed Forces during the Cold War. There can certainly be an anticipation of future behaviour based on past events. The question which naturally follows is what implications does the research have for current and future policy? This conclusion returns to the proposition that defence policy should be a response to the potential threats to the security of the nation which does not reflect the facts presented as the core of this research. Defence policy was not shaped by the threat, but rather by the amount of money realistically available, by answering the question of 'How little can we get away with?'[15] This was – and still is – a situation not conducive to long-term strategic thought and planning.

# SELECT BIBLIOGRAPHY

The following bibliography lists the most important works consulted. Other sources are cited in individual endnotes.

## National Archives

ADM 219   Admiralty: Directorate of Operational Research
CAB 129   Memoranda
CAB 130   Miscellaneous Committees: Minutes and Papers
CAB 175   War Books
DEFE 11   Chiefs of Staff Committee
DEFE 13   Private Office: Registered Files (all Ministers')
DEFE 24   Defence Secretariat Branches and their Predecessors
DEFE 25   Chief of Defence Staff
DEFE 48   Defence Operational Analysis Establishment, later Defence Operational Analysis Centre
DEFE 62   Defence Intelligence Staff
DEFE 70   Ministry of Defence (Army): Registered Files and Branch Folders
FCO 46    Defence Department and successors
HO 322    Civil Defence (Various Symbol Series) Files
PREM 16   Correspondence and Papers, 1974-1979
PREM 19   Correspondence and Papers, 1979-1997

## NATO

The North Atlantic Treaty, 4 April 1949. NATO.

NATO Medium Term Plan, 1 April 1950. DC 13. NATO.

A Report by the Military Committee to the Defence Planning Committee on Overall Strategic Concept for the Defense of the North Atlantic Treaty Organization Area, 16 January 1968. MC 14/3. NATO.

Annual Review 1953: Report on the United Kingdom. Paris: The North Atlantic Council, 24 November 1953. C-M(53)150, Part III, United Kingdom. NATO.

Final Communiqué, Defence Planning Committee. Brussels, 7 December 1977. NATO.

Final Communiqué, North Atlantic Council. New York: NATO, 26 September 1950.

Final Communiqué, North Atlantic Council. Oslo, 21 May 1976. NATO.

Force Goals 1952, 1953 and 1954. Lisbon: NATO Military Committee, 25 March 1952. MC-SG-SGM-0648-52. NATO.

Harmel, Pierre. Report of the Council on the Future Tasks of the Alliance. Brussels: NATO, 1967.

Lord Carrington. Final Communiqué of the Defence Planning Committee. NATO, 3 December 1985.

Measures to Implement the Strategic Concept for the Defence of the NATO Area, 8 December 1969. MC 48/3. NATO.

Overall Strategic Concept For The Defense Of The North Atlantic Treaty Organization Area, 23 May 1957. MC 14/2. NATO.

Strategic Guidance For The North Atlantic Regional Planning. Brussels, 28 March 1950. MC 14. NATO.

The Most Effective Pattern of NATO Military Strength for the next Few Years, 22 November 1954. MC 48 (Final). NATO.

## Government and Armed Forces of Great Britain

Ministry of Defence. Army Doctrine Publication – Training. Vol. 4. DGD&D/18/34/65. 1996.

BATUS Training Report, 1981.

Design for Military Operations: The British Military Doctrine. D/CGS/50/8. London: HMSO, 1989.

Statement on the Defence Estimates 1965. Cmnd 2592. London: HMSO, February 1965.

Statement on the Defence Estimates 1966, Part I. The Defence Review. Cmnd 2901. London: HMSO, February 1966.

Statement on the Defence Estimates 1968. Cmnd 3540. London: HMSO, February 1968.

Statement on the Defence Estimates 1975. Cmnd 5976. London: HMSO, 1975.

Statement on the Defence Estimates 1979. Cmnd 7474. London: HMSO, 1979.

Statement on the Defence Estimates 1980. Cmnd 7826. London: HMSO, 1980.

Statement on the Defence Estimates 1983. Cmnd 8951. London: HMSO, 1983.

Statement on the Defence Estimates 1984. Cmnd 9227. London: HMSO, 1984.

Statement on the Defence Estimates 1986. Cmnd 9763-1. London: HMSO, 1986.

Statement on the Defence Estimates 1989. Cmnd 675. London: HMSO, 1989.

Statement on the Defence Estimates 1991. Cmnd 1559-I. London: HMSO, July 1991.

Statement on the Defence Estimates 1993. Cmnd 2270. London: HMSO, July 1993.

Terms of Reference: Western Union Defence (Part 1) (Overseas Section); Final Version: Defence of the Western Union, 20 September 1948. DEFE 6/6/64. The National Archives.

The Falklands Campaign: The Lessons. Cmnd 8758. London: HMSO, December 1982.

The United Kingdom Defence Programme: The Way Forward. Cmnd 8288. London: HMSO, June 1981.

1(BR) Corps Battle Notes. BAOR HQ, 1981.

House of Commons Defence Committee. Allied Forces in Germany. HC 93. London: HMSO, 1982.

Defence Committee Tenth Report: Preliminary Lessons from Operation Granby. HC 287/I. London: House of Commons, 17 July 1991.

Implementation of Lessons Learned from Operation Granby. HC 43. London: House of Commons, 25 May 1994.

The Defence Requirement for Merchant Shipping and Civil Aircraft. HC 476. House of Commons Defence Committee, 7 June 1988.

The SA80 Rifle and Light Support Weapon. HC 728. London: HMSO, 1993.

Expenditure Committee. Second Report from the Expenditure Committee. HC 155. London: HMSO, 29 January 1976.

## Other Sources

Aldrich, Richard J., 'Intelligence within BAOR and NATOs Northern Army Group', Journal of Strategic Studies, 31, no. 1 (1 February 2008): pp.89–122

Allen, Charles, Thunder and Lightning: The RAF Tells Its Stories of the Gulf War (HMSO Books, 1991)

Badsey, Stephen, 'The Logistics of the British Recovery of the Falkland Islands, 1982', International Forum on War History: Proceedings, March 2014

Bowman, Martin W., *The English Electric Lightning Story* (Stroud: History, 2009)

Brown, David, *The Royal Navy and the Falklands War* (London: Arrow Books, 1989)

Carr, E H., *The Twenty Years Crisis, 1919-1939: An Introduction to the Study of International Relations* (London: Macmillan, 1946)

Clapp, Michael, and Ewen Southby-Tailyour, *Amphibious Assault Falklands: The Battle of San Carlos Water* (London: Leo Cooper, 1996)

Cordingley, Patrick, *In the Eye of the Storm: Commanding the Desert Rats in the Gulf War* (London: Hodder & Stoughton, 1996)

Coyle, Harold, *Team Yankee* (W.H. Allen, 1988)

Crawshaw, Steve, *Goodbye to the USSR: The Collapse of Soviet Power* (London: Bloomsbury, 1992)

Crick, Michael, *Michael Heseltine: A Biography* (London: Hamilton, 1997)

De la Billière, Peter, *Storm Command: A Personal Account of the Gulf War* (London: HarperCollins, 1992)

Dorman, Andrew, Michael Kandiah, and Gillian Staerck, eds., 'The Nott Review, 1981', *ICBH Witness Seminar Programme. Institute of Contemporary British History*, 2002

Eurogroup, *Western Defense: The European Role in NATO* (Brussels: Eurogroup, 1984)

Fortmann, Michel, and David G Haglund, 'Of Ghosts and Other Spectres: The Cold Wars Ending and the Question of the Next "Hegemonic" Conflict', *Cold War History* 14, no. 4 (2014): pp.515–532

Freedman, Lawrence, 'Alliance and the British Way in Warfare', *Review of International Studies* 21, no. 2 (1995): pp.145–158.

Freedman, Lawrence, 'British Defence Policy after the Falklands', *The World Today* 38, no. 9 (1982), pp.331–339.

Freedman, Lawrence, *The Official History of the Falklands Campaign. Vol. 2.* (Abingdon, Routledge, 2005)

Gray, Colin S., Strategy and Defence Planning. In *Strategy in the Contemporary World.*, 5th ed., (London: Oxford University Press, 2016), pp.157–174

Gray, Peter W, Air Power: Strategic Lessons from an Idiosyncratic Campaign. In *The Falklands Conflict Twenty Years On: Lessons for the Future* (The Sandhurst Conference Series. Abingdon: Frank Cass, 2005), pp.253–264

Grazebrooke, Major A M., Volunteers in BAOR. *British Army Review*, no. 62 (August 1979)

Hackett, General Sir John, *The Third World War* (London: Sphere Books, 1983)

Hegel, Georg Wilhelm Friedrich, *Lectures on the Philosophy of History*. Vol. 1. 3 vols, 1832.

Hellberg, Colonel I.J., An Experience with the Commando Logistic Regiment Royal Marines. In *The Falklands Conflict Twenty Years on: Lessons for the Future* (Sandhurst Conference Series. Abingdon: Frank Cass, 2005)

Hennessy, Peter, *Distilling the Frenzy: Writing the History of Ones Own Times* (London: Biteback, 2012)

Hennessy, Peter, *The Secret State* (London: Penguin Books, 2010)

Heuser, Beatrice, *NATO, Britain, France, and the FRG: Nuclear Strategies and Forces for Europe, 1949-2000* (New York: St. Martin's Press, 1997)

Hoffenaar, J., and Christopher Findlay, eds., *Military Planning for European Theatre Conflict During the Cold War: An Oral History Roundtable*. Zürcher Beiträge Zur Sicherheitspolitik, Nr. 79. Zürich: Center for Security Studies, ETH Zürich, 2007

Isby, David C., and Charles Kamps Jr., *Armies of NATOs Central Front* (London: Janes, 1985)

Locher, Anna, and Christian Nünlist. Internationale Sicherheitspolitik Im Kalten Krieg. Bulletin. Zurich: Parallel History Project on NATO and the Warsaw Pact, 2003. Centre for Security Studies

Macksey, Kenneth, *First Clash* (London: Book Club Associates, 1985)

Maguire, Richard, Jonathan Hogg, and Christoph Laucht, "Never a Credible Weapon": Nuclear Cultures in British Government During the Era of the H-Bomb. *British Journal for the History of Science* 45, no. 4 (2012): pp.519–533

Nott, John, *Here Today, Gone Tomorrow: Recollections of an Errant Politician* (London: Politicos, 2002)

Operation Corporate 1982: A Maritime Doctrinal Perspective. *Semaphore*, no. 6 (2012)

Price, Alfred, *Air Battle Central Europe* (London: Sidgwick & Jackson, 1986)

Privratsky, Kenneth L., *Logistics in the Falklands War* (Barnsley, Pen & Sword, 2014)

Quinlan, Michael, *Thinking About Nuclear Weapons: Principles, Problems, Prospects* (Oxford: Oxford University Press, 2009)

Reehal, P S. Transport and Movements. In *Gulf Logistics: Blackadders War* (London: Brasseys, 1995)

Rogers, Bernard W, The Atlantic Alliance: Prescriptions for a Difficult Decade. *Foreign Affairs* 60, no. 5 (1982): pp.1145–1156

Service, Robert, *The End of the Cold War* (London: Pan Books, 2016)

Tedder, Arthur William, *Air Power in War* (London: Hodder & Stoughton, 1948)

Thatcher, Margaret, *The Downing Street Years* (Harper Collins, 1995)

The Soviet "War Scare", Presidents Foreign Intelligence Advisory Board, 15 February 1990. George H W Bush Presidential Library.

Thompson, Major General Julian, *3 Commando Brigade in the Falklands: No Picnic* (Barnsley: Pen & Sword Military, 2007)

Thompson, Major General Julian, Force Projection and the Falklands Conflict. In *The Falklands Conflict Twenty Years on: Lessons for the Future*. Sandhurst Conference Series (Abingdon: Frank Cass, 2005)

Thompson, Major General Julian, *Lifeblood of War: Logistics in Armed Conflict* (London: Brasseys, 1994)

Vallance, Group Captain Andrew, Air Power in the Gulf War – The RAF Contribution. *Royal Air Force*, 20 January 2015. http://www.raf.mod.uk/history/AirPowerintheGulfWar.cfm

White, Kenton. "Effing" the Military: A Political Misunderstanding of Management. *Defence Studies* 17, no. 4 (2017): pp.1–13

Woodward, Sandy, and Patrick Robinson. *One Hundred Days* (London: Harper Press, 2012)

## TV Programmes

'Threads', BBC, 1984

A Gap in Our Defences. *Secret Society*. BBC, 1987

'The Day After', ABC, 1983

# NOTES

## Chapter 1

1 'A Report by the Military Committee to the Defence Planning Committee on Overall Strategic Concept for the Defense of the North Atlantic Treaty Organization Area', 16 January 1968, MC 14/3, NATO.

2 Richard J. Aldrich, 'Intelligence within BAOR and NATO's Northern Army Group', *Journal of Strategic Studies* 31, no. 1 (1 February 2008): pp.89–122.

3 Richard Maguire, Jonathan Hogg, and Christoph Laucht, '"Never a Credible Weapon": Nuclear Cultures in British Government During the Era of the H-Bomb', *British Journal for the History of Science* 45, no. 4 (2012): pp.519–533; Peter Hennessy, *The Secret State* (London: Penguin Books, 2010).

4 'Measures to Implement the Strategic Concept for the Defence of the NATO Area', 8 December 1969, MC 48/3, NATO.

5 Ministry of Defence, 'Terms of Reference: Western Union Defence (Part 1) (Overseas Section); Final Version: Defence of the Western Union', 20 September 1948, DEFE 6/6/64, The National Archives.

6 'The North Atlantic Treaty', 4 April 1949, NATO Article 3.

7 'Final Communiqué, North Atlantic Council' (New York: NATO, 26 September 1950).

8 'Strategic Guidance For The North Atlantic Regional Planning' (Brussels, 28 March 1950), para. 5, MC 14, NATO.

9 'MC 14', para. 7, Probable Strategic Intentions.

10 MC 3 and DC 6 series documents, 'The Strategic Concept for the Defense of the North Atlantic Area', were superseded by the MC 14 series, which included additional information for the Regional Planning Groups missing from the earlier documents. 'MC 14'.

11 'NATO Medium Term Plan', 1 April 1950, para. 57, DC 13, NATO.

12 'MC 14', 6.

13 'NATO Medium Term Plan', para. 2d.

14 Part III, 'NATO Medium Term Plan', para. 49.

15 'NATO Medium Term Plan', para. 54.

16 'MC 14', para. 8c. The North Atlantic Group consisted of all NATO member countries except Italy and Luxembourg.

17 'Force Goals 1952, 1953 and 1954' (Lisbon: NATO Military Committee, 25 March 1952), MC-SG-SGM-0648-52, NATO.

18 'The Most Effective Pattern of NATO Military Strength for the next Few Years', 22 November 1954, para. 5, MC 48 (Final), NATO.

19 'MC 14', Annex, para. 10.

20 'The Most Effective Pattern of NATO Military Strength for the next Few Years', para. 3.b.

21 Beatrice Heuser, *NATO, Britain, France, and the FRG: Nuclear Strategies and Forces for Europe, 1949-2000* (New York: St. Martin's Press, 1997), p.40.

22 'Overall Strategic Concept For The Defense Of The North Atlantic Treaty Organization Area', 23 May 1957, 9, MC 14/2, NATO.

23 'Overall Strategic Concept For The Defense Of The North Atlantic Treaty Organization Area', 10.

24 For fuller details of the Soviet nuclear test see Krzysztof Dabrowski, *Tsar Bomba* (Warwick: Helion & Company, 2021).

25 'A Report by the Military Committee to the Defence Planning Committee on Overall Strategic Concept for the Defense of the North Atlantic Treaty Organization Area', para. 19.

26 'Measures to Implement the Strategic Concept for the Defence of the NATO Area', para. 19.

27 Ministry of Defence, 'Statement on the Defence Estimates 1965', Cmnd 2592 (London: HMSO, February 1965), para. 1.

28 Ministry of Defence, 'Statement on the Defence Estimates 1966, Part I. The Defence Review', Cmnd 2901 (London: HMSO, February 1966), para. 4.

29 Ministry of Defence, 'Statement on the Defence Estimates 1975', Cmnd 5976 (London: HMSO, 1975), para. 7.

30 Ministry of Defence, para. 1.

31 Expenditure Committee, 'Second Report from the Expenditure Committee', HC 155 (London: HMSO, 29 January 1976), para. 140.

32 Expenditure Committee, para. 142.

33 Telegram from Sir John Killick (UKDELNATO) to FCO, 14th December 1976, 'Review of Defence Policies and Defence Expenditure', PREM 16/1186 (Kew: The National Archives, 1976 to 1977), TNA.

34 Memorandum by the Secretary of State for Defence 'NATO Defence Planning Long Term Programme', n.d., para. 6, DEFE 13/1411, TNA.

35 DUS(P) 236/78, Memorandum to Secretary of State for Defence from Michael Quinlan, 17th March 1978, 'NATO Defence Planning Long Term Defence Programme', paras 3–4.

36 Speech by the Rt Hon John Nott MP, Secretary of State for Defence at the IISS, 16th November 1981, 'NATO: UK Defence Policy', n.d., 2, FCO 46/2585, TNA.

37 Ministry of Defence, 'The United Kingdom Defence Programme: The Way Forward', Cmnd 8288 (London: HMSO, June 1981), para. 47.

38 House of Commons Defence Committee, 'Allied Forces in Germany', HC 93 (London: HMSO, 1982), p.vii.

39 'The Defence Programme', Letter from Michael Alexander, PM's Private Secretary, to Brian Norbury, MoD, 3rd June 1981, 'Defence Expenditure 1979-81', n.d., PREM 19/416, TNA.

40 DPN060/12, PQ2897C, Draft Answer, 8th April 1981, Annex C, 'NATO: UK Defence Policy', p.2.

41 Sir John Nott, KCB, in Andrew Dorman, Michael Kandiah, and Gillian Staerck, eds., *The Nott Review, 1981*, ICBH Witness Seminar Programme (Institute of Contemporary British History, 2002), p.35.

42 MO15/3, Defence of the United Kingdom, Memo from R Facer to B Cartledge, 11th May 1978, 'Defence against the Soviet Threat to the United Kingdom', n.d., PREM 16/1563, TNA.

43 Sir Colin Chandler, quoted in Michael Crick, *Michael Heseltine: A Biography* (London: Hamilton, 1997), p.274.

44 'Maritime Force Structure and the Determinant Case', April 1975, para. 14, ADM 219/704, TNA.

45 Ministry of Defence, 'Statement on the Defence Estimates 1991', Cmnd 1559-I (London: HMSO, July 1991), Introduction.

46 Ministry of Defence, 'Statement on the Defence Estimates 1993', Cmnd 2270 (London: HMSO, July 1993), p.7.

## Chapter 2

1 REFORGER was an anacronym for Reinforcement (or Return) of Forces in (or to) Germany.

2 Annex to MO 15/3, 23rd March 1977, 'JIC Assessment of Soviet Threat', 23 March 1977, PREM 16/2259, TNA.

3 3100/1, Memorandum to the Secretary of State for Defence from the Chief of the Defence Staff, 7th May 1973 Ministry of Defence, 'NATO Strategy', 1973, para. 4, DEFE 13/1036, TNA.

4 Dr J. Luns, 'Ministerial Guidance: Defence Planning Committee' (Brussels: NATO, May 1977), para. 2.

5 JIC(81)(N)10, quoted in DP12/81, An Assessment of UK Defence Programme Changes, 1981, 'NATO Logistics Policy General UK Logistics Assumptions' (Kew: The National Archives, n.d.), para. 4, DEFE 25/432, TNA.

6 COS 1146/434B, Attachment, Memorandum to the Chiefs of the Defence Staff from J Duxbury, 15th May 1980, 'NATO Planning and Strategy', n.d., 9, DEFE 70/722, TNA.

7 Defence Policy and Programme, Appendix A, Memorandum by the Secretary of State for Defence, 7th July 1980, 'UK Future Defence Planning', FCO 46/2171 (Kew: The National Archives, n.d.), para. 2, TNA.

8 M03/09/214/F.603, MC 161/81 (Final Draft): Warsaw Pact Strength and Capabilities and MC255 (Final Draft): The significance to NATO of Soviet Policy and activities in the Middle East and Peripheral areas, 8th June 1981, 'NATO Planning and Strategy', para. 4, DEFE 70/722, TNA.

9 Leonid Brezhnev, 'Statement' (United Nations Second Special Session on Disarmament, United Nations, New York, 16 June 1982).

10 *NATO and the Warsaw Pact: Force Comparisons* (Brussels: NATO Information Service, 1984), para. 8.

11 '1(BR) Corps Battle Notes' (BAOR HQ, 1981), 2-4–1.

12 DOP Note 713/74 (Final), Assumptions for Home Defence Planning, Chiefs of Staff Committee, 24th October 1975, 'Home Defence and Security of UK Base: Home Defence Organisation; Command and Control of Home Defence Forces, Pre-Strike Phase', n.d., para. 15, DEFE 11/879, TNA.

13 CAS 90544, Comment on MC 161/80 and MC 255 from the Chief of the Air Staff, 27th May 1980, 'NATO Planning and Strategy', DEFE 70/722, TNA.

14 'The Soviet Air Threat to the United Kingdom Base, 1980 – 2005', D/DIS(CS)17/20 (Ministry of Defence, 30 July 1980), para. 18, DEFE 62/3, TNA.

15 'A Forecast Warsaw Pact Air Order of Battle for Eastern Europe and Western Russia to 1989' (Defence Operational Analysis Establishment, 1979), 33, DEFE 48/968, TNA.

16 'The Soviet Air Threat to the United Kingdom Base, 1980 – 2005', para. 25, D/DIS(CS)17/20, DEFE 62/3, TNA, (Ministry of Defence, 30 July 1980).

17 The Tu-22M (NATO reporting name Backfire) was sometimes referred to in contemporary Western sources as the Tu-26.

18 Note of a conversation between the Prime Minister and the Secretary of State for Defence at 10 Downing Street on 20 February 1978, 'Defence against the Soviet Threat to the United Kingdom', n.d., PREM 16/1563, TNA.

19 DOP Note 713/74 (Final), 'Home Defence and Security of UK Base: Home Defence Organisation; Command and Control of Home Defence Forces, Pre-Strike Phase', para. 16, DEFE 11/879, TNA.

20 Letter from Captain J Moore, RN, to Mr Ian Gow MP, 20th December 1979, 'Defence Budget: Public Expenditure Cuts and Cash Limits; NATO Commitment; Part 1', n.d., PREM 19/161, TNA.

21 Annex A to MO15/3, 16th January 1978, 'Defence against the Soviet Threat to the United Kingdom', 2, PREM 16/1563, TNA.

## Chapter 3

1 Bernard W. Rogers, 'The Atlantic Alliance: Prescriptions for a Difficult Decade', *Foreign Affairs* 60, no. 5 (1982): p.1151.

2 'Final Communiqué, North Atlantic Council' (Oslo, 21 May 1976), para. 2, NATO.

3 There was also a Long Term Defence Programme undertaken by the UK Government in 1955. See TNA, DEFE 7/964 and AVIA 54/2171, Long term defence programme review, 1955.

4 MO9, Annex 'NATO Strategy', Memorandum from B Norbury (MoD) to G Walden (FCO), 10th March 1980, 'UK Future Defence Planning' (Kew: The National Archives, n.d.), B1, FCO 46/2171.

5 Enclosure 1 to ACDS(Ops) 8/52/1/4, 1st February 1978, 'NATO Long-Term Defence Programme: Task Force 1; Readiness', n.d., para. 10, DEFE 24/1660, TNA.

6 DUS(P) 236/78, Memorandum to the Secretary of State for Defence from Michael Quinlan, DUS(P), 17th March 1978, 'NATO Defence Planning Long Term Defence Programme', n.d., para. 3.i, DEFE 13/1411, TNA.

7 Striker was a light armoured vehicle in the CVR(T) family that included Scorpion and Scimitar. Striker mounted five ready to launch Swingfire missiles and another five reloads.

8 Lord Carrington, 'Final Communiqué of the Defence Planning Committee' (NATO, 3 December 1985), para. 5.

9 Lord Carrington, 'Final Communiqué of the Defence Planning Committee' (NATO, 3 December 1985), para. 5.

10 'Government War Book, Volume 2 – NATO Alert System' (Cabinet Office, n.d.), para. 4, CAB 175/24, TNA.

11 'Government War Book, Volume 2 – NATO Alert System' (Cabinet Office, n.d.), para. 4, CAB 175/24, TNA.

12 Operating Procedures, GWB Measures, January 1978, 'Government War Book, Volume 1', CAB 175/53 (Kew: The National Archives, 1985), para. 5, CAB 175/53, TNA.

13 D/DNW/100/1/7, NATO Alert Measures – Implementation Time, Memorandum from Director of Naval Warfare to DS12, 21st March 1980, 'Ministry of Defence (MOD) War Book', n.d., para. 2, DEFE 24/1418, TNA.

14 Defence Situation Centre, Standing Operating Procedure 35, Responsibilities of the Transition to War Team, ibid.

15 DOP Note 713/74, 'Home Defence and Security of UK Base: Home Defence Organisation; Command and Control of Home Defence Forces, Pre-Strike Phase', n.d., 5, DEFE 11/879, TNA.

16 'WINTEX-CIMEX 83 Committees', 1983, CAB 130/1249, TNA; 'Exercise Square Leg; Armed Forces Command and Control for Home Defence', 1981, HO 322/950 – 951, TNA; This is also the scenario used by General Sir John Hackett, *The Third World War* (London: Sphere Books, 1983).

17 'War Book Working Party: Post War Developments in the United Kingdom Transition to War Plans', CAB 175/32 (Cabinet Office, 11 November 1981), 14, CAB 175/32, TNA.

18 Statement by Secretary of Defense Harold Brown to the NATO Defense Planning Committee Ministerial Meeting, 11 – 12th December 1979, 'NATO Defence Planning Committee 1979' n.d., FCO 46/1987, TNA.

19 MO 15/3, 'JIC Assessment of Soviet Threat', 23 March 1977, PREM 16/2259, TNA.

20 'The Soviet "War Scare"' (President's Foreign Intelligence Advisory Board, 15 February 1990), 8, George H W Bush Presidential Library.

21 'Cabinet Office War Book, Volume 2', 1980, 1, CAB 175/31, TNA.

22 TO.2119/431/80, Annex A, 'Ministry of Defence (MOD) War Book', 8, DEFE 24/1418, TNA.

23 M09, United Kingdom Defence Policy, The Present Options, 6th April 1979, 'Defence Expenditure – Defence Budget Reductions – Overstretch in the British Army – 1974 to 1978', n.d., para. 8, PREM 16/1987, TNA.

## Chapter 4

1 COS 43/68, Annex A, Chiefs of Staff Committee, 'Revision of NATO Strategy' (MoD, 1968), 55, DEFE 13/635, TNA.

2 COS 43/68, Annex A, ibid., p.49.

3 Ministry of Defence, 'Statement on the Defence Estimates 1968', Cmnd 3540 (London: HMSO, February 1968).

4 Ministry of Defence, 'Statement on the Defence Estimates 1980', Cmnd 7826 (London: HMSO, 1980), para. 616.

5 'Statement on the Defence Estimates 1980', 25 January 1980, para. 616, CAB 129/208/8, TNA.

6 Major A M Grazebrooke, 'Volunteers in BAOR', *British Army Review*, no. 62 (August 1979): p.62.

7 D/DMO/70/6/1/MO3 (4), 23rd February 1978, Manning levels of Standing Forces, 'NATO Long-Term Defence Programme: Task Force 1; Readiness', n.d., paras 3–6, DEFE 24/1660, TNA.

8 MILAN was a crew-served anti-tank guided missile used at the battalion level; the initial issue was 16 per infantry battalion and later increased to 24. Some 'Light Role' Regular battalions would still have only six launchers. LAW80 was a man-portable disposable anti-tank weapon designed to replace both the 66mm LAW (M72) and 84mm Carl Gustav at the section level; it was only slowly introduced to the Regular forces in the very late 1980s.

9 Ministry of Defence, 'Statement on the Defence Estimates 1983', Cmnd 8951 (London: HMSO, 1983), para. 337.

10 Article for NATO review by the Secretary of State for Defence, Draft, 20th September 1979, 'United Kingdom and NATO', n.d., para. 7, FCO 46/1993, TNA.

11 PUS/81/1188, Defence Programme, Memorandum from Sir Frank Cooper, 22nd July 1981, 'NATO Logistics Policy General UK Logistics Assumptions' (Kew: The National Archives, n.d.), para. 3, DEFE 25/432, TNA.

12 D/DMO/77/18/1/MO3, Memorandum to the Director of Operations NATO, Readiness in the Central Region, 25th March 1980, 'NATO Allied Command Europe and Mobile Land Force', n.d., para. 2, DEFE 24/1462, TNA.

13 Ministry of Defence, 'Statement on the Defence Estimates 1989', Cmnd 675 (London: HMSO, 1989), p.28.

14 D/MIN/JG/7/11, 21st December 1977, Annex A, Ministry of Defence, 'War Reserve Stocks', n.d., DEFE 13/1059, TNA.

15 DP 12/81, An Assessment of UK Defence Programme Changes, Draft, 'NATO Logistics Policy General UK Logistics Assumptions', DEFE 25/432, TNA, (Kew: The National Archives, n.d.).

16 Extract from 'The Training of the Army for War' by Brigadier AP Wavell, CMG, MC, Ministry of Defence, *Army Doctrine Publication – Training*, vol. 4, DGD&D/18/34/65 (Ministry of Defence, 1996), p.24.

17 DP 12/81, An Assessment of UK Defence Programme Changes, Draft, 'NATO Logistics Policy General UK Logistics Assumptions', para. 39, DEFE 25/432, TNA, (Kew: The National Archives, n.d.).

18 MO 8/2/12, Memo from Francis Pym to John Biffen, 25th September 1980, 'UK Future Defence Planning' (Kew: The National Archives, n.d.), 2, FCO 46/2171.

19 Ministry of Defence, 'Statement on the Defence Estimates 1979', Cmnd 7474 (London: HMSO, 1979), para. 138.

20 Serial EL48, 'NATO Force Proposals 1979 – 1984', n.d., DEFE 70/435, TNA.

21 Study into Training and Preparation for Operation GRANBY, Ministry of Defence, *Army Doctrine Publication – Training*, 4:4–4, vol. 4, DGD&D/18/34/65, (Ministry of Defence, 1996).

22 D/DMO/77/7/100/A/MO3, CINCNORTH's call on CGS – 24 Jul 84, Memorandum from Colonel Hyde, MO3, 28th July 1984, 'NATO Planning and Strategy', n.d., para. 3, DEFE 70/722, TNA.

23 MO3/513/F.823, 6th Field Force ORBAT, April 1976, 'Army Organisation and Structure – United Kingdom Mobile Force (UKMF) Organisation' (Kew: The National Archives, n.d.), para. 4, DEFE 70/431.

24 MO3/513/F.823, 6th Field Force ORBAT, April 1976, ibid.

25 TO.2119/431/80, Memorandum from Captain Vallings, Director of Naval Operations and Trade, 'Ministry of Defence (MOD) War Book', n.d., para. 6, DEFE 24/1418, TNA.

26 D/DMO/77/37/MO3, 24th August 1978, 'NATO Allied Command Europe and Mobile Land Force', 'NATO Allied Command Europe and Mobile Land Force', para. 1, DEFE 24/1462, TNA.

27  ACDS(OPS) S/52/1, Rationalisation of Common Defence, Appendix G, Task Team 1B, 7th March 1978, 'NATO Defence Planning Committee Meetings', n.d., G-3, FCO 46/1700, TNA.

28  D/DPS B 56/14, Annex A, Loose Minute, SACEUR OPLAN 10002 (Second Draft) Rapid Reinforcement Plan (RRP), 25th March 1981, 'NATO Rapid Reinforcement Planning', n.d., para. 4.D.3, FCO 46/2583, TNA.

29  D/DMO/77/18/1/MO3, Rapid Reinforcement Plan, Memorandum from Colonel Thorne, Annex A, 16th March 1981, ibid., para. 3.c.

30  D/MIN/JG/7/11, Army War Reserves, Ministry of Defence, 'War Reserve Stocks', para. 6, DEFE 13/1059, TNA.

31  ACDS(Ops) 8/52/1, 7th March 1978, Long Term Defence Programme – Task Force 1 – Final Report, Annex G, 'NATO Defence Planning Committee Meetings', 16, FCO 46/1700, TNA.

32  Ministry of Defence, 'SDE 1968', 50, Cmnd 3540, (London: HMSO, February 1968), War Contingency and Stocks.

33  D/MIN/JG/7/11, War Stocks, Memorandum from the Private Secretary to the Minister of State for Defence, 21st December 1977, Ministry of Defence, 'War Reserve Stocks', DEFE 13/1059, TNA.

34  VCGS 50-3, 10th June 1977, Attachment, ibid., para. 7.

35  D/MIN/JG/7/11, Memorandum to the Minister of State for Defence, 21st December 1977, ibid., para. 3.

36  D/MIN/JG/7/11, 21st December 1977, in Ministry of Defence, 'War Reserve Stocks', DEFE 13/1059, TNA.

37  N/224/5/2, Attachment to VCNS 10/32, War Reserves, 9th June 1977, ibid.

38  Major General Julian Thompson, *Lifeblood of War: Logistics in Armed Conflict* (London: Brassey's, 1994), p.281.

39  'Ammunition Rates and Scales: Comparison of Review of Ammunition Rates and Scales (RARS) Stage 2 and DOAE Study 236' (Kew: The National Archives, 1977), para. 52, DEFE 48/1030.

40  Ibid., p.3.

41  D/MIN/JG/7/11, War Reserves, Army, 22nd July 1977, Ministry of Defence, 'War Reserve Stocks', para. 2, DEFE 13/1059, TNA.

42  Major R W Attoe et al., 'Direct Fire Anti-Armour Ammunition Requirements for the 1(BR) Corps Battle' (Defence Operational Analysis Establishment, 20 January 1977), para. 48, DEFE 48/994, TNA.

43  'Annual Review 1953: Report on the United Kingdom' (Paris: The North Atlantic Council, 24 November 1953), 21, C-M(53)150, Part III, United Kingdom, NATO.

44  D/MIN/JG/7/11, War Reserves, 21st December 1977, Ministry of Defence, 'War Reserve Stocks', para. 4, DEFE 13/1059, TNA.

45  'Final Communiqué, Defence Planning Committee' (Brussels, 7 December 1977), para. 5, NATO.

46  D/MIN/JG/7/11, Annex A, Memorandum to the Minister of State for Defence from the Private Secretary, 21st December 1977, Ministry of Defence, 'War Reserve Stocks', DEFE 13/1059, TNA.

47  Ministry of Defence, 'Statement on the Defence Estimates 1979', para. 127, Cmnd 7474, (London: HMSO, 1979).

48  Bernard W. Rogers, 'The Atlantic Alliance: Prescriptions for a Difficult Decade', *Foreign Affairs* 60, no. 5 (1982): p.1151.

49  *Eurogroup. Western Defense: The European Role in NATO* (Brussels: Eurogroup, 1984), p.8.

50  Ministry of Defence, 'Statement on the Defence Estimates 1989', para. 328, Cmnd 675, (London: HMSO, 1989).

51  Memorandum to the Minister of State for Defence, 21st December 1977, Ministry of Defence, 'War Reserve Stocks', DEFE 13/1059, TNA.

52  N/224/5/2, Navy Department Paper on War Reserves, June 1977, B James, 'Weapon Weighting Vectors in the Battlegroup Model', DOAE Working Paper (DOAE, October 1975), paras 6–7, DEFE 48/803, TNA.

53  N/224/5/2, Navy Department Paper on War Reserves, June 1977, Ministry of Defence, 'War Reserve Stocks', para. 19, DEFE 13/1059, TNA.

54  VCGS 50-3, Attachment, Loose Minute, War Reserves, from the VCGS to the Minister of State, 10th June 1977, ibid., para. 11. B Vehicles are non-combat types, usually transport and logistic such as lorries and Land Rovers.

55  VCDS(P&L) 203, Memorandum on the State of Logistics, from VCDS(P&L) to COS, 20th March 1981, 'NATO Logistics Policy General UK Logistics Assumptions', para. 3, DEFE 25/432, TNA, (Kew: The National Archives, n.d.).

56  The State of Logistics, Memo from CDS (draft) to the Secretary of State for Defence, April 1981, 'NATO Logistics Policy General UK Logistics Assumptions', DEFE 25/432, TNA, (Kew: The National Archives, n.d.).

57  Speaking Notes (Speaker not known), War Reserves and Stock levels, 27th October 1981, ibid., 2.

58  VCDS(P&L) 203, Holding of War Reserves, 1981, ibid., para. 5.

59  VCGS 50-3, 10th June 1977, Ministry of Defence, 'War Reserve Stocks', para. 10, DEFE 13/1059, TNA.

60  VCGS 50-3, 10th June 1977, ibid., para. 11.

61  D/MIN/JG/7/11, War Reserves, Navy, 22nd July 1977, ibid., para. 5.

62  VCNS 10/32, War Reserves, Memorandum from VCNS to Minister of State, 9th June 1977, ibid., para. 3.

63  ACDS(Ops) 8/52/1, Annex A, Long Term Defence Programme – Task Force 1 – Final Report, 7th March 1978, 'NATO Defence Planning Committee Meetings', 3, FCO 46/1700, TNA.

64  ACDS(Ops) 8/52/1, Annex G, Long Term Defence Programme – Task Force 1 – Final Report, 7th March 1978, ibid., p.7.

65  D/MIN/JG/7/11, War Reserves, 22nd July 1977, Ministry of Defence, 'War Reserve Stocks', para. 3, DEFE 13/1059, TNA.

66  VCGS 50-3, 10th June 1977, ibid., para. 20.

67  D/MIN/JG/7/11, Annex B, Army Review of Ammunition Expenditure Rates and Scales, 21st December 1977, ibid., para. 7.

68  D/DMO/70/6/1/MO3, LTDP, Annex C, Task Team 1C, Accelerate implementation of Forward Storage Programme, 23rd February 1978, 'NATO Long-Term Defence Programme: Task Force 1; Readiness', 1, DEFE 24/1660, TNA.

69  Brief for VCDS(P&L)'s meeting with CDS, 3rd April 1981, 'NATO Logistics Policy General UK Logistics Assumptions', para. 3.d, DEFE 25/432, TNA, (Kew: The National Archives, n.d.).

70  Sir John Nott KCB was Secretary of State for Defence between January 1981 and January 1983.

71  John Nott, *Here Today, Gone Tomorrow: Recollections of an Errant Politician* (London: Politico's, 2002), p.210.

72  Taken from Ministry of Defence. 'Statement on the Defence Estimates 1979', Cmnd 7474.

## Chapter 5

1  'NATO Medium Term Plan', 1 April 1950, para. 2d, DC 13, NATO.

2  DCINC/100, 'Haul-down' report by Air Chief Marshal Sir Peter Le Cheminant GBE KCB DFC RAF – Deputy Commander-in-Chief, Allied Forces Central Europe, 1st May 1979, 'NATO Allied Command Europe and Mobile Land Force', 7, DEFE 24/1462, TNA.

3  OD(80), Tank Policy, Note by the Secretary of State for Defence, Draft, 27th June 1980, 'UK Future Defence Planning', FCO 46/2171, (Kew: The National Archives, n.d.).

4  The JP233 was a large submunition dispenser system designed to be carried by Tornado. Its primary role was to damage runways with concrete-piercing bombs and to disperse anti-personnel mines to delay subsequent repair.

5  Pierre Harmel, 'Report of the Council on the Future Tasks of the Alliance' (Brussels: NATO, 1967).

6  The US Navy and several allies had adopted the Vulcan Phalanx system in this role; this consisted of a six-barrelled 20mm gun system designed to destroy incoming missiles or aircraft at very short ranges.

7  Mr Keith Speed, Hansard, House of Commons Debate 19 May 1981 vol 5 cc160-242, col 181-182

8  Interview with Capt Dr David Reindorp RN, Assistant Head (Analysis) / Joint Warfare Directorate, 10th December 2014

9  Andrew Dorman, Michael Kandiah, and Gillian Staerck, eds., *The Nott Review, 1981*, ICBH Witness Seminar Programme (Institute of Contemporary British History, 2002), p.27.

10  Ministry of Defence, 'The United Kingdom Defence Programme: The Way Forward', Cmnd 8288 (London: HMSO, June 1981), para. 23.

11  Note of a conversation between the Prime Minister and the Secretary of State for Defence at 10 Downing Street on 20th February 1978, 'Defence against the Soviet Threat to the United Kingdom', n.d., PREM 16/1563, TNA.

12  Measure 4.11, 'Government War Book, Volume 1', CAB 175/53 (Kew: The National Archives, 1985), CAB 175/53, TNA.

13  DN Plans 75/3/2, Defence of Ports and Anchorages, 16th December 1977, 'War Planning: Defence of Ports and Anchorages around the UK', n.d., DEFE 24/1721, TNA.

14  D/AUS(NS)15/81, Questions and Answers Brief, 41 Commando, 'Defence Estimates, Working Papers 1981 to 1982', n.d., FCO 46/2557, TNA.

15  MO 15/3, Annex, Part II, Memorandum to the Prime Minister from Fred Mulley, 16th January 1978, 'Defence against the Soviet Threat to the United Kingdom', para. 9, PREM 16/1563, TNA.

16  The Foreign Policy aspects of major changes in UK Defence priorities, Report from D Gillmore, Defence Department, 13th March 1981, 'NATO: UK Defence Policy', n.d., 3, FCO 46/2585, TNA.

17    DP 14/81, Report by the Defence Policy Staff, NATO Force Goals 1981 – 1986 and Long Term Defence Programme, Annex A, 'NATO Long Term Defence Planning', FCO 46/2586 (Kew: The National Archives, 1981), A6, TNA.

18    Martin W Bowman, *The English Electric Lightning Story* (Stroud: History, 2009), p.6.

19    AUS(DS)/BF12/1 (21/81), Estimates 1981/82 – Announcement of Measures, Memorandum to DUS(P) from J Stewart AUS(Defence Staff), Annex B, 13th January 1981, 'Defence Estimates, Working Papers 1981 to 1982', l. 4, FCO 46/2557, TNA.

20    These squadrons were manned by the RAF Regiment though paid for by the USAF.

21    Ministry of Defence, 'Statement on the Defence Estimates 1989', para. 330, Cmnd 675, (London: HMSO, 1989).

22    Interview with Air Chief Marshall Sir Peter Harding, CINC UKAF, 'A Gap in Our Defences', *Secret Society* (BBC, 1987).

23    D/DS9/2869/657/1/2, Loose Minute, Background Note, 'Defence Estimates, Working Papers 1981 to 1982', FCO 46/2557, TNA.

24    Annex C to D/DASD/105/121, 18th November 1977, 'Army Organisation and Structure – United Kingdom Mobile Force (UKMF) Organisation', C–1, DEFE 70/431, (Kew: The National Archives, n.d.).

25    48903 G3 (Ops), 15th October 1981, 'British Army of the Rhine: Ground Defence Plan' (Kew: The National Archives, 1976), 4, DEFE 70/1276.

26    D/DASD/67/99, 10th November 1978, 'British Army of the Rhine' (Kew: The National Archives, 1978), 1, FCO 46/1735.

27    Ministry of Defence, 'Statement on the Defence Estimates 1980', para. 315, Cmnd 7826, (London: HMSO, 1980).

28    D/DS12/48/16/1, Danish Defence: Reinforcement (Draft), 22nd September 1981, 'NATO Rapid Reinforcement Planning', para. 4, FCO 46/2583, TNA.

29    DUS(P) 336/80, 27th June 1980, Tank Policy, 'UK Future Defence Planning', para. 4, FCO 46/2171, (Kew: The National Archives, n.d.).

30    In practice, the only LRATGW in service with ground troops at this point in time was Swingfire mounted on FV438 or Striker vehicles.

31    DP 14/81(Final), Appendix 2, Annex A, Serial EL05, NATO Force Goals 1981-1986 and Long Term Defence Programme, 6th October 1981, 'NATO Long Term Defence Planning', FCO 46/2586, TNA, (Kew: The National Archives, 1981).

32    AB/P(77)13, Annex A, Serial EL07, 'NATO Force Proposals 1979 – 1984', DEFE 70/435, TNA.

33    David C. Isby and Charles Kamps Jr, *Armies of NATO's Central Front* (London: Jane's, 1985), p.292.

34    Lawrence Freedman, *The Official History of the Falklands Campaign*, vol. 2 (Abingdon, 2005), p.733.

35    Ministry of Defence, 'Statement on the Defence Estimates 1984', Cmnd 9227 (London: HMSO, 1984), para. 424.

36    Ministry of Defence, 'Statement on the Defence Estimates 1986', Cmnd 9763-1 (London: HMSO, 1986), para. 424.

37    UKCICC 1252/1, Plan for the Home Defence of the United Kingdom in the setting of General War, 1st January 1975, 'Home Defence and Security of UK Base: Home Defence Organisation; Command and Control of Home Defence Forces, Pre-Strike Phase', n.d., para. 2, DEFE 11/879, TNA.

38    DOP Note 713/74 (Final), Chiefs of Staff Committee, Defence Operational Planning Staff, Assumptions for Home Defence Planning, 24th October 1975, ibid., para. 6.

39    'Measures to Implement the Strategic Concept for the Defence of the NATO Area', 8 December 1969, para. 17, MC 48/3, NATO.

40    'The Soviet Air Threat to the United Kingdom Base, 1980 – 2005', D/DIS(CS)17/20 (Ministry of Defence, 30 July 1980), 1, DEFE 62/3, TNA.

41    Interview with Captain Dr David Reindorp, RN, 3rd July 2014

42    Appendix A, 'Measures to Implement the Strategic Concept for the Defence of the NATO Area', paras 19 and 20, MC 48/3, NATO.

43    D/DMO/70/6/1/MO3, Annex B, 'NATO Long-Term Defence Programme: Task Force 1; Readiness', B1, DEFE 24/1660, TNA.

44    D/DMO/70/6/1/MO3, Task Team 2A, Recategorisation of Forces, 23rd February 1978, 'NATO Long-Term Defence Programme: Task Force 1; Readiness', DEFE 24/1660, TNA.

45    Enclosure to A/BR/214/2/MO3, Draft Paper on The Incorporation of the UK into NATO as a Land Region of Allied Command Europe (ACE), 21st February 1977, 'NATO Allied Command Europe and Mobile Land Force', para. 2, DEFE 24/1462, TNA.

46    D/DS7/10/7, Memorandum from MJV Bell, Head of DS7, to Head of DS12, 27th April 1977, ibid., para. 3.

47    UKCICC 1252/1, United Kingdom Commanders-in-Chief Committee (Home) Plan for the Home Defence of the United Kingdom in the setting of General War, 1st January 1975, 'Home Defence and Security of UK Base:

48    Home Defence Organisation; Command and Control of Home Defence Forces, Pre-Strike Phase', para. 2, DEFE 11/879, TNA.

48    UKCICC 2/75, The Function of the United Kingdom Commanders-in-Chief Committee (Home) in Transition to War, May 1975, 'Home Defence and Security of UK Base: Home Defence Organisation; Command and Control of Home Defence Forces, Pre-Strike Phase', DEFE 11/879, TNA.

49    DOP Note 713/74 (Final), Assumptions for Home Defence Planning, 24th October 1975, 'Home Defence and Security of UK Base: Home Defence Organisation; Command and Control of Home Defence Forces, Pre-Strike Phase', para. 21, DEFE 11/879, TNA.

50    Chiefs of Staff Committee, Assumptions for Home Defence Planning, DOP Note 713/74 (Final), ibid., para. 9.

51    DP12/81, An Assessment of UK Defence programme changes, Draft, 15th July 1981, 'NATO Logistics Policy General UK Logistics Assumptions', para. 34, DEFE 25/432, TNA, (Kew: The National Archives, n.d.).

52    Measure 3.86, 'Government War Book, Volume 1', CAB 175/53, CAB 175/53, TNA, (Kew: The National Archives, 1985).

53    DOP Note 713/74 (Final), Assumptions for Home Defence Planning, 24th October 1975, Annex A, 'Home Defence and Security of UK Base: Home Defence Organisation; Command and Control of Home Defence Forces, Pre-Strike Phase', para. 2, DEFE 11/879, TNA.

54    CDP/70 263/36/3, memo from J F D Buttery, Home Office, 25th September 1974, 'Army Command Organisation in the UK' (Kew: The National Archives, n.d.), HO 322/802.

55    DOP Note 713/74 (Final), 'Home Defence and Security of UK Base: Home Defence Organisation; Command and Control of Home Defence Forces, Pre-Strike Phase', para. 17, DEFE 11/879, TNA.

## Chapter 6

1    'British Army of the Rhine: Ground Defence Plan' (Kew: The National Archives, 1976), DEFE 70/1276.

2    MO 15/3, Annex A, 16th January 1978, 'Defence against the Soviet Threat to the United Kingdom', n.d., 2, PREM 16/1563, TNA.

3    TO.2119/431/80, Annex A, 'Ministry of Defence (MOD) War Book', n.d., 8, DEFE 24/1418, TNA.

4    Measure 3.39, 'Government War Book, Volume 1', CAB 175/53 (Kew: The National Archives, 1985), CAB 175/53, TNA.

5    Colonel IJ Hellberg, 'An Experience with the Commando Logistic Regiment Royal Marines', in *The Falklands Conflict Twenty Years on: Lessons for the Future*, Sandhurst Conference Series (Abingdon: Frank Cass, 2005), p.110.

6    Ministry of Defence, *Design for Military Operations: The British Military Doctrine*, D/CGS/50/8 (London: HMSO, 1989), p.3.

7    DP12/81, An Assessment of UK Defence Programme Changes, Strategic Implications, 'NATO Logistics Policy General UK Logistics Assumptions' (Kew: The National Archives, n.d.), para. 44, DEFE 25/432, TNA.

8    Beatrice Heuser, *NATO, Britain, France, and the FRG: Nuclear Strategies and Forces for Europe, 1949-2000* (New York: St. Martin's Press, 1997), p.144.

9    'DEFE 70/1276', DEFE 70/1276, (Kew: The National Archives, 1976). Letter to General Bagnall from General Gow, 8th June 1982.

10    'Data Assumptions, Method of Analysis and Study Programme for DOAE Study 288 (1 (BR) Corps Concept of Operations 1985 – 2005)', D/DOAE/44/616, 23 January 1980, para. 3, DEFE 48/1095, TNA.

11    Annex C to Section 2, Ministry of Defence, 'BATUS Training Report', 1981, 2C – 1.

12    Quoted in Alfred Price, *Air Battle Central Europe* (London: Sidgwick & Jackson, 1986), p.4.

13    'The Effect on Maritime Operations of Warsaw Pact Air Attacks on NATO Land Bases and Installations' (Ministry of Defence, 1979), para. 21, DEFE 48/1092, TNA.

14    House of Commons Defence Committee, 'Implementation of Lessons Learned from Operation Granby', HC 43 (London: House of Commons, 25 May 1994), para. 77.

15    '1(BR) Corps Battle Notes' (BAOR HQ, 1981), chap. 7.

16    Ibid., chap. 5.

17    No 136/81, Britain's Defence Policy, December 1981, 'NATO: UK Defence Policy', n.d., 10, FCO 46/2585, TNA.

18    Ministry of Defence, 'The United Kingdom Defence Programme: The Way Forward', Cmnd 8288 (London: HMSO, June 1981), para. 23.

19    Michael Clapp and Ewen Southby-Tailyour, *Amphibious Assault Falklands: The Battle of San Carlos Water* (London: Leo Cooper, 1996), p.4.

20    UKCICC 1252/1, United Kingdom Commanders-in-Chief Committee (Home) Plan for the Home Defence of the United Kingdom in the setting of General War, 1st January 1975, 'Home Defence and Security of UK Base:

Home Defence Organisation; Command and Control of Home Defence Forces, Pre-Strike Phase', n.d., para. 2, DEFE 11/879, TNA.

21 Reading War Room ('The Citadel'), University of Reading, https://historicengland.org.uk/listing/the-list/list-entry/1393194

22 1252/1, 'Home Defence and Security of UK Base: Home Defence Organisation; Command and Control of Home Defence Forces, Pre-Strike Phase', para. 52, DEFE 11/879, TNA.

23 Kenneth Macksey, *First Clash* (London: Book Club Associates, 1985).

24 General Sir John Hackett, *The Third World War* (London: Sphere Books, 1983); Harold Coyle, *Team Yankee* (W.H. Allen, 1988).

25 Mick Jackson, 'Threads' (BBC, 1984).

26 'WINTEX-CIMEX 83 Committees', 1983, CAB 130/1249, TNA.

27 'Protect and Survive' was a programme intended to provide basic advice to householders on building simple fallout shelters and surviving a nuclear attack and its aftermath.

28 The *Kirov* was a large, nuclear-powered battle cruiser extensively armed with conventional and nuclear anti-ship missiles and had an impressive anti-air warfare capability. Four such vessels with minor variations were built under the Soviet Project 1144 Orlan. Such a vessel would form the centre of a group of up to half-a-dozen escorts and could itself serve as escort to one of the Kiev-class carriers.

## Chapter 7

1 Peter W Gray, 'Air Power: Strategic Lessons from an Idiosyncratic Campaign', in *The Falklands Conflict Twenty Years On: Lessons for the Future*, The Sandhurst Conference Series (Abingdon: Frank Cass, 2005), p.253.

2 Personal note to Margaret Thatcher from the First Sea Lord, 18th May 1981, 'Defence Expenditure 1979-81', n.d., PREM 19/416, TNA.

3 Lawrence Freedman, 'British Defence Policy after the Falklands', *The World Today* 38, no. 9 (1982): p.333.

4 MA Strategic Studies Lecture, University of Reading, Dr G Sloan, 2013. See also 'Operation Corporate 1982: A Maritime Doctrinal Perspective', *Semaphore*, no. 6 (2012).

5 Small numbers of 20mm Oerlikon and 40mm Bofors guns were in service aboard some Royal Navy vessels, though these types had very limited capabilities versus fast jests or modern missiles.

6 Ministry of Defence, 'The Falklands Campaign: The Lessons', Cmnd 8758 (London: HMSO, December 1982), para. 229.

7 Phalanx and Goalkeeper were 20mm and 30mm, respectively, multi-barrelled cannon designed to provide a last line of defence against sea-skimming missile attack. Phalanx was already in service with the US Navy and Goalkeeper was a design produced in the Netherlands.

8 The Way Ahead, Draft, 'NATO UK Programme and Budget', n.d., para. 29, FCO 46/2572, TNA.

9 Kenneth L. Privratsky, *Logistics in the Falklands War*, 2014, p.120.

10 Major General Julian Thompson, *3 Commando Brigade in the Falklands: No Picnic* (Barnsley: Pen & Sword Military, 2007), p.4.

11 Hellberg, 'An Experience with the Commando Logistic Regiment', 111, in *The Falklands Conflict Twenty Years on: Lessons for the Future*, Sandhurst Conference Series, (Abingdon: Frank Cass, 2005).

12 Ibid., 117; Privratsky, *Logistics in the Falklands War*, p.39.

13 Hellberg, 'An Experience with the Commando Logistic Regiment', 110, in *The Falklands Conflict Twenty Years on: Lessons for the Future*, Sandhurst Conference Series, (Abingdon: Frank Cass, 2005).

14 Hellberg, 'An Experience with the Commando Logistic Regiment', 110, in *The Falklands Conflict Twenty Years on: Lessons for the Future*, Sandhurst Conference Series, (Abingdon: Frank Cass, 2005), p.111.

15 David Brown, *The Royal Navy and the Falklands War* (London: Arrow Books, 1989), p.68.

16 Stephen Badsey, 'The Logistics of the British Recovery of the Falkland Islands, 1982', *International Forum on War History: Proceedings*, March 2014, p.113.

17 Thompson, *3 Commando Brigade in the Falklands*, 126, (Barnsley: Pen & Sword Military, 2007).

18 Ibid., p.13.

19 'Maritime Force Structure and the Determinant Case', April 1975, para. 16, ADM 219/704, TNA.

20 Sandy Woodward and Patrick Robinson, *One Hundred Days* (London: Harper Press, 2012), p.387.

21 Sandy Woodward and Patrick Robinson, *One Hundred Days* (London: Harper Press, 2012), p.387.

22 Patrick Cordingley, *In the Eye of the Storm: Commanding the Desert Rats in the Gulf War* (London: Hodder & Stoughton, 1996), p.9.

23 Study into Training and Preparation for Operation GRANBY, Ministry of Defence, *Army Doctrine Publication – Training*, 4:4–4, vol. 4, DGD&D/18/34/65, (Ministry of Defence, 1996).

24 Peter De la Billière, *Storm Command: A Personal Account of the Gulf War* (London: HarperCollins, 1992), p.96.

25 4th and 7th Armoured Brigades had a total of three Armoured regiments and three Armoured Infantry battalions between them, however, there were significant contributions from many other regiments, battalions and supporting arms from across the Army, ready formed casualty replacement units and units dedicated to prisoner of war handling.

26 House of Commons Defence Committee, 'Defence Committee Tenth Report: Preliminary Lessons from Operation Granby', HC 287/I (London: House of Commons, 17 July 1991), para. 10.

27 P S Reehal, 'Transport and Movements', in *Gulf Logistics: Blackadder's War* (London: Brassey's, 1995), p.69.

28 Ibid.

29 Major General Julian Thompson, *Lifeblood of War: Logistics in Armed Conflict* (London: Brassey's, 1994), p.344.

30 House of Commons Defence Committee, 'HC 43', para. 39, HC 43, (London: House of Commons, 25 May 1994).

31 Ibid., para. 44.

32 Lawrence Freedman, 'Alliance and the British Way in Warfare', *Review of International Studies* 21, no. 2 (1995): p.155.

33 House of Commons Defence Committee, 'HC 43', para. 55, HC 43, (London: House of Commons, 25 May 1994).

34 House of Commons Defence Committee, 'The Defence Requirement for Merchant Shipping and Civil Aircraft', HC 476 (House of Commons Defence Committee, 7 June 1988).

35 House of Commons Defence Committee, 'HC 287/I', para. 14, HC 287/I, (London: House of Commons, 17 July 1991).

36 Ibid., para. 33.

37 Major General Julian Thompson, 'Force Projection and the Falklands Conflict', in *The Falklands Conflict Twenty Years on: Lessons for the Future*, Sandhurst Conference Series (Abingdon: Frank Cass, 2005), p.82.

38 House of Commons Defence Committee, 'The SA80 Rifle and Light Support Weapon', HC 728 (London: HMSO, 1993), para. 32.

39 Charles Allen, *Thunder and Lightning: The RAF Tells Its Stories of the Gulf War.* (HMSO Books, 1991), p.53.

40 It should be noted that whilst four RAF Tornadoes were lost in action in 1991 none was actually employing the JP233 system at the time it was lost. One aircraft lost was carrying the JP233 but had already used this and was on the return leg of its sortie.

41 Group Captain Andrew Vallance, 'Air Power in the Gulf War – The RAF Contribution', *Royal Air Force*, 20 January 2015, http://www.raf.mod.uk/history/AirPowerintheGulfWar.cfm.

42 House of Commons Defence Committee, 'HC 43', para. 42, HC 43, (London: House of Commons, 25 May 1994).

43 Margaret Thatcher, *The Downing Street Years* (Harper Collins, 1995), p.153.

## Chapter 8

1 Albert Sorel, L'Europe et la Révolution Française, p. 474, quoted in E H Carr, *The Twenty Years Crisis, 1919-1939: An Introduction to the Study of International Relations* (London: Macmillan, 1946), p.11.

2 Defence Policy and Programme, Appendix A, Memorandum by the Secretary of State for Defence, 7th July 1980, 'UK Future Defence Planning' (Kew: The National Archives, n.d.), para. 2, FCO 46/2171.

3 Michael Quinlan, *Thinking About Nuclear Weapons: Principles, Problems, Prospects* (Oxford ; New York: Oxford University Press, 2009), p.22.

4 COS 43/68, Annex A, The British Contribution to NATO in the Long Term, Part IV – Capabilities Required by NATO, Conventional Capabilities, Chiefs of Staff Committee, 'Revision of NATO Strategy' (MoD, 1968), para. 114, DEFE 13/635, TNA.

5 Admiral Sir John (Sandy) Woodward, GBE, KCB, in Andrew Dorman, Michael Kandiah, and Gillian Staerck, eds., *The Nott Review, 1981*, ICBH Witness Seminar Programme (Institute of Contemporary British History, 2002), p.71.

6 DP12/81, An Assessment of UK Defence Programme Changes, Strategic Implications, 'NATO Logistics Policy General UK Logistics Assumptions' (Kew: The National Archives, n.d.), para. 44, DEFE 25/432, TNA.

7 Arthur William Tedder, *Air Power in War* (London: Hodder & Stoughton, 1948), p.25.

8 'WINTEX-CIMEX 83 Committees', 1983, 59, CAB 130/1249, TNA.

9    Kenton White, '"Effing" the Military: A Political Misunderstanding of Management', *Defence Studies* 17, no. 4 (2017): 1–13, doi:10.1080/1470243 6.2017.1351879.

10   This phrase has been adopted from Peter Hennessy, *Distilling the Frenzy: Writing the History of One's Own Times* (London: Biteback, 2012), p.83. Hennessy used it in relation to the Beveridge Report of 1942.

11   Anna Locher and Christian Nünlist, 'Internationale Sicherheitspolitik Im Kalten Krieg', Bulletin (Zurich: Parallel History Project on NATO and the Warsaw Pact, 2003), Centre for Security Studies; J. Hoffenaar and Christopher Findlay, eds., *Military Planning for European Theatre Conflict During the Cold War: An Oral History Roundtable*, Zürcher Beiträge Zur Sicherheitspolitik, Nr. 79 (Zürich: Center for Security Studies, ETH Zürich, 2007).

12   TIALD was the Thermal Imaging Airborne Laser Designator; though already developed these were rushed into service by GEC-Marconi.

13   Steve Crawshaw, *Goodbye to the USSR: The Collapse of Soviet Power* (London: Bloomsbury, 1992); Robert Service, *The End of the Cold War* (London: Pan Books, 2016); Michel Fortmann and David G Haglund, 'Of Ghosts and Other Spectres: The Cold War's Ending and the Question of the Next "Hegemonic" Conflict', *Cold War History* 14, no. 4 (2014): p.515–532.

14   Georg Wilhelm Friedrich Hegel, *Lectures on the Philosophy of History*, vol. 1, 1832, sec. II.

15   This is discussed in detail in Colin S. Gray, 'Strategy and Defence Planning', in *Strategy in the Contemporary World.*, 5th ed. (London: Oxford University Press, 2016), p.162.

# ABOUT THE AUTHOR

Kenton White is a lecturer in Strategic Studies and International Relations at the University of Reading. He also is an active organiser for the Ways of War Centre at Reading. His main areas of research are British defence policy over the last 200 years, the Peninsular War, and the study of strategy through history, and is also keen wargamer. *Never Ready* is his second book for Helion and his first in the @War series.